Arab Spring, Libyan Winter

Vijay Prashad

AK Press Publishing & Distribution
Chico | Oakland | Baltimore | Edinburgh

Arab Spring, Libyan Winter
By Vijay Prashad

© 2012 Vijay Prashad

This edition © 2012 AK Press (Edinburgh, Chico, Oakland, Baltimore)

ISBN: 978-184935-112-6

e-ISBN: 978-1-84935-113-3

Library of Congress Control Number: 2012933066

AK Press   AK Press UK

370 Ryan Ave. #100   PO Box 12766

Chico, CA 95973   Edinburgh EH8 9YE

USA   Scotland

www.akpress.org   www.akuk.com

akpress@akpress.org   ak@akdin.demon.co.uk

The above addresses would be delighted to provide you with the latest AK Press
distribution catalog, which features several thousand books, pamphlets, zines, audio
and video recordings, and gear, all published or distributed by AK Press. Alternately,
visit our websites to browse the catalog and find out the latest news
from the world of anarchist publishing:

www.akpress.org | www.akuk.com

revolutionbythebook.akpress.org

Cover design by Tim Simons | www.timsimonsgraphics.com
Interior by Kate Khatib | www.manifestor.org/design
Cover image by Daisy Rockwell
All rights reserved, unless otherwise specified.

"He who has not lived in the years before the revolution cannot know what the sweetness of living is."
— Talleyrand, via Bertolucci, *Prima della Rivoluzione*, 1964.

This book is for Brinda Karat.

بچوں کی ہنستی آنکھوں کے
جو آنے چکناچور ہوئے
اب ان کے ستاروں کی لو سے
اس شہر کی راتیں روشن ہیں

"Those shattered mirrors once were
The smiling eyes of children
Now are star-lit
This city's nights are bright."
— Faiz, *ek nagma karbala-e Beirut ke liye*, 1982.

And for Anthony Shadid (1968–2012).
Most humane of reporters.

Openings.

Revolutions have no specified timetable. Karl Marx used the image of the Mole to stand in for Revolutions to explain their hard-working yet unreliable nature. The Mole spends its time making tunnels underground, and then, when you least expect it, breaks the surface for a breath of air. "Well burrowed, Old Mole," Marx wrote; the breaking free to the surface is the spectacular part of the Revolution, but it is the burrowing, the preparing, that is the most important part. The least prepared Mole is the easiest to defeat because it has not groomed its subterranean space effectively enough. Such is true of the Revolution: if it has not taken the grievances of the people and produced organizations capable of withstanding the counter-revolution—if it has not harnessed these grievances to the discipline of revolutionary force—then it is easily defeated. It is the burrowing that is essential, not simply the emergence onto the surface of history.

A process of preparation has been long afoot in West Asia and North Africa, all at a different tempo. In Tunisia and Egypt there have been many constitutional challenges to the one-party state, by which I mean challenges within the bounds of the constitution: protests and attempts to forge independent political platforms, including through the Muslim Brotherhood in Egypt, as well as attempts to found a new human rights sensibility (for example, in the campaigns of people like Ayman Nour). All of this is prologue, the work of building movements and a new vision for their societies. Much the same process was underway in Bahrain, via political parties like al-Wefaq, mainly, but also in the human rights redoubts, such as the Bahrain Centre for Human Rights and in the secular outposts that linger in the shadows of a theocratic state.

Libya was not fated for an easy Arab Spring. As Aijaz Ahmad once put it, "every country gets the fascism it deserves." In that spirit, every country gets the rebellion it deserves. Libya did not deliver the uplifting narrative of Tunisia or Egypt. It faced a complex situation, with a leader who could speak with the rhetoric of his own 1969 revolution but whose state had moved a long way towards the opposite of what he promised. Working-class protests in the industrial suburbs of Tripoli conjoined with political Islamist unrest in the eastern part of the country. These were the rumbles from below. They were harnessed by human rights lawyers from Benghazi and by neoliberal "reformers," who were disheartened by the pace of change in the Qaddafi regime. It was this latter, these neoliberal "reformers" who were able to set the pace of the Libyan revolt. Such people were not central to the revolts in Egypt and Tunisia, where the people, as a mass, stood up and were fortunate that the military stood down.

The Atlantic powers, led by the United States, France and Britain, saw the pillars of their regional stability wear thin by the developments in Tunisia and Egypt as well as Bahrain and Yemen. Libya provided a unique opportunity. The Atlantic states did not intervene on the side of the people in any of the other struggles. Rather they stood by their old pillars of stability, concrete and trowels in hand. As the University of Tehran scholar Yaghoob Javadi put it, the Atlantic states preferred "regime rehabilitation" to regime change. With Libya, things were different. Even though Qaddafi had given his regime over to the Atlantic states as an ally in the War on Terror and as a provider of oil, the erratic nature of his decision-making and the blocked transit to a full neoliberal dispensation inside the country earned him few friends in the Atlantic capitals. The Gulf Arab emirs hated Qaddafi for his frequent outbursts against them (most recently at a summit in Doha, Qatar, in 2006 when Qaddafi said that the Saudi monarch was "made by Britain and protected by the US," embarrassing the emir of Qatar and angering the Saudis). Personal animosity plays a role when it comes to absolute monarchs, whose whims are not to be discounted. But the turn against Libya was not about whim alone. Interests in oil and in political stability played their part.

The Atlantic powers made a deal with the Saudis and the Gulf Arab states that allowed the latter to silence dissent on the Arabian Peninsula (Bahrain and Yemen), if they would deliver the Arab League, and thus the United Nations, for a NATO-led intervention in Libya. The spotlight shone on Qatar, which did the leadership work for the Gulf Arabs. Its emir could remarkably draw the shine from the Arab Spring, dent its republicanism and fashion himself as a *rebel* in Libya, not in Doha. The oil is a central issue with Libya, but so too was its political significance. That the Atlantic states and their Gulf Arab partners decided to intervene in Libya and not in Bahrain or Yemen, and certainly not in Syria, tells us something. It is what this something is that I will unravel in this brief book.

No revolt or revolution is capable of being rendered mute by the attempt of a clique to seize control of it. Tendencies to a better future continue and thrive. The Libyan revolt was certainly hijacked by the neoliberal "reformers," but the people of Libya have not surrendered the wider aspirations that motivated them to risk everything in this battle. Tensions remain in the country. Qaddafi has been killed, his son Saif al-Islam is in custody, and much of the formal regime has collapsed. The neoliberal reformers remain in the shadows, running the Central Bank and the oil ministry. But they have to contend with the fighters who are not willing to transfer authority over to the reformers. The fighters comprise equal parts of Islamists and amateurs, with their roots as much in their cities of origin as in the global *ummah*. They have their own agendas. This book will appear at the anniversary of the start of the Libyan revolt. It is too early to tell how things will pan out. This book does not risk more than a few general remarks. *Arab Spring, Libyan Winter* is less about predicting the future and more about showing us how the Atlantic powers insinuated themselves into the Arab Spring, to attempt to create a Libyan Winter to the advantage of their national interests, the interest of the multinational oil firms and the neoliberal reformers within Libya.

Part I: Arab Spring.

I. Bread

When the unwashed began to assert themselves in France, the royalty scoffed at them. What they wanted was bread, whose price skyrocketed in 1774–75. Taking to the streets in remarkable numbers, the people demanded fair prices for bread, their main staple. In reaction to *la guerre des farines*, the flour war, Marie Antoinette proposed that the poor "eat cake." After the Revolution removed the monarchy and its *élèves* from the thrones of power, the new government hastened to subsidize bread. Hunger broke the back of fear. It is the lesson for the ages.

It was a lesson for North Africa in late 2010. In the last two quarters of 2010, the IMF Food Price Index rose by thirty percent. Grain prices soared by sixty percent. Protestors in Tunisia came onto the streets in December with baguettes raised in the air. In Egypt, protestors took to the streets in January chanting, "They are eating pigeon and chicken, and we are eating beans all the time." Hunger and inequality drove the protests. Their governments hastened to up their subsidies, but it was too little, too late.

The question of bread reveals a great deal about the delinquent states in Egypt and Tunisia. The Nasserite state in Egypt well understood the importance of a bread subsidy, and it encouraged the domestic production of wheat for the bread needs of the citizenry. When Anwar Sadat came to power in the 1970s, he gradually cut off the bread subsidy, what the Tunisian intellectual Larbi Sadiki calls a "democracy of bread" (*dimuqratiyyat al-khubz*). This was part of the wave of "reforms" in North Africa against the economic policies that favored national development. In Egypt, these "reforms" were part of the phase of *infitah*, the openness of Egyptian society to the Atlantic world's economic needs. Sadat opened a correspondence with the IMF: the Law of the New Economic Measures (1974) was the opening gambit, sealed in a Letter of Intent to the IMF (May 1976) and a second Letter of Intent (June 1978). Robust national development went by the wayside. More important was the will of the IMF and the international bond markets. Nationalization and subsidies ended, and free enterprise zones were created by February 1974. Sadat wanted a "blood transfusion" for the Egyptian economy, and so the Atlantic banks began to draw pints of blood from the ailing Egyptian working-class and peasantry. The "democracy of bread" was a casualty of the new thinking. In 1977, the Egyptian people rose up in a "bread intifada," with additional targets being the nightclubs and liquor stores, symbols of the "openness." The regime's guns killed 160, and shut down the protests. Lessons were hastily learned. Subsidies returned.

The new regimes tried to maintain the subsidies along with the new "openness." There was to be no subsidy to the small farmer, the *fellahin* of the Nile's fertile plains. Instead, the Egyptian regime, for instance, relied upon US Agency for International Development assistance that amounted to $4.6 billion over the next three decades. This money was used to buy the massive output of the industrial farms in the United States. Wheat came into the country, but at the expense of the restive peasantry, now increasingly under-employed. In 2010, Egypt was the leading importer of wheat in the world. Egypt relied upon its rent income for survival (remittances from payment for privatization, among others). The ruling clique diverted a substantial part of the rent into the coffers of the Swiss banks. Democracy did not live within this economy. The tyrant here was the ruling clique but not operating alone. It had close collaborators in the IMF, the World Bank, the Banks, the bond markets and the multinational corporations.

Oil did not flow liberally under the sands of Tunisia and Egypt, but it did in the rest of the Arab world, from Libya to the Arabian Peninsula. It has long been a question of the Arab Revolution that opened in the 1950s: When will the economies of the Arab region be able to sustain their populations rather than fatten the financial houses of the Atlantic world, and offer massive trust funds for the dictators and monarchs? Cursed with oil, the Arab world has seen little economic diversification and almost no attempt to use the oil wealth to engender balanced social development for the people. Instead, the oil money sloshed North, to provide credit for overheated consumers in the United States and to provide the banks with the vast funds that are otherwise not garnered by populations that have stopped saving (in the United States wages have been stagnant since 1973 but cultural expectations for lifestyle have not declined, which means that the credit provided by the petro-dollars artificially closed the gap between empty coffers and lavish dreams). The oil money also went toward the real estate boom in the Gulf, and the baccarat tables and escort services of Monaco (the Las Vegas of Europe, which has another decrepit monarch, Albert II, at its head). It did not flow into the pockets of the Arab Street.

The contradictions of the neoliberal security state in Egypt were plainly exhausted by 2008, when the "bread intifada" returned in force (protests in much smaller scale were seen across the Arab world, from Morocco to Syria). The pressure was such that lines for bread increased, and by March 2008 about a dozen people died in scuffles or from exhaustion, waiting on bread. Hosni Mubarak, the heir to Sadat's policies, sent in the army to quell protests over these "bread martyrs." On April 6, 2008, a mass protest in al-Mahalla al-Kubra went from the issue of bread to unemployment and onward to the normal excesses of the security state. Mahalla is no backwater. In 2006, twenty-four thousand workers went on strike in the textile mills of this industrial town not more than a few hours drive north of Cairo. They were the backbone of the 2008 events.

US Ambassador Francis Ricciardone arrived in Cairo in 2007. This Turkish speaker and veteran of the Foreign Service was confounded by the "paranoia of the Egyptian dictatorship" (cable sent on May 14, 2007). A year later, Ricciardone sent his assessment of

Mahalla and of the tremors underfoot to his superiors at the State Department in Foggy Bottom: "Although not on the scale of the 1977 or 1986 riots, Mahalla is significant. The violent protests demonstrated that it is possible to tear down a poster of Mubarak and stomp on it, to shout obscene anti-regime slogans, to burn a minibus and hurl rocks at riot police. These are unfamiliar images that lower-income Egyptians thrill to. In Mahalla, a new organic opposition force bubbled to the surface, defying current political labels, and apparently not affiliated with the MB [Muslim Brotherhood]. This may require the government to change its script" (cable sent on April 16, 2008). The government did not change its script. This new opposition, strengthened by factory workers and students, the unemployed and the embittered, would take the name of April 6—and eventually find themselves in Tahrir Square by January 2011.

In 2010, twenty-first century plagues reduced the Russian wheat harvest to a third. As the journalist Annia Ciezadlo put it, "a combination of factors—droughts, wildfires, ethanol subsidies, and more—converged into a global food crisis." The epicenter of this was North Africa. World wheat prices rose beyond imagination. Tunisia and Egypt, both importers of wheat, could not maintain the "democracy of bread." Inequality flourished in Egypt, and neoliberal policies produced an *haute bourgeoisie*, fanned on by Mubarak's son Gamal, with more investment in London than in Alexandria. In October 2010, the courts directed the government to raise the minimum wage from \$70/month to \$207/month. Unbalanced by the rising tide of discontent, Mubarak tried to return to the "democracy of bread." It was far too late. As the economic belt tightened, the Egyptian population inhaled for a political battle.

II. Dignity

On January 4, 2011, Mohamed Bouazizi, a street vendor in the central Tunisian town of Sidi Bouzid, set himself on fire and died. Bouazizi was the breadwinner of his family, and well known in his modest neighborhood for distributing food from his cart to the poor. Harassment by the Tunisian police over his inability to pay their bribes or purchase their permits dogged Bouazizi through his life. This was the mandate of the hard-working informal sector, to be ceaselessly humiliated by the security state for the mere fact of existence. When the dejection got too much for him, he poured gasoline on his body in front of the governor's office, set himself alight and yelled, "how do you expect me to make a living?"

An act of immolation in central Tunisia would normally matter very little to the intelligence and diplomatic corps in Washington, London, Paris and elsewhere in the advanced financial world. But Bouazizi's suicide before the town hall had an electric effect. It galvanized the people of Tunisia against their suave and ruthless leader, Zein el-Abidine Ben Ali, who had been praised by the governments of France and the United States, by the International Monetary Fund and by the bond markets. In 2010, the World Economic Forum's *Global Competitiveness Report* picked Tunisia as the leading country for investment in Africa.

Neoliberal policies pleased everyone but the Tunisian working people, who took Bouazizi's sacrifice as the spark to rise up and send Ben Ali into his Saudi exile.

Astronomic poverty rates bedevil the region (in Egypt, half the population is under the $2/day poverty level). The *infitah* "reforms" crushed the social possibilities of the organized working-class and the peasantry, who drifted into the world of informal work. More and more Bouazizis inhabit the streets and the *souqs* of North Africa. A decline in rent incomes and a reduction in tax rates reduced the budgets of the state governments, who then cut subsidies and social services to the people. Less income and less services produced slumlands whose frustrations led in two directions, as the Cairo-based scholars Helmi Sharawy and Azza Khalil noted: "acquiescence or revolt."

Revolts of various kinds were the order of the day, since at least 2006. Egyptian society sprouted a series of organizations in addition to the April 6 Movement: March 20 Movement, March 9 Movement for the Independence of Universities, Egyptian Movement for Change (*Kefaya*), Women for Change (*Mesreyat Maa al-Tagheer*), the Coordination Committee for the Defense of Worker Rights, Committee for the Defense of Insurance Funds, Centre of Manual Workers of Egypt, Federation of Pensioners, Engineers Against Sequestration, the Mahallah Committee for Workers' Consciousness, Workers for Change and so on.

Rural Egypt did not sit passive, waiting for urban Egypt to act. Over the past decade, peasant struggles in Sarando, Bhoot and Kamshish have been commonplace. The latter, Kamshish, is not twenty kilometers

15

from the birthplace of Mubarak (Kafr el-Meselha) and only eight kilometers from that of Sadat (Mit Abu al-Kum). In May 2011, as Tahrir Square remained the focal point of the Arab Spring, the farmers of Kamshish honored the forty-fifth anniversary of the death of Salah Hussein who led the charge against the local landlord al-Fiqi family by founding the Union of Egyptian Farmers. The doctors at the Zazazig Hospital and the lawyers of Port Said and Cairo, as well as the school principals of Minieh inspired other professionals to toss aside their hesitancy for dignity. "In Egypt," economist Omar Dahi writes in the *IDS Bulletin*, "some 1.7 million workers took part in over 1,900 strikes between 2004 and 2008, before the financial crisis, when the number of strikes and work stoppages reached into the thousands. The laboring classes were reacting in fury not only to their higher cost of living, but also to the mounting extravagance and conspicuous consumption of the elite." It was the rate of social inequality and the neoliberal consumerism of the upper ranks that unshackled the people's hesitancy.

In Tunisia, the depth of an obvious political society such as in Egypt is not apparent. Nonetheless, as political scientists Laryssa Chomiak and John Entelis point out in the *Middle East Report*, "Tunisia's disenfranchised masses developed mechanisms for dodging the tentacles of the authoritarian state, including tax avoidance, illegal tapping of municipal water and electricity supplies, and illicit construction of houses. Within this atmosphere of circumvention, moments of contentious politics nonetheless occurred eventually leading to the precipitous puncturing of Ben Ali's system of control." One of the most spectacular punctures took place in the southwestern mining town of Redayef (near the mining area of Gafsa) in January 2008. The state-owned phosphate company conducted a fraudulent hiring process, cashiering the unconnected and hiring eighty-one people with connections to the upper state apparatus. Redayef is the Tunisian Mahallah. The street protests of the workers and the unemployed expanded to include students in Tunis, Sfax and Sousse, and the broadest of the social classes from the Gafsa governorate. The main axis here was the underground cadre of the banned Workers' Communist Party, whose cells among the Tunisian diaspora in France hummed with solidarity activity. Wives and widows of the imprisoned workers captured the streets in April, and the police responded with their own habits. In June, two protestors were killed. The dynamic smoldered, not erupting, but not dying down either. Bouazizi's action would oxygenate it.

It has been a long-standing question in the Arab world: When will we rule ourselves? Not long ago, France's Nicolas Sarkozy and America's Hillary Clinton offered praise for their "democratic" friends, Tunisia's Ben Ali and Egypt's Mubarak. To top the obscenity, during the capture of Tahrir Square, Obama conferred with the Saudis on the democratic transition in Egypt: this is like asking a carnivore how to cook tofu.

In 1953, the aged King Farouk of Egypt set sail on his yacht, *al-Mahrusa*. Guarded by the Egyptian navy, he waved to people who he considered his lesser: Nasser, son of a postman, and Sadat, son of small farmers. Their Colonel's Coup was intended to break Egypt away from monarchy and imperial domination.

Nationalization of the commanding heights of the economy came alongside land reforms. But these were ill conceived, and they were not able to throttle the power of the Egyptian bourgeoisie (whose habit for quick money continued, with three quarters of new investments going to inflate a real estate bubble). The economy was bled to support an enlarged military apparatus, largely to fight the US-backed armies of the Israelis. Egypt's defeat in the 1967 War led Nasser to resign on June 10. Thousands of people took to the streets of Cairo, and filled Tahrir Square, this time to ask Nasser *to return to office*, which he did, although much weakened.

The democratic opening of 1952 was, however, unable to emerge. Military officers, even if temperamentally progressive, are loathe to hand over the reins of power. The security apparatus went after the Muslim Brotherhood certainly, but it was fiercest against the Communists. Nasser did not build up a strong, independent political culture. "His 'socialism,'" as the historian L. S. Stavrianos put it, "was socialism by presidential decree, implemented by the army and police. There was no initiative or participation at the grass-roots level." For that reason, when Sadat moved the country to the Right in the 1970s there was barely any opposition to him. Nasserism after Nasser was as hollow as Perónism after Perón.

The revolt that broke out in 2011 was against the regime set up by Sadat and developed by Mubarak. The Sadat-Mubarak regime was a national security state that had no democratic pretensions. In 1977, Sadat identified Nasserism with "detention camps, custodianship and sequestration, a one-opinion, one-party system." Sadat allowed three kinds of political forces to emerge, but then hastily defanged them (the leftist National Progressive Grouping Party), co-opted them (the Arab Socialist Party and the Socialist Liberal Party), or tolerated their existence (Muslim Brotherhood). Cleverly, Sadat put in place what he accused Nasser of building. It was under Sadat, and Mubarak (with his own Oddjob, Omar Suleiman, in tow) that the detention camps and torture centers blossomed. Egypt's 2006 budget provided $1.5 billion for internal security. There is about one police officer for every thirty-seven Egyptians. This is extreme. The subvention that comes from the United States of $1.3 billion per year helps fund this monstrosity. This archipelago of torture would be essential when the United States needed to send those who had been placed in the "extraordinary rendition" program after 9/11 to sing their songs under distress.

The revolt of 2011, in addition, was egged on by sections of the business elite who were disgusted with the neoliberal consumerism of the clique around Gamal Mubarak, the president's son. This repulsed national bourgeoisie was no match for multinational capital and understood that the cannibalization of the country would not be a benefit to them in the long term: it would simply cut the heart out of the vast masses, whose anemic social condition would mean that the Egyptian economy would not be able to demand any of the goods produced and sold by the national bourgeoisie. No wonder then that on January 31 notable businessman Naguib Sawiris joined the Tahrir Square dynamic. As Paul Amar put it at *jadaliyya.com*, "Sawiris and his allies had become threatened by Mubarak-and-son's extreme neoliberalism and their favoring of Western, European and Chinese investors over national businessmen. Because their investments overlap with those of the military, these prominent Egyptian businessmen have interests literally embedded in the land, resources and development projects of the nation." Their interests paralleled those in the military who were also disgusted by the corruption and a policy of privatization that was plainly the defenestration of the national economy. That is why Gamal Mubarak and his cronies were ejected from the cabinet on January 28, and this is why the military gleefully put Gamal, his brother and his now hapless father on trial in August 2011.

In Tahrir Square, twenty-two year old Ahmed Moneim told the BBC, "The French Revolution took a very long time so the people could eventually get their rights." His struggle in 2011 is to repeal the national security state and to bring into place a dignified society. That is the basic requirement, to return to the slogan of the French Revolution. The dynamic that Ahmed identifies returns Egypt to the original movement of 1952, but this time it asks that democracy be a fundamental part of the equation, and the military remain in its barracks. That is one of the lessons of history that was clear in the battlements of Tahrir Square.

The other lesson emerges as it often does in the midst of modern revolts: that women form a crucial part of the waves of revolt, and yet when the revolt succeeds women are set aside as secondary political actors. It was after all the twenty-six year old member of the April 6 movement, Asmaa Mahfouz, who posted a video challenge on January 18, "If you think yourself a man, come with me on 25 January. Whoever says women shouldn't go to protests because they will get beaten, let him have some honor and manhood and come with me on 25 January. Whoever says it is not worth it because there will only be a handful of people, I want to tell him, 'You are the reason behind this, and you are a traitor, just like the president or any security cop who beats us in the streets.'" Women such as Mahfouz and Azza Soliman of the Centre for Egyptian Women's Legal Assistance, and the thousands of women who took to the streets in rural and urban Egypt were central to the revolt. "What are the possibilities for a democratization of rights in Egypt," asked Nadine Naber at *jadaliyya.com*, "in which women's participation, the rights of women, family law, and the right to organize, protest and express freedom of speech remains central?" Naber repeats a question raised in 1957 at the Afro-Asian People's Solidarity Conference by Karima el-Said, the deputy minister of Education of the United Arab Republic (the confederation of Egypt and Syria), "In Afro-Asian countries where people are still suffering under the yoke of colonialism, women are actively participating in the struggle for complete national independence. They are convinced that this is the first step for their emancipation and will equip them to occupy their real place in society." It is history's second lesson, that the democracy that emerges be capacious.

One of the curious manifestations of Americanism is to try to bring control of every dynamic into its own circuit. The Tunisians and Egyptians rose up, and the establishment media in the United States wanted to give the glory to Facebook or Obama's 2009 Cairo

speech or the handbook by philosopher Gene Sharp—
not to the ordinary people of North Africa themselves.
In Cairo, Obama said, "we will extend a hand if you
are willing to unclench your fist." During the Tahrir
Square standoff, protestors chanted, "we have extended our hand, why have you clenched your fist?" Their
words came as they foisted in the air tear gas canisters
that read Made in the USA. They fully grasped the hy-
pocrisy of imperial liberalism. Facebook certainly allowed for some creative organizational work amongst
the literate, but it was not significant.

On January 28, Mubarak, along the grain of
this kind of Americanism, hastily cut Internet and
cellphone service. It had little impact on the protests.
As Navid Hassanpour shows in a paper presented
to the American Political Science Association meeting in 2011, "The disruption of cellphone coverage
and Internet on the 28th exacerbated the unrest in at
least three major ways. It implicated many apolitical
citizens unaware of or uninterested in the unrest; it
forced more face-to-face communication, i.e., more
physical presence in streets; and finally it effectively
decentralized the rebellion on the 28th through new
hybrid communication tactics, producing a quagmire
much harder to control and repress than one massive
gathering in Tahrir." In fact, the closing down of Facebook provided new opportunities to reach new con-
stituencies and to broaden the movement. It would be
a surprise to the workers of Suez or the cadre of the
Muslim Brotherhood or even the students of Cairo's
universities that they were unwitting pawns of some-
one else's dreams. This was an Egyptian Revolution.
It did not seek permission from elsewhere.

The Arab revolt that began in Tunisia and spread to Egypt and onwards seemed on the surface like a "1968" for the Arab World. Sixty percent of the Arab population is under the age of thirty (seventy percent in Egypt). Their slogans are about dignity and employment. The resource curse brought wealth to a small percentage of their societies, but little economic development. Social development came to some parts of the Arab world: Tunisia's literacy rate is seventy-five percent, Egypt's just over seventy percent and Libya's at ninety percent. The educated lower middle class and middle class youth have not been able to find decent jobs. The concatenation of humiliations disgust these young people: no job, no respect from an authoritarian state, and then to top it off the general malaise of being second class citizens on the world stage (the suppression of the Palestinians and the crushing of Iraq are indices of the Arab gloom; it was the solidarity committees for the second intifada of the Palestinians and of the anti-war rally of March 20, 2003 that formed *Kefaya* and the March 20 Movement): all this was overwhelming. The chants on the streets of Tunisia and Egypt were about this combination of dignity, justice and jobs.

III. God

The Muslim Brotherhood came onto the Cairene streets. It set its own ideology to mute. Its spokesperson, Gamal Nasser, said that they are only a small part of the protests in Tahrir Square. This is a protest about Egypt, he said, not Islam. Much the same kind of statement came from the *mullahs* in Iran during the massive protests of 1978–79, the precursor of the creation of the Islamic Republic. Organized into a panoply of organizations, the Egyptian people filled their squares and refused to leave. When the camel-riding thugs of the Mubarak regime entered the square on February 2, the organized and disciplined Brotherhood gathered in formation to defend the square. As Dyab Abou Jahjah pointed out on his blog on that day, "Today the revolution needs structured organizations to form a fighting machine, and the Brotherhood has experience, resources, and the will to play that role. And they are doing it for the movement without claiming it." That evening the Brotherhood's spiritual leader, Sheikh Yusuf Abdullah al-Qaradawi spoke to *al-Jazeera* from his Qatar exile, "The Egyptians know that their peaceful democratic revolution, their remarkably responsible and intelligent mass movement, is being crushed by America and Israel as much as by Mubarak's dictatorship. I will make a prediction: if this revolution fails, America will face an unprecedented wave of Arab anger, and Egypt will be plagued by violence from now on. The Muslim Brothers who have escaped from prison, for instance, know that their fate in the coming weeks is to be rearrested and tortured to death. They will fight."

Much the same sort of attitude was struck in Tunisia. The no. 2 in the Islamist Nahda Party, Abdelfattah Mourou told *al-Jazeera* on March 10 that his party was out on Avenue Habib Bourguiba for the sake of all of Tunisia. He used the term *sha'b*, the people, not Islam or Muslims. "When asked about Nahda's position toward partisan politics, often considered to contradict

Islamists' ideal of unity," Nadia Marzouki points out at the *Middle East Report*, "Mourou insisted on 'the right of the people to its self' (*haqq al-sha'b li-nafsihi*)." "The people may have different feelings," Mourou conceded, "but the only parties that will win will be those chosen by the people." The deep desire and commitment to some form of democracy is underlined.

We tend to exaggerate the authority of the clerics, or at least to treat it as natural, as eternal. Al-Qaradawi came to Tahrir Square in late February, once Mubarak went to the seaside at Sharm al-Sheikh for his enforced retirement (and where he would later be brought before a court, in his gurney). Rather than offer himself as an Islamic leader alone, he first asked for blessings from the youth (a reversal itself) and then greeted the Christians and others, saying, "In this Square, sectarianism died." These were brave words, but also frayed at the edges since some sectarian attacks had already begun and others would follow (it had become commonplace to blame these on remnants of the Mubarak regime, eager to sow suspicion and fear). "The revolution isn't over. It has just started to build Egypt," announced the cleric, "guard your revolution." Raymond Baker and Karen Aboul Kheir were right to point out at *ZNET* that al-Qaradawi's son is a supporter of the liberal political figure Mohamed ElBaradei, and his granddaughter had joined the brigades busy with the cleaning of the square. They had secular affiliations.

Since the 1970s, clericalism in the Arab World and in Iran has had the upper hand in oppositional struggles. This has everything to do with the calcification of the secular regimes of the national liberation era (the new states formed out of the export of Nasserism: from Egypt to Iraq, Syria, Yemen and into Libya by 1969), the deterioration of the Third World Project (especially the fractures in the oil cartel OPEC that opened up in the summer of 1990 and fed into the Iraqi invasion of Kuwait), and the promotion and funding of the advance guard of Islamism through the World Muslim League by the Saudis from Chechnya to Pakistan and Indonesia, with its greatest impact through small Salafist bands across North Africa and the Middle East.

If you go back and look at the period when Nasserism and the Third World Project were dominant, what you will find are the clerical intellectuals in the midst of ideological battles against radical nationalism and Marxism, all the while borrowing from Bolshevik techniques of party building to amass their own organizational strength. For example, in Iraq, it was the Communist Party that dominated the working-class regions of Baghdad. Unable to fully confront this political force, the clerics of working-class Shi'ism, such as the al-Sadr family, had to evoke a politics through and against the Communists. Baqir al-Sadr's intellectual work took on Marxism (his *Iqtisaduna* was a critique of *Capital*, vol. 1) and his organizational work (through the al-Da'wah al-Islamiyah) was modeled on the Iraqi Communist Party. Clericalism, on the back-foot, had to engage with the dominant tendency, which was radical nationalism and Marxism. If you go farther East you would run into Haji Misbach, an Indonesian cleric, also known as Red Haji, who confronted the dynamic Indonesian Communist Party with his own brand of Islamic Communism in the sugar belt of central Java. Like Baqir al-Sadr, Misbach was perplexed by the popularity of the CP in his society. He wanted to find a way to bring the spiritual to socialism. These are all precursors of Ali Shariati, the great Iranian thinker who was influenced by the Third World Project, and by Marxism, but once more wanted to bring Islam into it. For all these thinkers, the problem was quite the opposite of what it is today: the workers seemed ascendant, driven by the science of secular socialism at least in the domain of politics and production. It terrified the clerics.

The Communists and the radical nationalists crumbled under the weight of several factors. Preeminent among them was the pressure from the camp of imperialism, led by the United States, but with the Europeans and the Gulf Arabs in eager tow. Economic pressure combined with commitments made to Salafi opposition figures (via the World Muslim League) undermined the attempt to create new foundations for these societies. It did not help that the radical nationalists had little solidarity with the Communists, and nor did the Soviet Union, which routinely sold out their local fraternal parties for better relations with the nationalist strongmen, the megalomania of *realpolitik* eclipsing social justice and internationalism. Repression of the Communists (in Sudan, Iraq and Egypt for example) weakened the left pole in these societies. Additionally, the Atlantic powers built up a strong network of sympathetic countries, the Gulf Arabs at the top of the list at the center of West Asia and North Africa, but with a Maghrebian pro-Atlantic bloc of Tunisia and Libya (the treaty of January 6, 1957) and the Mashriqain Baghdad Pact of Iran, Iraq, Pakistan and Turkey (the treaty of February 25, 1955). The Pacts and the bloc would wither (after the Iraqi coup of 1958 and the Libyan coup of 1969), but the Atlantic world hastened to create new alliances and allegiances, rooted mainly in the implacable Gulf Arab region (the Gulf Cooperation Council, the Arab NATO, was formed in 1979, and provided the most resolutely loyal force for the interests of the Atlantic world, and decisively opposed radical nationalism, Communism and eventually the post-1979 Iranian Revolution).

Such pressure from the outside world exaggerated and sharpened the failures of statecraft within the Arab governments. The new regimes were unable to found their society on a platform that included the widest spectrum of rights and responsibilities, from the requirements of decent employment to the provision of safe and stimulating social life, from the imperatives for political freedom to the decency of intellectual development. Paranoid about genuine threats from outside and from the oxygenation of toxic forces within, they held back on political rights and attempted to stifle political and intellectual freedom. They provided social welfare, but did not fully recreate the realm of production to facilitate worker and peasant control over their economic lives. The growth of the neoliberal security state in Egypt is emblematic of this failure to engender a new society that would be able to withstand external threats and to model an alternative path for social development for the other post-colonial states.

The collapse of the national liberation project by the 1980s came alongside the slow demise of the USSR, and its role as the upholder of the Utopian horizon of socialism. With the eclipse of that horizon, it became harder to assert the need for people to risk their lives in struggle for what appeared to be in fundamental retreat, namely socialism. The idea of the inevitability of socialism inspired generations to give themselves over to the creation of the Jacobin force, the Party that would, under relentless pressure, lead the working-class and peasantry to certain revolution. As well, the failure of the national liberation project meant the whittling down of the realm of production, and so the organized working-class found itself cast into the unsavory and unpredictable world of informal work. The main organization force of the Communist parties, the organized working-class, began its slow disappearance from world history.

It is this combustive situation that amputated the socialist dream in the Arab lands, and drew the now informal workers of hitherto Communist strongholds such as al-Thawra (Baghdad) and Haret Hreik (Beirut) into the parties of God, such as the Sadrites and Hezbollah. Religion has an unshakable eschatology, which a post-utopian secular politics lacks. No wonder that religion has inspired action in the Arab lands, even if destructive rather than revolutionary, whereas secular politics has become less inspirational.

With Mubarak gone and the squabbles of the post-Mubarak era in the open, the Muslim Brotherhood seeks its place at the table. It has long turned its back publicly on violence, which was why Ayman al-Zawahiri founded the Islamic Jihad, to absorb the extremist, terrorist space abjured by the Brotherhood. The Brotherhood's Issam al-Aryan laid out the line for his organization years ago, saying, "The Brothers consider constitutional rule to be closest to Islamic rule. We are the first to call for and apply democracy. We are devoted to it until death." Which is indeed what one saw at the borderlands of Tahrir Square when it was attacked. As the electoral process unfolded in 2011, it was inevitable that the Brotherhood's Freedom and Justice Party and the Salafi Al-Nour party would do well. Mubarak's electoral machine had no more legitimacy. The persecuted left had little of its previous mass character. The liberals generally eschew any mass organizing, and had only a moral claim to make on the population. It was left to the Brotherhood and the Salafis, who did not initiate the protests but who participated in them, to stake an electoral claim. Their activists were familiar with the interior of Mubarak's prisons, but their parties were tolerated by the state — used when it suited Mubarak, jailed when he willed it. The avuncular support of money and *al-Jazeera* from the emirate of Qatar also helped the Islamists. In other words, the political Islamists captured a considerable amount of the political space in Egypt.

Election results from Tunisia also followed the predictable path. The Islamist party, Harakat an-Nahda (or Ennahda) faced brutal repression from Ben Ali, with Ennahda's leader, Rashid Ghannouchi going from prison to exile to prison to exile without losing his political stamina. Before his return from exile in London, Ghannouchi stopped off in Qatar. Even as Ghannouchi has been outspoken against the Saudis (calling the decision to let in US troops in 1990 a "colossal crime"), the Gulf Arabs provided Ghannouchi and Ennahda with the monetary and institutional support essential for its rapid re-emergence in Tunisian society. There was no question that it would trounce the enfeebled left and liberals in an election that catapulted it to victory in November 2011.

Little wonder that the Iranian Ayatollah Khamenei proclaimed confidently on February 4, 2011 that the uprisings would spur on an "Islamic Awakening" across the region.

The calculation for how to deal with the parties of God is fairly simple. They are certainly a legitimate part of the political process, and their role in political life cannot be banned into oblivion. They also appear to be somewhat committed to democratic developments, even if these are narrowed when it comes to their own program. For example, in a place such as Lebanon, as Fawwaz Trabulsi points out, Hezbollah largely restricts its charity to its own sect, and within that sect it promotes private religious education and the obligatory veil at the same time as it erases all awareness of social rights. It is important to offer a scrupulous and forthright criticism of the shortcomings and social degeneration of the parties of God. In 2007, the Communist Parties in India held an anti-imperialist meeting in Delhi. A Hezbollah representative, Ali Fayyad, came for it. At the plenary, Aijaz Ahmad lit into Fayyad regarding Hezbollah's position on women's rights. It is just what should be done. The parties of God have virulence at their fingertips, particularly as it relates to matters of social equity and economic policy. That has to be scorched. Clara Zetkin warned that the emergence of fascism could be laid partly on the failure of the workers, their intellectual allies and their revolutionary parties to form tactical alliances that are also founded on honest and serious criticism of those alliances. That is how one moves effectively toward the future, particularly when the context is such that the left pole is weak and the national-popular domain is largely in the hands of the parties of God.

Most indications point to the fact that the parties of God are unable to fully take on board the grievances and needs of the people. The Muslim Brotherhood in Egypt hastily came to an accommodation with the neoliberal agenda and suggested that it would not be averse to the Camp David treaty with Egypt. The United States reached out to the Brotherhood, and in the interests of expediency and in their lust for power, the Brotherhood reached back and made these concessions. Such departures from the popular agenda will turn the Brotherhood into a more socially cruel force (to shore up its base) and so might make it marginal to the political process. If the Brotherhood goes fully in this direction, suggests the University of Tehran's Seyed Mohammad Marandi, it "will probably at some point split into two or more separate parties, which will then provide competing interpretations of how society should be run." Or, if the parties of God entirely fail to make their mark on the world of today, this might provide an opening to more authentic working-class and peasant parties that are yet to make themselves manifest.

The clerics do not command the total field. In Egypt, hope vested for a while in the emergence of a secular bloc. But here the catapult would not shoot hopes too far out of the fortress of the military and neoliberal consumerism. Mohamed ElBaradei flew into Tahrir Square from his diplomatic exile in Geneva. In 2010, he returned to his native Egypt to declare his intention to bring "good governance" with him. If this meant the removal of Mubarak and the opening of political space, it was welcome. ElBaradei sounded like one of many World Bank advisors, who had come to terms with the fact that neoliberal consumerism had failed to bring positive change, and had now articulated Structural Adjustment, part 2, with "good governance" as the leading edge. No sense in opening up the economy if the politics is not also opened up was the new mantra. But when Tahrir filled up, ElBaradei seemed enthused. With Ayman Nour in poor health, he took up the mantle of the liberals. The fact that he spent the better part of his career and the worst years of Mubarak's rule outside Cairo gave him credibility. A man of his class would have been co-opted into the Mubarak web. Only an outsider like him could be both of the ruling bloc (in terms of class position and instinct) and outside the ruling apparatus (that is, of Mubarak's cabinet circle). It was a point of great privilege.

People like ElBaradei cannot be reduced to being more sophisticated puppets for the Atlantic world. Early in his career, in the 1960s, he served in the Nasserite Ministry of External Affairs. He then moved to the Foreign Ministry under Ismail Fahmi, one of the most impressive of the Nasser-era bureaucrats. When Sadat went to Jerusalem and then to Camp David, Fahmi resigned from his cabinet. For one year, ElBaradei served with Boutros Boutros Ghali at the Foreign Ministry. Unwilling to bend to the wiles of Sadat, both ElBaradei and Boutros Ghali fled into the UN bureaucracy. It was this Nasserite training that schooled both of them, and forged them as strong pillars of international law and the rights of all nations. No wonder that ElBaradei would not wither before US pressure as the Director of the International Atomic Energy Agency during the lead-up to the war on Iraq (2002–2003). It is the reason why the IAEA and ElBaradei as its head won the Nobel Peace Prize in 2005. ElBaradei's residual Nasserism shows us that the threats to the US pillars of stability (pliancy to US will, protection of Israel) are real whether the Brotherhood wins the democratic process of not. In this regard, the gap between ElBaradei's liberal bloc and the Islamist bloc is narrower than one might expect. ElBaradei's 2012 suggestion that he would not enter the presidential election because the military has yet to fully open space for civilian politics is welcomed, but it also suggests that ElBaradei recognizes that the liberals would at this time only have a shallow support base compared to the far more popular Islamists.

The Tunisian trade unions (the Union Générale Tunisienne du Travail or UGTT) and the Egyptian labor and peasant movement played essential roles in the uprisings of 2011. Millions of people participate in these platforms, and millions more are loyal to them. Yet, these organizations have not asserted themselves into the electoral domain, even though they were major political actors during the uprisings. There are rumbles of discontent amongst the unions of the dangers of letting political Islam command the electoral field, and therefore government. The danger is not only social. Most of the forces of political Islam are quite comfortable with neoliberal economic policies, and with making adjustments of various kinds (bro-

kered through Qatar) with the capitals of Atlantic imperialism. The recognition of the political limitations
of political Islam are not unknown to the labor leadership of North Africa. Habib Jerjir, a leader of the
Regional Workers' Union of Tunis, told the AP, "I'm
against political Islam. We must block their path."
Whether this sentiment will translate into the creation
of a mass working-class political party is to be seen.
It would provide the only alternative to neoliberalism
and social suffocation in the region.

IV. Ben Ali and Mubarak Go to the Seaside

On January 14, 2011, Zein el-Abidine Ben Ali fled
with his family to the Red Sea port city of Jeddah,
Saudi Arabia. He was welcomed by King Abdullah,
and told he could stay as long as he kept out of politics. Uganda's Idi Amin lived on the top two floors of
the Novotel Hotel in Jeddah and then in a luxurious
villa, but these are no longer available. Ben Ali was
provided with a vast palace, surrounded by high walls
and tall palm trees, accessed by seven gates guarded
by armed guards. It is a sumptuous prison.

On February 11, after thirty years at the helm of
Egypt, Hosni Mubarak and his family departed for
the resort town of Sharm el-Sheikh on the southern
tip of the Sinai. Sixteen days of resolute protest by
a cross-section of the Egyptian public put enormous
pressure on the Egyptian military. It is the institution
that held the keys to Mubarak's future. Most auto-
cratic societies hollow out political institutions that

might balance power in the State. That is why the legislature is weak, and that is why there are no legal political parties apart from Mubarak's façade of a party (when its headquarters were burnt down, the party effectively ceased). Absent of other political challenges, the tussle came down to a test of wills between the protestors and the military.

The rank and file and the divisional commanders had the closest ties to the protestors, and they signaled their willingness to see Mubarak leave. The top generals, who served alongside Mubarak in the armed forces and then in the government, were less happy to send him off. It was this internal struggle in the army that delayed matters. Fear that the Tunisian contagion would spread even more rapidly if Egypt fell to it made the Royal Families of the Gulf burst into shivers. They pledged to back Mubarak to the hilt. The Saudi offer in particular gave Mubarak the confidence for his bizarre television address on February 10, where even his translator seemed hesitant, embarrassed to have to render the clichés into English.

Eventually, the Saudi money and the loyalty of the Generals were not sufficient. The tide from below prevailed. Mubarak and his family boarded a helicopter and went off.

History is filled with bizarre analogies. February 11, Mubarak's day of departure, is also the day when the Shah of Iran's regime fell in 1979. The emergence of an Ayatollah Khomeini in Egypt had given pause to some outside the country; would the Muslim Brotherhood take over, they suggested? Iran has a well-organized clergy who had taken a defiant position against the Shah. These clergy also had a charismatic leader, exiled in Paris, whose return to Tehran was greeted by millions of people. No such clergy exists in Egypt, and nor is there a person such as Khomeini. Iran is a bad analogy for Egypt.

Better yet is South Africa. On February 11, Nelson Mandela was finally released after twenty-seven years in jail. I remember watching television in 1990, as Mandela hesitantly walked out of the prison in Paarl. Egypt has had its own exit from Babylon moment: its jailer has departed. It has walked into the light.

For the Arab lands, the events of early 2011 were not the inauguration of a new history, but the continuation of an unfinished struggle that is a hundred years old. Some people already despair, discounting the remarkable victory of ejecting Ben Ali and Mubarak. The military remain in power in Egypt, the older social classes of property and power are not dislodged in Cairo and Tunis. But their figureheads have been jettisoned. Such acts raise the confidence of the people and propel other struggles into motion. The old order might yet remain, recasting itself in different clothes, speaking a different vocabulary. But it knows that its time is at hand. In *Gladiator* (2000), the Germanic barbarians sever the head of a Roman soldier and toss it in front of the Roman battle lines. One of the Roman generals says, "People should know when they are conquered." He means the barbarians. The dictators of the Arab world, our barbarians, might yet throw some heads before the advance of the people. But they know that they are defeated. Faith and fear in them has now ebbed. It is simply a matter of time: a hundred years, or ten. *'U'balna kulna, is the phrase: may we all be next.*

The tidal wave that lifted Ben Ali and Mubarak out of their palaces to their exiles inspired millions across West Asia and North Africa. Protests had already broken out on the Arabian Peninsula, in Yemen and Bahrain, protests would soon break out in Libya and Syria, and a new energy manifested itself among the Palestinians in exile and in the occupied territories. Historical grievances combined with inflationary pressures now met with the subjective sense that victory might be at hand—this was not simply a protest to scream into the wind, but a protest to actually remove autocrats from their positions of authority. The facts of resistance had given way to the expectation of revolutionary change.

V. Bagman of the Empire

Washington was convulsed by Tahrir Square. The tidal wave of protests threatened its prejudice toward stability. Events had run out of control. The main features of US power in the region seemed on the horizon of being compromised. If the Mubarak regime fell, what would this mean to Israel? If enthusiasm about Mubarak and Ben Ali's ousters escalated the protests in Bahrain and Yemen, what would this mean for Saudi Arabia and the Gulf emirates? Something had to be done to manage what had begun to seem like a revolutionary situation.

From inside the bowels of Washington's power elite, Frank Wisner emerged, briefcase in hand. He had met the President, but he was not his envoy. He represented the United States, but was not the Ambassador. What was in his briefcase was his experience: it includes his long career as bagman of Empire, and as bucket-boy for Capital. Pulling himself away from the Georgetown cocktail parties and the Langley power-point briefings, Wisner found his way to the Heliopolis cocktail parties and to the hushed conferences in Kasr al-Ittihadiya. Mubarak (age 82) greeted Wisner (age 72), as these elders conferred on the way forward for a country whose majority is under thirty.

Obama came to Cairo in 2009, and said, "America does not presume to know what is best for everyone." Those words should have been cast in gold and placed in the portico of the White House. Instead, they drift like wisps in the wind, occasionally cited for propaganda purposes, but in a time of crisis, hidden behind the clouds of imperial interests (or those of Tel Aviv and Riyadh). America presumes to know, and presumes to have a say equivalent to those of the millions who thronged Egypt's squares, streets and television sets (one forgets about the protests of the latter, too tired to get to the square, nursing sick children or adults, a bit fearful, but no less given over to anger at the regime).

The Republicans have their own ghouls, people like James Baker, who are plucked out for tasks that require the greatest delicacy. They are like diplomatic hit-men, who are not sown up by too much belief in the values of democracy and freedom, but to the imperatives of "stability" and Empire. The Democratic bench is lighter now, as the immense bulk of Richard Holbrooke has departed for other diplomatic assignments. He had been given charge of Pakistan and Afghanistan, where he found little traction. The Taliban could not be cowered, and nor could the Pakistani military. Holbrooke had much easier times in the Balkans, where, according to Diana Johnstone, he instigated the conflict by refusing the road of peace. Wisner comes out of the same nest as Holbrooke. He is the Democrat's version of James Baker, but without the pretend gravity of the Texan.

Wisner has a long lineage in the CIA family. His father, Frank Sr., helped overthrow Arbenz of Guatemala (1954) and Mossadeq of Iran (1953), before he was undone in mysterious circumstances in 1965. Frank Jr. is well known around Langley, with a career in the Defense and State Departments along with ambassadorial service in Egypt, the Philippines and then India. In each of these places Wisner insinuated himself into the social and military branches of the power elite. He became their spokesperson. Wisner and Mubarak became close friends when he was in the country (1986–1991), and many credit this friendship (and military aid) with Egypt's support of the United States in the 1991 Gulf War. The delusions are many. George H. W. Bush calls his presidential counterpart, Hosni, in the afternoon of January 21, 1991. They are discussing their war against Iraq. "How is public support there," Bush asks him. Mubarak answers hastily, "It is still good." For Mubarak, "public" meant his clique, not the eighty odd million. Not once did the US provide a criticism of Egypt's human rights record. As Human Rights Watch put it in their 1992 World Watch Report, the George H. W. Bush regime "refrained from any public expression of concern about human rights violations in Egypt." Instead, military aid increased, and the torture system continued. The moral turpitude (bad guys, aka the Muslim Brother-hood and democracy advocates, need to be tortured) and the torture apparatus set up the system for the regime followed by Bush's son, George W. after 9/11, with the extraordinary rendition programs to these very Egyptian prisons. Wisner should be considered the architect of the framework for this policy.

Wisner remained loyal to Mubarak. In 2005, he celebrated the Egyptian (s)election (Mubarak "won" with 88.6% of the vote). It was a "historic day" he said, and went further in a report for the Baker Institute, "There were no instances of repression; there wasn't heavy police presence on the streets. The atmosphere was not one of police intimidation." This is quite the opposite of what came out from election observers, human rights organizations and bloggers such as Kareem Suleiman and Hossam el-Hamalawy. The Democratic and Republican specters came together in the James Baker Institute's working group on the Middle East. Wisner joined the Baker Institute's head, Edward Djerejian, and others to produce a report in 2003 that offers us a tasty statement, "Achieving security and stability in the Middle East will be made more difficult by the fact that short-term necessities will seem to contradict long-term goals." If the long-term goal is Democracy, then that is all very well because it has to be sacrificed to the short-term, namely support for the kind of neoliberal security state embodied by Mubarak. Nothing more is on offer. No wonder that a "Washington Middle East hand" told *The Cable*, "[Wisner's] the exact wrong person to send. He is an apologist for Mubarak." But this is a wrong view. Wisner was just the exact person to send

VIJAY PRASHAD

to protect the short-term, and so only-term, interests of Washington. The long-term had been set aside.

I first wrote about Wisner in 1997 when he joined the board of directors of Enron Corporation. Where Wisner had been, to Manila and New Delhi, Enron followed. As one of his staffers said, "if anybody asked the CIA to help promote US business in India, it was probably Frank." Without the CIA and the muscle of the US government, it is unlikely that the Subic Bay power station deal or the Dabhol deal would have gone to Enron. Here Wisner followed James Baker, who was hired by Enron to help it gain access to the Shuaiba power plant in Kuwait. Nor is he different from Holbrooke, who was in the upper circle of Credit Suisse First Boston, Lehman Brothers, Perseus and the American International Group. They used the full power of the US state to push the private interests of their firms, and then made money for themselves. This is the close nexus of Capital and Empire, and Wisner is the hinge between them.

One wonders at the tenor of the official cables coming from Cairo to Washington during January 2011. Ambassador Margaret Scobey, a career official, had been once more sidelined. The first time was over rendition. She is known to have opposed the tenor of it, and had spoken on behalf of human rights champion Ayman Nour and others. This time Obama did an end run around her, sending Wisner. Scobey went to visit ElBaradei. Similar treatment was meted out to Ambassador Anne Patterson in Islamabad. Her brief was narrowed by Holbrooke's appointment. What must these women in senior places think, that when a crisis erupts, they are set-aside for the men of Washington?

Wisner urged Mubarak to concede. It was not enough. More was being asked for in the Egyptian streets. Emboldened, Mubarak's supporters came onto the streets with bats in hand, ready for a fight. This was probably sanctioned in that private meeting. It is what one expects of Empire's bagman. At a security conference in Munich shortly after his Cairo trip, Wisner made a historic gaffe. Mubarak needed time to sort out his legacy, Wisner intimated, and whatever should take place must keen a keen eye on stability. "You need to get a national consensus around the preconditions of the next step forward, and the president must stay in office in order to steer those changes through," he said via satellite feed. This embarrassed the Obama administration, which wanted to appear both for stability and for change. Secretary of State Hillary Clinton's team dismissed Wisner for his poor choice of words, at the same time as Clinton seemed to pursue his suggestion. She recommended an "orderly transition," and proposed that Mubarak leave and give the keys to the state to his deputy Omar Suleiman. Such an "orderly transition…takes some time," she noted, "There are certain things that have to be done in order to prepare."

VI. Edicts of the Status Quo

"[The Arab Revolt] aroused mixed feelings
and made strong friends and strong enemies,
amid whose clashing jealousies its affairs
began to miscarry."
—T. E. Lawrence, Seven Pillars of Wisdom, 1922.

Ululations of joy broke out in Tel Aviv when it became clear in late January 2011 that neither the United States nor the Egyptian ruling elite wanted to succumb to the torrents from below. It was all very well to allow managed democracy in Eastern Europe or in Central Asia, but such illusions were out of the question for the Middle East. A cobwebbed tradition of Orientalist scholarship had proclaimed the Arab incapable of Enlightenment inventions such as democracy (a convenient example is Raphael Patai's *The Arab Mind*, 1973). Their policy cousins, in the diplomatic hovels of Foggy Bottom and in Kiryat Ben Gurion, absorbed this twaddle. For them, the Arab World would only ascend to Democracy in the long-term. In the short-term, where we all live, it would have to make do with Stability. When the masses gathered in Tahrir Square, they were not harbingers of Democracy for Washington and Tel Aviv: instead, they augured something worse than Mubarak—rule by the Muslim Brotherhood. Visions of Iran, Hezbollah and Hamas ran through their future plans. Israel would be encircled by cartoon character Ayatollahs who resembled Jafar, the Grand Vizier of Agrabah (from Disney's 1992, *Aladdin*). It was all too much to bear.

Obama's White House and State Department seemed unable to keep up with the pace of events in Egypt and in the Arab world in general. One revolutionary wave after another put various scenarios for diplomacy and intervention into the shredder. The popular uprisings did not keep to any timetable, and their phases seemed hard to predict. The intransigence of the people in Tahrir Square, in particular, dazzled the planners. Frank Wisner's friendly chat with Mubarak got the old man to agree to leave by September. In his place came Intelligence chief Omar Suleiman, an old friend of Israel and the United States. But the people in Tahrir Square seemed to know that if they went home and disbanded the fist that they had created, in the dark night Suleiman's agents would swoop into their homes, take them to Abu Zaabal to be hung upside down and beaten. Too much is known of the ways of the secret police to allow the dynamism of Tahrir Square to be so easily broken. Mubarak's gambit was patently insufficient.

But this is all that the United States could offer. Too much was at stake. The four pillars of US foreign policy had to be allowed to remain intact. If they fell, then the US would lose the Middle East in the same way as it has substantially lost South America. These defeats and retreats portend the collapse of US hegemony.

The first pillar is US reliance upon this region for oil, which must be allowed to flow freely into the car culture of Europe and the United States. The second pillar is that its allies in the Arab World (such as Ben Ali, Mubarak, the Saudis and Qaddafi) must stand firm with the Atlantic powers in its war on terror. Omar Suleiman had opened his jails to the CIA "ghost prisoners" and Qaddafi had closely collaborated with the US intelligence services and with Suleiman in the transit and torture of suspected al-Qaeda members (such as Ibn al-Shaykh al-Libi). The third pillar is, of course, that the Arab allies have to tether their own populations' more radical ambitions vis-à-vis Israel. Egypt accepted a US annual bribe of $1.3 billion in order to honor its 1979 peace agreement with Israel, and this has allowed the Israelis to conduct their asymmetrical warfare against the Palestinians and the Lebanese. The fourth pillar is related to the previous three. It is to circumvent what the US State Department calls "Iranian revisionism" against the status quo. The maintenance of these four pillars is a fundamental goal of US foreign policy in the Arab world. Little needs to be said about pillar no. 1. It is the obvious one. The other three are less established.

Oil.

> "Middle East oil was as essential to mutual
> security as atomic warheads."
> —US Treasury Secretary Robert Anderson,
> National Security Council, July 15, 1960.

Industrial society relies upon oil to power itself, and to derive materials for much of its industrial production (it is a crucial raw material for plastics, for example). The United States is the world's largest consumer of oil, a fourth of the total, but most of its oil is not from the Middle East. Rather, it gets its oil from the Americas (Canada, Brazil, Mexico, Venezuela and domestic production), from Africa (Nigeria and Angola), as well as from Saudi Arabia and Iraq. Reliance upon Middle Eastern oil is a global phenomenon, and its production affects global oil prices—it is not the physical delivery of Middle East oil to the United States that is the issue, simply that the oil must be kept flowing to maintain low oil prices and to enable industrial society to proceed at its exponential pace. It is also an imperative for the private multinational oil corporations who require their protection costs to be borne by the public sector, namely to the US armed forces. That is the reason why the United States, as the world's largest economy since the 1920s and the world's most powerful military since at least the 1990s, has become the de facto policeman of the world's oil supply.

After the Iranian Revolution of 1979, the United States pledged through the Carter Doctrine that the defense of the Saudi realm was tantamount to the defense of the United States, and that the full might of the US military would be used to counter any attempt by "any outside force to gain control of the Persian Gulf region." The "outside force" referred equally to the Soviets and to the Iranians (ironic, considering that the name "Persian Gulf" is given to the waters from the ancestors of the Iranians). The Atlantic powers joined with the Carter Doctrine in principle, knowing full well that the weight of the responsibility would fall on the United States. It had to counter the Soviets and the Iranians, and it would do it with its Gulf allies. The French and the British did not want to get their hands dirty. This was unseemly work.

When Saddam Hussein's armies invaded Kuwait in 1990, it threatened the delicate balance that the Atlantic powers held over the oil lands. Earlier in that year, Saddam went to claim his prize for going to war against Iran during the 1980s. He went to OPEC to raise the target oil price, to censure Kuwait for lateral drilling into Iraqi oil fields and to suggest that the oil profits no longer be held in dollars. This was unthinkable. On August 10, 1990, US Secretary of State James Baker went to NATO to underscore that the alliance "could not allow any hostile power to gain a stranglehold over its energy resources. Now

Saddam Hussein poses just such a threat. Given the central importance of Gulf oil to the global economy, all of us share an interest in thwarting this dictator's ambitions. We all have a critical stake in this." Two days later, Thomas Friedman wrote in the *New York Times*, "The United States has not sent troops to the Saudi desert to preserve democratic principles. The Saudi monarchy is a feudal regime that does not even allow women to drive cars. Surely it is not American policy to make the world safe for feudalism. This is about money, about protecting governments loyal to America and punishing those that are not and about who will set the price of oil." No more need be said. America went to war, clobbered Iraq, put in place a garrisoned sanctions regime till 2003, when its armies returned to overthrow Saddam Hussein. Misery came to Iraq because of its oil underfoot.

Arab Friends.

The second pillar is to maintain Egypt as a firm ally in the US-led war on terror. Here the Mubarak regime was not following the United States. It had interests that parallel those of Washington. The secular regime set up by Gamal Abdul Nasser was already at war with political Islam within Egypt. Nasser's popularity held the Muslim Brotherhood in check. Nasser's aide, Anwar Sadat, had been the Egyptian military's liaison with the Muslim Brotherhood since the 1930s. When he took over from Nasser, Sadat tried to outflank the Brotherhood from the right, calling himself the Believer President (*al-rais al-mou'min*), and bringing the *shari'a* into the constitution of 1971. Sadat could not complete the job. The Islamists killed him in 1981.

Sadat's successor, Mubarak, also tried to dance with the Islamists, but was not successful. In 1993, Mubarak picked a career military man, General Omar Suleiman, to run his internal security department, the *Mukhabarat el-Aama*. Two years later, Mubarak was to go to a meeting in Addis Ababa. Suleiman insisted that an armored car be flown to Ethiopia. Suleiman sat beside Mubarak when the Islamist gunmen opened fire on the car. The armor saved them. Mubarak signed legislation that made it a crime to even sympathize with Islamism, and his regime built five new prisons to fill with Brotherhood members. Some of these prisons became the torture chambers after 9/11 run by Suleiman on behalf of the CIA. Mubarak and Suleiman matched Bush and his clique in their hatred of the Brotherhood, as has been shown by Lisa Hajjar at *al-Jazeera*. They were natural allies.

But Egypt's willingness to be a partner had been strained by the Iraq War. In 2008, Ambassador Margaret Scobey worried that Egypt's eagerness had flagged. "The Egyptians have lost confidence in US regional leadership. They believe that the US invasion of Iraq was an unmitigated disaster that has unleashed Iranian regional ambitions and that the US waited far too long to engage in Arab-Israeli peacemaking efforts." Ambassador Scobey worried in a diplomatic cable leaked by WikiLeaks that "Egypt's aging leadership" was averse to change. Defense Minister Field Marshall Mohammed Hussein Tantawi had been in office since 1991, and he had "been the chief impediment to transforming the military's mission to meet emerging security threats." Mubarak "is in solid health," she wrote, and would run and win in the 2011 election. "Despite incessant whispered discussions, no one in Egypt," she noted, "has any certainty about who will eventually succeed Mubarak."

The US had long considered Omar Suleiman to be the best bet. In 2006, the Cairo Embassy wrote, "Our intelligence collaboration with Omar Soliman [*sic*] is now probably the most successful element of the relationship."

Suleiman saw Iran under the hood of every Brotherhood car. In 2009, he met General David Petraeus in Cairo. Ambassador Scobey wrote a note back to the State Department on July 14. "Soliman [*sic*] stressed that Egypt suffers from Iranian interference, through its Hezbollah and Hamas proxies, and its support for Egyptian groups like Jamaat al-Islamiyya and the Muslim Brotherhood," she wrote. "Egypt will confront the Iranian threat, he continued, by closely monitoring Iranian agents in Hamas, the Muslim Brotherhood, and any Egyptian cells." This was music to the ears of the Washington Hawks. Suleiman was a reliable upholder of Pillar no. 2.

Wisner's visit to Cairo was not idiosyncratic. It was to put some stick about in the Arab World's most important capital, Cairo. If Mubarak had to go, then Mubarak's regime had to remain in place and the public outcry had to be slowly silenced. The Egyptian military, well-funded by the US, came in to do the work, but it had to be pressured. State Department Undersecretary of State for Political Affairs Bill Burns and National Security Council's Senior Director David Lipton hastily traveled to Cairo. They needed to shore up people like Mohammed Hussein Tantawi, the head of Egypt's Higher Military Council (and later the Supreme Council of the Armed Forces, the SCAF). When the Tahrir Square protests began, Mubarak sent Tantawi to Washington to seek support for his regime, and for anti-riot equipment. Tantawi was an old war-horse of the Mubarak regime, and in 2008 the US State Department said of him that he wanted to make sure that the US would not "reduce military assistance to Egypt in the future." He is committed, in other words, to the US-Egypt alliance, which means to the dispensation with Israel (the cable from the Cairo embassy said that Tantawi is "frozen in the Camp David paradigm," good news for Tel Aviv).

Israel's Supremacy.
The third pillar of US foreign policy in the region is to protect Israel. Israel has faced no existential threat since the 1973 war, when Egypt's powerful army took it on. The Egypt-Israel peace treaty of 1979 allowed Israel to pivot its entire security strategy to face off against much weaker actors, such as Lebanon and the Palestinians. Egypt's withdrawal has allowed Israel to exert itself with overwhelming force against the Palestinians, in particular. As well, Egypt's *volte-face* in 1979 allowed Israel to reduce its defense spending from 30% of its Gross National Product to 7% of its GNP.

As part of this deal, the United States has provided each country with a large bursary each year over the past thirty years: Israel receives about $3 billion and Egypt receives $1.5 billion. Most of this money goes toward the military and security services of these two allies. The US subvention and the Egypt-Israel peace treaty create an exaggerated asymmetry between the Israeli armed forces and the Palestinian fighters.

Protests in Egypt, with the Muslim Brotherhood as part of the action, sent a tremor through Tel Aviv's establishment. If a new government came to power with the Brotherhood in alliance, this might lead to the abrogation of the 1979 treaty. If this were to occur, Israel would once again be faced with the prospect of a hostile Egypt, and its Goliath stance against the Palestinians would be challenged.

In 2008, Israeli Defense Minister Ehud Barak visited the Egyptian leadership in Cairo. When his team returned to Tel Aviv, his adviser David Hacham debriefed the US embassy's Luis G. Moreno. Hacham said that the team was "shocked by Mubarak's appearance and slurred speech." They talked about Iran and Mubarak and Barak agreed, "Israel and Egypt have a common strategic interest in stopping the expansion of Iranian influence in the region, as well as a common view of the threat posed by Iran's nuclear program." Then, strikingly, Moreno wrote a parenthetical note, "We defer to Embassy Cairo for analysis of Egyptian succession scenarios, but there is no question that Israel is most comfortable with the prospect of Omar Soliman [*sic*]."

If Suleiman took the reins, in other words, the third pillar of US interests would remain stable.

The actions of US foreign policy have not progressed much from the inclinations of Teddy Roosevelt. In 1907, he wondered if "it is impossible to expect moral, intellectual and material well-being where Mohammedanism is supreme." The Egyptians were "a people of Moslem fellahin who have never in all time exercised any self-government whatever." This was disingenuous. Roosevelt knew of course that the British ruled over Egypt. The Egyptians rose in revolt in 1881 under Ahmed Arabi against the Khedive (the British puppet Twefik Pasha), and once more in Alexandria in 1882. These rebellions, or the urge for self-government, were interpreted cynically by the British as its opposite: a reason to stay, to tame the passions of the population. The British would withdraw, the Foreign Office wrote, "as soon as the state of the country and the organization of the proper means for the maintenance of the khedivial authority will admit it." This promise was repeated almost verbatim sixty-six times between the early 1880s and 1922. It was Nasser who tossed them out in the 1950s. Roosevelt threw in his lot with the British consul, Lord Cromer. Cromer, he said, "is one of the greatest modern colonial administrators, and he has handled Egypt just according to Egypt's needs." This is what Omar Suleiman said in those February days, that Egypt is too immature for democracy in the Enlightenment sense. Wisner whispered just this nonsense in his ear when he was in Cairo.

Tahrir Square burst with enthusiasm and resilience on February 8. The US hastily told the Egyptian authority to make a few more concessions. Anything would do as long as the three pillars remained intact. Joe Biden called Suleiman and told him to make "immediate, irreversible progress." The US and Israel wanted Suleiman to take the reins at least four years ago. The protests simply hastened the script. The people of Egypt wanted to write a new play. But Suleiman was not to their taste. He had to be jettisoned. It was Suleiman who announced that Mubarak was to leave, and as Vice President he hoped to step into his shoes, to be Mubarak II. It was not to happen. The next day, the Armed Forces Supreme Council, led by General Tantawi, took over. Suleiman was not a member. He had to retire.

Matters were not so easily left to chance. In late February, much to the consternation of the Israelis, General Tantawi's military council allowed an Iranian frigate, the *Alvand*, to use the Suez Canal for the first time since 1979. More surprises were to follow. Tantawi chose as foreign minister a very conventional figure, Nabil Elaraby, who has worked at the Ministry of Foreign Affairs since the 1970s (he was ambassador to India in the 1980s). In this period, Elaraby led the legal team to Camp David (1978) and to the Taba Conference (1985–89) to settle the terms of the Egyptian-Israeli peace. Nonetheless, right after the February ouster of Mubarak and the entry of Elaraby into office, the old legal advisor sought out Hamas and began to talk about a new strategy for Egyptian-Palestinian relations. Some of this was driven by the role of Kefaya, one of the core organizations of the Tahrir protests whose own roots are in the Palestinian solidarity work during the second intifada of 2000. One outcome of the talks was the freeing up of restrictions on the Rafah Border Crossing between Egypt and Gaza on May 28. There is pressure on the parties that are now part of the political class to revoke the peace agreement and to pressure Israel to forge a lasting peace with those whom they should really be talking to, the Palestinians. Absent a genuine dialogue, the Egyptian people released their frustrations with the 1979 treaty on the Israeli embassy in Cairo in September 2011. Such a move is obviously detrimental to peace, and a violation of the sanctity of diplomacy. Nevertheless, it revealed an Egyptian public whose views on Israel have been suffocated by the enforced peace deal. There is little public support for the 1979 peace deal, and whatever patience existed in Cairo vaporized when Israel conducted its campaign to prevent the Palestinians from taking their case to the United Nations in late September.

Money and threats from Washington fall daily on Tantawi's head. The direction of the Egyptian revolution in the future will have to settle this central question of the core pillar of Atlantic stability in the region, Israel.

The character of the settler-colonial Israeli state and its security are certainly under threat. If it is to be a Jewish State and yet not make a comprehensive and real deal toward the creation of a Palestinian State, it is fated to be mired in a fatal demographic contradiction: by 1976, in the Koenig Memorandum, it was clear that there was going to be an increase in the Arab population (now about 20%) and a flattening or even decrease in the Jewish population (hence the insistence on bringing into Israel the Russian Jewish migrants and others from the Diaspora). The only way to seal off a Jewish State, for those who are so inclined, is to ensure that the Palestinians have their own state. But that is not going to happen unless Israel concedes certain fundamental demands, namely questions of security for the new Palestinian State and reasonable borders. Unless Israel is willing to allow certain demands for the creation of Palestine, it is going to run up against a serious threat to the character of Israel as a Jewish State, as the Koenig Memo made clear. Israel is unwilling to grasp this contradiction. Its elites are in denial. They think that the security (or military) solution is going to be adequate to preserve their hopes. These are rancid, particularly if the non-violent mass demonstrations like those in the first Intifada begin again.

The Arab Spring has provoked three new elements in the Palestinian struggle: first, a surface political unity between Hamas and Fatah; second, the non-violent protests on the Israeli-Syrian border; third, the push by the Palestinians to go to the United Nations General Assembly and ask for a formal declaration of statehood. The nonviolent protests are a real threat to Israel. In February 2010, Israel's military chief Amos Gilad told the US embassy in Tel Aviv, "We don't do Gandhi very well." If more peaceful protests continue, the Israeli Defense Force warned that they would turn to harsher techniques (given the IDF's track record, one wonders what would be harsher than firing into crowds). It was to undercut this that President Obama tried to offer a concession, the declaration of a state of Palestine based on the 1967 border, with swaps to preserve Israel's sense of security. Obama wanted to make a few modest concessions to circumvent the Palestinian positive dynamic (it would look appalling in the context of the Arab Spring for the US to have to wield its veto against the Palestinians in the Security Council). Netanyahu had none of this. He chose to hold fast, believing that the US had to follow his lead as long as Israel remains a major pillar of the old order in the West Asia and North Africa. He was not wrong. The US has a hard time pulling itself away from the most outrageous positions taken by Israel in its dealings with its neighbors, and with the Palestinians. If these three new elements (the unity of the political forces, the nonviolent protests, and the move to the UN) continue, it is going to make things very difficult for the Israelis and for the US—they have gotten used to Hamas' rockets, which are easy to manipulate. It is much harder to legitimize what Baruch Kimmerling calls the "politicide" of the Palestinians because of peace marches toward the Israeli line of control.

Over the question of the Palestinian case to the UN, the pillars of stability rub against each other. The United States fought off a bid by the Palestinians to make their case before the UN Security Council. The Israelis won that gambit. UNESCO accepted the Palestinian Authority as a full member, and the United States declined to honor its fiscal contributions to the cultural agency. To rebuke the Palestinian state rebukes the Arab Spring. To do so also threatens the viability of the other pillars of stability, such as the Saudi monarchy. Hence, in the tumult over the UN vote, Prince Turki al-Faisal wrote in the *New York Times* (September 12), if the US did not support the Palestinians it would lose Saudi Arabia. "With most of the Arab world in upheaval," he wrote, "the 'special relationship' between Saudi Arabia and the United States would increasingly be seen as toxic by the vast majority of Arabs and Muslims, who demand justice for the Palestinian people." If Saudi Arabia remained a pillar of stability, it would lose its own people. If the United States abandoned Israel, it would gain Saudi friendship and it would have an opportunity to "contain Iran and prevent it from destabilizing the region." This is a dilemma: it gave the White House sleepless nights.

By August 2011, Israel was in ferment. The pathways along Rothschild Boulevard in Tel Aviv were packed with Israelis furious at their government for its refusal to engage with their real lives. Inflation and a housing crisis dogged the lives of Israelis, and following the example of Egypt, they convened in their squares, manifesting their discontent. Netanyahu had bragged during the high point of the Arab Spring that such events could not take place in Israel, the "only democracy in the Middle East." Musician Noy Alooshe's video took that line about the world shaking and remixed it with images of crowds in Tel Aviv shouting with the spirit of the Spanish *indignados*, "The People Want Social Justice." Shake Bibi Shake, goes the video, a sort of Ibiza on the Rothschild Blvd. There was no indication that these protests had more than economic goals. There was no link between the unemployment question and the permanent warfare state. There was no open frustration with a government that is keen to bash Palestinians on the head and call that governance. If Israeli political life is able to cleave out a genuine dynamic against its settler-colonial situation, this pillar of stability might make its own accommodation with its neighbors.

Encircle Iran.

Geopolitical ambitions easily overcame any dedication to values of human dignity. Political scientists whose writings are legible to Washington bureaucrats have long divided the Middle East along a simple cardinal line: the status quo powers and the revisionist powers. The status quo powers are those who enable the imperial interests of the Euro-American capitals, and the revisionists are those who threaten these interests.

From 1952 to 1979, the principle status quo power in the Middle East was Iran, with the Shah as the bastion of Progress against the revisionism of the Arab renaissance, under the star of Nasser. Nasser's Free Officers coup of 1952 sent a tremor through the Arab world. The creation of the United Arab Republic (Egypt and Syria) in February 1958 pushed Lebanon into almost terminal civil chaos in May, and in July the Iraqi Free Officers overthrew their feeble king. Inside the palaces of Saudi Arabia, the Free Princes formed a battalion to diminish the autocracy of King Saud. The fusion of Egypt with Syria was not a progressive action in itself. It was done, largely, to eliminate the dynamic Communist Party and the pro-Communist General Afif al-Bizri. The anti-Communism of Nasser was not sufficient to ingratiate him with the bureaucrats in Washington. They despised his anti-imperialism, and later, his unrelenting position on Israel. To be a status quo power, then, was to be a defender of the interests of Washington and London (with Paris in tow) and to be an ally of Israel's erratic strategy for its singular objective. The Shah of Iran stood fast against Nasserism.

A geo-political earthquake tore open the foundation of this map. The first event took place in 1973, when the Yom Kippur War turned out to be a fiasco for the Arab states. Sadat had already turned his back on Nasser's economic and political policies in 1971; foreign investment was being courted and Egypt's constitution adopted a more Islamic tone. Now, Sadat turned tail for Camp David in March 1979, where he accepted an annual American bribe for a peace treaty with Israel. Sadat took home the Nobel Peace Prize, which went on the altar of the new dispensation. A few months before Sadat went to Camp David, his friend Reza Pahlavi, the deposed Shah of Iran, arrived at Assuan, Egypt to begin his long exile around the world before he returned to Egypt's Al-Rifa'i mosque to be buried. The Shah's departure from Iran and Sadat's return from Camp David set in motion the new alliances. Washington now saw Iran under the Mullahs as the leading revisionist power. The bulwark for the United States and Israel was now Sadat's Egypt and Saddam Hussein's Iraq, which was hastily sent off with a pot of money to begin hostilities against Iran (the war lasted from 1980 to 1988, with little territorial gain but a massive loss of life and treasure).

Washington's steady ally before and after this cataclysmic shift was of course Saudi Arabia, and its satellite Gulf emirates. The Saudis' deal with the US goes back to the 1950s, when the steady stream of oil from the Gulf lanes to the gas stations of the heartland was guaranteed as long as the US pledged to protect the shaky monarchies from their hostile neighborhood, and their often hostile populations (by the Saudi Arabian National Guard, heavily armed and often trained by the United States). Nasserism came into the palaces with the Free Princes, who were ejected to exile in Beirut. Then, after 1979, an older danger threatened the Royals. The working-class in eastern Saudi Arabia and in the cities that run from Kuwait to Muscat along the eastern rim of the peninsula are mainly Shi'a. Oil worker protests in Qatif (also called

Little Najaf, the religious city in Iraq) date back to the emergence of the oil industry in the Kingdom. In 1979, after the Iranian Revolution, the workers in the area again went out on strike, but were beaten back ferociously. The *New York Times* did not complain. It was as it should be.

Since 1979, any attempt to move a democratic agenda forward in the Arab world has been tarred with the brush of *Iranianism*, what is generally called "Islamic fundamentalism." It is not Islam or autocracy that worries the planners of the World Order. If that were the case, they should be apoplectic about the Saudi monarchy, whose *Sharia* laws would make the Iranian mullahs blush. What drives Langley and The Harold Pratt House crazy is the issue of Iranian influence, and so of the revision of the power equation in the Middle East. These intellectual bureaucrats stretched the short, tight skin of Shi'ism over the gigantic body of the Arab world. Hamas and Hezbollah are treated as Iranian mailboxes in Palestine and Lebanon respectively.

The Iranian Revolution certainly gave the historically oppressed Shi'a population of the Arabian Peninsula courage to call for self-respect. Eager to live dignified lives, these populations took refuge in religious organizations that provided them with a framework to make their call for dignity comprehensible. Bahrain's al-Wefaq National Islamic Society is, as a US State Department cable candidly noted (September 4, 2008), neither a fundamentalist nor a sectarian party, but it "continues to demand a 'true' constitutional monarchy in which elected officials make policy decisions, the prime minister is accountable to the parliament, and the appointed upper house loses its legislative power." These are elementary, civic claims. But they cannot be honored because they come from al-Wefaq against the power of a King who allows the US to base its Fifth Fleet in his archipelago, and who is fiercely against Iran. It is far easier to tar parties like al-Wefaq as Iran's proxies, and to categorize the simple demands of the people for dignity as "the Shia revival" (as Vali Nasr does in his 2006 blockbuster, *The Shia Revival*).

The uprisings in Tunisia, Egypt, Bahrain, Yemen, Libya and elsewhere threw the geo-political equation into disarray. If Hosni Mubarak looked out of his villa in Sharm el-Sheikh a few days after his arrival there, he would have seen two Iranian vessels (a frigate and a supply ship) power around the bend at Ras Moham-med, up the Gulf of Suez and cross into the Mediter-ranean Sea through the Canal. These two "war ships" docked in Syria on February 24. That Egypt allowed the Iranians to use the Canal for the first time since the 1979 revolution threatened the architecture of US power in the region.

Alireza Nader, of RAND, told the *New York Times*, "I think the Saudis are worried that they're encircled—Iraq, Syria, Lebanon; Yemen is unstable; Bahrain is very uncertain." The US war in Iraq hand-ed the country over to a pro-Iranian regime. In late January, the Hezbollah-backed candidate (Najib Mi-kati) became Prime Minister of Lebanon, and Hamas' hands were strengthened as the Palestinian Author-ity's remaining legitimacy came crashing down when *al-Jazeera* published the Palestine Papers. Ben Ali and Mubarak's exile threw Tunisia and Egypt out of the column of the status quo states. Libya's Qaddafi and Yemen's Saleh have been loyal allies in the War on Terror. Their fall was preordained.

As the status quo withered, its loyal dogs tried out the old chant about the threat of Islamic Fundamentalism. Mubarak's chorus about the Muslim Brotherhood was off key. When Sheikh Yusuf al Qaradawi returned from his exile in Qatar, he did not play the part of Khomeini. The Sheikh opened his sermon in Tahrir Square with a welcome to both Muslims and Christians. Qaddafi's shrieks about a potential al-Qaeda in the Maghreb being formed in the eastern part of Libya repeated the paranoid delusions of the AFRICOM planners. Bahrain's Hamad al-Khalifa hastened to kiss the hem of King Abdullah's substantial *jalabiya*, and to plot together about the Shi'a challenge to the Sunni monarchs. They wished to convert their sectarian histrionics onto their dissenting populations, but al-Wefaq's Khalil Ibrahim al-Marzooq quickly warned that the Saudis might try to flood Bahrain with the kind of mercenary thugs that they would send into Yemen to disrupt the Marxist republic in the 1970s. He was prescient. This is exactly what happened, as we shall see.

In 2008, during the armed confrontation between the Lebanese government and Hezbollah, the Saudi Foreign Minister Saud al-Faisal met with the US Ambassador David Satterfield. Saud feared an "Iranian takeover of all Lebanon." He wanted armed intervention. The Lebanese Armed Forces were not up to the task. Nor was the UN force in south Lebanon, "which is sitting doing nothing." What was needed was for the US and NATO to provide "naval and air cover"

63

and for an "Arab force" drawn from the "Arab periph-
ery." It did not come to pass. But the idea percolates
on the surface of Riyadh's palaces.

The Saudis, the anchor of anti-Iranianism, did not
believe that the US had the spine to act as it must. The
uprisings in Bahrain and Yemen had to be crushed. It
would look bad if this was sanctioned in the name of
the preservation of the monarchy. Far better to see the
protesters as terrorists (as in Yemen) or Iranianists
(as in Bahrain). Or even better yet, to turn this largely
peaceful wave into a new military confrontation. The
hawks of Order had every incentive to enchain the
doves of Change.

VI. On the Rim of Saudi

When Ben Ali flew to Saudi Arabia, he brought with
him to the peninsula the magic of the wave. That's
where events ran into some trouble. The Saudi monarchy found it intolerable that democracy dare to
make its presence felt on its borders. The various
sheikhdoms, some that predate the Saudi one (such as
Bahrain, 1783 to al-Saud's 1932), are ideological and
practical buffer zones. The idea of the Arab monarchy
would be harder to sustain if the only such were in
Riyadh, however rich. It becomes easier to point the
royal finger toward Manama and Kuwait, to suggest
that it is in the temperament of Arabs to be ruled by
their royals, or their tribal chiefs. Saudi Arabia was
prepared to go to any length to vanquish the protests
in Bahrain, which it did with armed force after doing
a monumental deal to which we shall return eventu-

ally. In Yemen, matters were simplified. There was no need to do a deal to send in troops. The president, Ali Abdullah Saleh, is clever. He played the crowds carefully, holding his own support base together with tribal blandishments and with threats about the fear of the notorious South, once home to Marxism and now, by his lights, home to al-Qaeda. Saleh had two other cards in his pocket: (1) that the Saudis did not want instability on the Peninsula, and besides, after attempting to overthrow him in 1994 they have now come to terms with his rule; (2) that the United States and Saudis are petrified of al-Qaeda in the Arab Peninsula (AQAP). Yemen remained on the front pages of the newspapers of the region, and on the inside pages of the Atlantic papers *only* because of the courage of the Yemeni people. But there was *no real* pressure for regime change from either Riyadh or Washington. In fact, Saleh was allowed to get away with murder, as the Saudis have in Manama, because there are limits to what Power is willing to concede in the region. Bahrain and Yemen illuminate the manuscript of Imperialism, a concept that many have increasingly come to deny or misrepresent.

Such protests appear unlikely only because the wave of struggle that broke out on the Peninsula in the late 1950s and peaked in the 1970s was crushed by the early 1980s. Encouraged by the overthrow of the monarch in Egypt by the coup led by Nasser, ordinary people across the Arab world wanted their own revolts. Iraq and Lebanon followed. On the peninsula, the people wanted what Fred Halliday called "Arabia without Sultans." The People's Front for the Liberation of the Occupied Arab Gulf emerged out of the Dhofar (Oman) struggle. It wished to take its local campaign to the entire peninsula. In Bahrain, its more timid branch was the Popular Front. It did not last long. With Nasserism in decline by the 1970s, the new momentum came to this Arabian republican-ism from the Iranian Revolution of 1979. The Islamic Front for the Liberation of Bahrain attempted a coup in 1981. They had the inspiration, but not the organi-zation. This Arab archipelago could not go the way of Yemen, where a revolution allowed a Marxist organi-zation to seize power in 1967. Yemen's Marxists faced ceaseless pressure from the Saudis, their Yemeni allies and the forces of the Atlantic world. In 1990, with the Soviet Union on the wane, the North (led by Saleh) absorbed the South. It was the peninsula's *Die Wende*, the turning point, at about the same time as the two Germanys were united. The pendulum swung in favor of the status quo.

Rumbles have been heard in Saudi Arabia itself over the years. Liberals and Islamists held the cen-ter of the opposition to the regime. The former were constrained by threats and material advances, while if the latter were not susceptible to bribes they were sent off to do *jihad* elsewhere or to contemplate their errors in prison and re-education camps. One has to only look at the kleptocracy that goes by the name Al Saud Inc. to understand the frustrations of the peo-ple. Each of the major royals gets a monthly bursary of $270,000 while minor royals get $800 per month (with a bonus of $3 million at marriage and at the con-struction of a palace). Of the total Saudi budget of $40 billion, $2 billion goes to the core of the al-Saud family itself, who are, the US Embassy in Riyadh complained, "more adept at squandering than accumulating wealth." Popular revulsion against this kind of expenditure is quite general. As Egypt rumbled, the regime put into place its typical maneuvers. Preemptive arrests removed some of the typical culprits. Interior Minister Prince Nayef bin Abdul Aziz met with Saudi newspaper editors and told them that the events in Egypt were the work of outsiders, a theme familiar to tyrants. His half-brother, the King, hastily opened the family's treasury and disbursed $36 billion to quell the economic worries. The official opposition formed a platform of unity: it included the Islamic Umma Party (led by ten well-regarded clerics), the National Declaration of Reform (led by Mohammed Sayed Tayib), al-Dusturieen (a lawyers movement led by Prince Talal bin Abdul Aziz) and a host of reform websites (such as dawlaty.info and saudireform.com). The Islamic Umma Party's Abdul Aziz Mohammed al-Wohaibi told the *Christian Science Monitor*, "We think the royal family is not the only one who has the right to be leader of the country. We should treat the royal family like any other group. No special treatment." This was heresy.

A Facebook group called for a "Days of Rage" protest on March 11. On March 2, one administrator of the site, Faisal Ahmed Abdul-Ahadwas, was killed. The Saudi National Guard was busy with sharp, and barely reported upon, repression. The Days were anemic in the western cities, but stronger in the Eastern Provinces. There the population are much more restive, feeling the bite of social oppression (they are largely Shi'a in an aggressively Sunni state) and of social exploitation (the economic climate has been very rough over the past few years). Cleverly, the governor of the province, Prince Muhammed bin Fahd bin Abdul Aziz al-Saud, met with the dissident leadership, released a few prisoners and spread the King's largess around. It was enough to keep things in check. The only threats on the peninsula that remained were in Yemen and Bahrain.

In October, the hardline Interior Minister Prince Nayef became the Crown Prince. He is now heir to the Saudi throne. The pillar is strengthened by his iron fist.

Yemen.

> "We have a problem called Yemen."
> —Saudi Prince Mohammed bin Nayef,
> Assistant Minister of the Interior to US Ambassador Richard Holbrooke, May 16, 2009.

Events in Yemen escalated faster than anyone could have assumed. In January, street protests opened up the Yemeni struggle in the capital, Sana'a. Quickly protests moved to the south of the country, long an incubator for rebellion, with the cities of Aden and Ta'izz in ferment. The economic crisis provided the early slogans, but these morphed quickly into the reason for unemployment and distress—the political autocracy that smothered the ability of the people to identify their own policies for their country. Within weeks, the demand mimicked that in Tunisia and Egypt, with the very large crowds now calling for the ouster of President Saleh. Opposition leader Tawakel Karman, head of the Women Journalists Without Chains, called for "days of rage." Karman and her fellows have held a weekly protest, every Tuesday, since 2007. They are part of a movement that wishes to change the political dispensation in Yemen, where Saleh has ruled since 1978, one year more than Mubarak. "The combination of dictatorship, corruption, poverty, and unemployment has created this revolution," she pointed out. She and her group of people had been prepared, and as the popular anger came out onto the streets in 2011, they tried to offer leadership. "It's like a volcano. Injustice and corruption are exploding while opportunities for a good life are coming to an end." Karman feared that Saleh's constitutional amendments had converted Yemen into a virtual monarchy. Under pressure, Saleh said he would not seek re-election in 2013. That was a ploy that Mubarak had used. It was already worthless to an enthusiastic population.

Twenty-thousand people flooded Taghyir (Change) Square in Sana'a on February 3. The Common Front, a political alliance that included the main opposition parties (such as Islamist leaning al-Islah and the Yemeni Socialist Party, which was the former ruling party in South Yemen), threw their lot with the protestors. They called for regime change, and were met with tear gas and live ammunition. Mediation between the opposition and Saleh came to nothing.

The tide began to turn in late February, when most of the major tribal heads threw their lot in with the opposition. Sheikh Hussein bin Abdullah al-Ahmar, the head of the Hashid tribal confederation, resigned from the government "in protest at the repression." His act was welcomed by the Baqil, whose leadership also made similar remarks. Sheikh al-Ah-

mar is the brother of Hamid al-Ahmar, a leader of the
Islamist al-Islah party, one of the main groups in the
Joint Meeting Party (the opposition coalition, where
al-Islah commands about forty percent of the seats).
The Hashid defection threatened Saleh's control over
the army, as the loyalty of General Ali Muhsin al-Ahmar, in charge of the northwest division, was no longer certain. He would soon defect to the opposition.
Muhsin al-Ahmar had a reason to fear and despise his
old comrade, Saleh. In 2009, it is rumored that Saleh
colluded with the Saudis to kill Muhsin al-Ahmar
during his wars against the Zaydi Huthi rebels (Saleh
apparently gave the Saudis the coordinates of al-Ahmar, but their air force failed to get him). It is also alleged that Saleh wanted to remove al-Ahmar, the only
credible force preventing the transition of power from
Saleh to his son, Ahmed Ali. Al-Ahmar's defection to
the opposition was credible.

Saleh recognized the signs. He called for a national reconciliation government. This was denied.
Then Saleh refused a proposal for a peaceful transition.
Deaths continued, as the security services routinely
opened fire on the population (forty-five shot dead in
Sana'a on March 18). The tribal armies entered the
cities, confronted by the security services and national
army. Saleh wanted to blame them for the instability,
but Amal al-Basha, head of the Arab Council for Human Rights, would have none of it. "He is the one who
committed crimes and violated the law in the first place.
He is the one who broke the constitution and dragged
the country into violence. He is the one who practiced
state terrorism." By the end of March, the government
lost control of a third of the country.

On March 27, US Defense Secretary Robert Gates reiterated the importance of Saleh to the counter-terrorism offensive in Yemen, against al-Qaeda in the Arabian Peninsula (AQAP). "If the government collapses," Gates told ABC television, "or is replaced by one that is dramatically more weak, then I think we'd face some additional challenges out of Yemen, there's no question about it." AQAP has indeed operated out of Yemen, threatening Saudi Arabia as much as the United States. It was the site of the attack on the USS Cole, and it is from somewhere in Yemen that the Yemeni American cleric Anwar al-Awlaki sent his dispatches and his bombers (including Umar Farouk Abdulmutallab, the "underwear" or Christmas bomber). It was also orders from Yemen that sent the "anus" bomber Abdullah al-Asiri to kill Saudi interior minister Prince Mohammed bin Nayef in September 2009.

Gates' fears also stemmed from actions in Abyan governorate on March 22, when AQAP declared the creation of an Islamic emirate in the province, with strict measures to restrict the movement of women. According to an essay in the *Sydney Morning Herald* written by Sarah Phillips, a scholar of contemporary Yemen, "The declaration overlooks the complexities of Abyan's local landscape, particularly the fact that much of its farming economy relies upon the labour of women. If women are really to remain in their homes the local modes of production will have to shift radically. It is one thing to say that Abyan is an Islamic emirate, but another matter entirely to administer it accordingly without attracting local hostility." Because of this complex landscape, Phillips cautions, neither the Saleh regime nor the AQAP should be taken at their word. "Doing so gives oxygen to sentiments that are abhorred by most Yemenis and constricts the options of those who are committed to genuine change. Real change will be slow, unstable, and non-linear, but it is inevitable."

Despite what Phillips argues, the entanglements between the Saleh regime, the US counterterrorism operation and the Saudis are going to be very difficult to unravel. Over the last few years, Yemen has become a central front in the War on Terror, and a central location in Droneland. In December 2009, General David Petraeus, head of Central Command, came to visit Saleh and talk about the War and Droneland. Saleh gave the US permission to bomb his territory, even if the strike kills civilians alongside *jihadis*. "Yemen insisted it must 'maintain the status quo' regarding the official denial of US involvement," Ambassador Stephen Seche wrote in his role as stenographer. "Saleh wanted operations to continue 'non-stop until we eradicate the disease.'" "We'll continue saying the bombs are ours, not yours," Saleh told Petraeus. His Deputy, Rashad al-Alimi said that he had just lied to parliament, telling it that the bombs are American, but fired by Yemenis. Petraeus pointed out that Saleh must tell the Yemeni customs to stop "holding up Embassy cargo at the airport, including shipments destined for the [Yemeni government] itself, such as equipment of [Yemen's Counter Terrorism Unit]." Meanwhile, Saleh wanted money (he got millions) and equipment (helicopters and IED-jamming devices). Petraeus was less eager about the equipment. Saleh was angry. Americans are "hot blooded and hasty when you need us," he said presciently, "but "cold blooded and British when we need you." On September 30, a US drone strike assassinated al-Awlaki and his associate the Yemeni American al-Qaeda journalist Samir Khan somewhere between the provinces of Marib and al-Jawf. Both were American nationals.

The United States was wrong-footed over the Yemen protests. It could not afford to alienate Saleh, who still remained in control of the counter-terrorism apparatus. Nor could it go ahead of the Saudis, who remained happy with Saleh (he has a close ally in bin Nayef, the deputy interior minister of the Saudis).

Enter the Gulf Cooperation Council, the Arab NATO. In late April, as events seemed at a bloody standstill, the GCC entered with a proposal that Saleh pledge to leave and the opposition stand down. Saleh refused to sign the proposal thrice, and after his May 22 refusal, the GCC walked out. The violence escalated, until Saleh was injured in a 3 June bombing of his compound. Wounded, Saleh fled to Saudi Arabia for medical treatment leaving his deputy Abd al-Rab Mansur al-Hadi in charge, his son Ahmed in charge of the Republican Guard and his brother Khaled in a position of decisive authority over the army. These are the people whom the protestors called the "Orphans of Saleh."

The military is split into two factions: Ahmed Ali holds the Yemeni government for his father, via his command over the Republican Guard (his cousins Yahya and Ammar hold the Central Security Forces and the National Security Bureau respectively); Ali Muhsin al-Ahmar, Saleh's main military man is now with the rebellion. The Saudis hedged their bets between Saleh's return and al-Ahmar's accession to the presidency.

The protests continued. In mid-September, the First Armored Division under the command of al-Ahmar clashed with the Republican Guard of the Saleh family. Shells fell between Taghyir Square, where the opposition created a tent city, and the Kentucky Roundabout, held by the Republican Guard. The fear was that under cover of the tumult of the Arab Spring, and taking advantage of the massive civilian protests against Saleh, al-Ahmar might conduct a conventional coup.

By early January 2012, Saleh pushed through an amnesty law. Granted immunity from prosecution, and given allowance for his family to maintain control over the forces of repression, Saleh withdrew on behalf of his Vice-President Hadi. Protests broke out once more against the immunity deal that was pushed through the parliament. Amnesty International and Human Rights Watch agreed with the protestors. The draft law, noted Amnesty, is a "smack in the face for justice, made all the more glaring by the fact that protesters have been calling for an end to impunity since mass protests began in early 2011."

Saudi machinations are rumored. The United States remains silent. There is no call for any human rights investigation or for the withdrawal of the amnesty deal. There is no discussion of substance in the United Nations. Silence descends upon Yemen.

In October, Tawakel Karman won the Nobel Peace Prize. The committee wanted the prize to deliver "an important signal to women all over the world," removing Karman from her precise context. She would have none of it. This prize, she pointed out, "is a victory for Arabs around the world and a victory for Arab women…. I am so happy, and I give this award to all of the youth and all of the women across the Arab world, in Egypt, in Tunisia…. The fight for democratic Yemen will continue."

Bahrain.

> *"Give us back our Bahrain.*
> Return this country to its people;
> to *us*, its people.
> *Our Bahrain is ours."*
> —Ayat al-Qurmezi, Bahraini poet,
> February 23, Pearl Square.

On Valentine's Day, a protest march in Manama, Bahrain, had no love for the al-Khalifa royal family. It wanted to deliver a message. They did not pick the day for obvious reasons, but because it was the anniversary of the vote on a National Charter delivered by the monarch on February 14, 2002. That vote, ninety-eight percent in favor, was recorded, and its meaning filed into the royal archives. It was enough to make the promise and have the people ratify it. Not much was done to put it into action. "Our demand is a constitution written by the people," the protestors chanted. Opposition leader Abdul-Wahab Hussain said, "The number of riot police is huge, but we have shown using violence against us only makes us stronger." The police fired rubber bullets and dispersed the as yet small crowd on February 14. "This is just the beginning," Hussain said after he was beaten off the streets. The main leadership found itself behind bars: Hassan Mushaima (Haq movement), Ibrahim

Sharif (Waad Society) and Hussain (Wafa). Sheikh Ali Salman of the al-Wefaq Party urged the people to return to their protests.

Haq, Waad, Wafa, al-Wefaq: these are the contours of the contemporary revolt in Bahrain. They are the children of the protests of the 1990s, when a reform movement formed to push King Hamad bin Isa al-Khalifa to follow the stipulations of the 1973 Constitution. The al-Khalifa regime met these protests with stiff resistance. The new ruler, Hamad (a graduate of Cambridge University), was smart. He knew a thing or two about hegemony. Not enough to smash the heads of the Islamists or the Shi'a parties, he hastily called for an elected parliament, allowed women to vote, and released some political prisoners (this was the grandly named National Charter of Bahrain, 2001). It was enough to please Washington, where the liberal internationalists smiled to hear of these paper reforms, and where the oil companies nodded their heads sagely, for they do not like disturbances to their business. Nothing like stability that looks like democracy.

The Egyptian virus of 2011, however, overcame the façade of democracy erected by Hamad. Protests returned and on February 19, large numbers came and occupied Pearl Square in Manama.

On February 23, a young poet, Ayat al-Qurmezi read out her impassioned poem for Bahrain. "Our Bahrain is Ours," she bravely intoned. She was arrested and jailed, one of many to taste the hospitality of the al-Khalifa family's considerable prisons. "Bahrain's phony veneer of a progressive, liberal form of rule has been crushed before the world," said Ali Jawad, a member of the AhlulBayt Islamic Mission.

The regime went after doctors and hospitals (such as Dr. Sadeq Abdullah at the Salmaniya Medical Centre) where victims of the repression were being treated, and the state arrested human rights lawyers (such as Mohammed al-Tajer) who were representing the grievances from below.

The contagion was not only political. It was also, and perhaps decisively, economic. Bahrain relies upon oil for its wealth. Oil money spawned real estate speculation (the Dubai model). The beneficiaries of this process have been the royal family and a crony clique. In 2009, US-based Occidental Petroleum, UAE-based Mubadala Development and the National Oil and Gas Authority of Bahrain formed the Tatweer Petroleum firm to secure about $20 billion as investment toward doubling Bahrain's oil and natural gas production. It is an ambitious plan.

Bahrain's oil was discovered in 1932 and by 1934 it was the first country to export its oil to Europe. A British protectorate against the Ottoman Empire, Bahrain provided oil and protection for the sea-lanes from powers that sought to rival British dominion over the Indian Ocean. In December 1934, a group of educated Bahrainis drafted a petition to their titular ruler, Sheikh Hamad bin Isa al-Khalifa (who answered to Sir Charles Dalrymple Belgrave, who fashioned himself as Belgrave of Bahrain). No real reforms were forthcoming, and so in 1938, Shi'a and Sunni leaders (educated merchants and intellectuals) joined with the oil workers (who went on strike) to call for an elected legislature and the other trappings of democracy (including legal trade unions). They were crushed. Their leaders were sent to India. A second revolt, this time helped along by Nasserism, between 1954 and 1956 was equally beaten back (its leaders were sent to the cell in St. Helena that once housed Napoleon). There was little of religion in these movements from below. They wanted a better share of the oil profits, and respect.

Independence from Britain in 1971 was greeted by a new struggle for constitutionalism. The al-Khalifa ruler went to visit the leading Shi'a cleric, Ayatollah Mohsin al-Hakim in his base in Najaf (Iraq), to urge him to moderate the "Shi'a demands." It was in the interest of the al-Khalifas to color the demands from below as sectarian. A toothless constitutionalism was set up. Frustration with the pace of reform was heightened after the Iranian Revolution, and the older (Akhbari Shi'a) traditions found themselves marginalized by the more aggressive political Shi'ism that emanated from Qom (Iran). Sheikh Ali Salman, the current head of the al-Wefaq party, comes from this latter tradition, schooled in King Saud University (chemistry) and then in the famous al-Hawzah al-Arabiyyah in Qom (he was there during the first Gulf War). A renewed constitutional attempt in the early 1990s was once more crushed and Ali Salman had to leave Bahrain. It set the stage for the King's new constitution of 2002 that made the King truly sovereign and the various bodies purely advisory. The Shi'a leader of the time, Sheikh Abdul Amir al-Jamal said of it, "this is not the type of parliament we had demanded." Al-Jamal died in 2006, leaving the field to Sheikh Isa Ahmed Qassim and his protégé, Ali Salman.

The vast mass, mainly Shi'a, are enraged that Bahrain's wealth has had almost no social outlet. Afraid of the Shi'a population, the monarch imported 50,000 foreign workers to reconfigure the demographic landscape. This Bahranization policy was a smokescreen to pit the (local) labor against the (foreign) labor. It has not worked. To top it off, an outcome of the credit crunch since 2007 has been the Bahrain government's proposal to cut subsidies of food and fuel. These cuts had to be hastily withdrawn because of popular anger. Young people are at the forefront of the revolts because they have the most to lose from the austerity cuts, and from the policies that mortgage their futures.

Money is the oil that lubricates the counter-revolution. The Saudi royal family threw out its billions. The Gulf Cooperation Council decided to turn over $20 billion to the beleaguered monarchies of Bahrain and Oman. Recycled cabinets are not enough for this popular upsurge, and the bullets fired into the crowd have failed to have the required pedagogical effect. The people will not stop their obligation to democracy. Money was effective, but not enough for many who wanted regular access to the fruits of their labor not charity to quell disquiet.

The emirs stoked the fires of the Shi'a Revival. Their response to the Pearl Square protests was to inaugurate what Nabeel Rajab of the Bahrain Centre for Human Rights calls a "campaign for sectarian cleansing." Shi'a areas and mosques became targets, even as the ordinary population refused to be drawn into the masquerade of sectarianism. They are not alone. US Defense Secretary Robert Gates left a testy meeting with King Abdullah of Saudi Arabia in early April with his talking points reaffirmed. "We already have evidence that the Iranians are trying to exploit the situation in Bahrain," he said, "And we also have evidence that they are talking about what they can do to try and create problems elsewhere as well." That elsewhere was probably the Eastern Province of Saudi, the area that gives nightmares to the residents of Yamama Palace in Riyadh.

The Baharnah, the indigenous Shi'a of Bahrain, have a political party, the al-Wefaq, that certainly speaks for the Shi'a working class and middle class who feel a great sense of alienation from Bahrain's institutions. However, this alienation was not always so. In other words, it is not a sectarian alienation whose roots might be found in the eighth century. Rather, the Shi'a distress in Bahrain has modern roots, even if these are refracted through older lineages. It is an alienation from oil more than a theological dispute against the Sunnis. The al-Wefaq Party has its spiritual roots, no doubt, but its social base grows out of grievances that have a much more mundane foundation.

Whatever their temperament, the Wefaq Party led by Ali Salman is not in a position to create the *vilayat-e faqih*, the guardianship of the clerics. In collaboration with six other parties, it had made a reasonable demand, that the current government resign and that a new transition government "whose hands have not been stained with the blood of the martyrs" help "pave the way for the transition to real reforms." They point to housing and income, to corruption and monarchical excess as their spurs. Also here is talk of discrimination, and the "exclusion of competent national talent." The party is backed by the clerics of Bahrain. This association leads al-Wefaq to often take very peculiar positions (against the hanging of underwear in the University of Bahrain, and for segregated housing between Bahraini nationals and South Asian contract workers). The party does, however, command the loyalty of a very large number of people, a fact admitted by US Ambassador Adam Ereli on September 4, 2008 in a dispatch to Washington, "The Wefaq party remains the most popular party among the majority Shi'a underclass and advocates non-violent political activism on behalf of the Shi'a community."

The counter-revolution counts on sectarianism to tear apart the Arabian resistance. During Israel's war on Lebanon in 2006 and the Shi'a-Sunni conflict in Iraq, the establishment Sunni clerics in Saudi Arabia went on an anti-Shi'a rampage. Clerics such as Safar al-Hawali and Nasir al-'Umar preached exclusively through an anti-Shi'a lens. 'Abd al-Rahman al-Barrak produced a *fatwa* in December 2006 that declared the Shi'a to be *takfir*, enemies of the Sunnis. In the last months of 2006, Toby Jones notes in the *International Journal of Middle East Studies*, the security forces "arrested Shi'is from Qatif and the surrounding areas, reportedly for supporting Hezbollah." Ten years before, in Bahrain, the minister for justice and Islamic Affairs, Sheikh Abd Allah bin Khalid al-Khalifa, threatened "some Islamic movements" for "taking an extremist path," and so allowed his security agencies to take the violent path against them, mainly Shi'a. It was a convenient way to pollute the waters of grievance.

In 1845, a British official watched unrest take hold in Bahrain. He wrote, "Numbers of the principal and most wealthy inhabitants, to avoid the effects of increased anarchy and confusion, fled upon the commencement of actual hostilities to Koweit on the Arabian and to Lingah and other places on the Persian Coast, where they have since temporarily located themselves, in order to watch the course of events, and return with the first signs of peace and established government, and consequent security to life and property." The forces of counter-revolution in 2011, similarly, watched and waited for its agents to do its work for it. It too wants to preserve life and property, but not those of the masses; only its own life and its own property. It counts on its allies in the North to bring the cavalry if things turn dire.

The Pearl Square protests sent a shiver through the Washington establishment for two reasons. Firstly, the archipelago on the eastern flank of the Arabian Peninsula is home to the US Navy's Fifth Fleet. It is just a few miles off the coast of Iran, and able to fully support the US adventures in West Asia and in East Africa. If the monarchy in Bahrain falls, there is every indication that a civilian government led by al-Wefaq will ask the Fleet to depart. An economically strapped Dubai might welcome a base, but that would look poorly for its desire to be a Global City. The velvet glove of Commerce likes to distance itself from the iron fist of Military force. Qatar already hosts the al-Udeid Air Base, but the US must share this with the ever expanding Qatari air force's own needs. Secondly, the US does not wish to allow the domino of republicanism to begin in Bahrain. US Assistant Secretary of State Jeffrey Feltman and the chairman of the Joint Chiefs of Staff Admiral Mike Mullen went on a tour of the emirates' capitals, declaring their unconditional support. The US stands for "universal human rights," Feltman told the emirs, but of course since "every country is unique" these rights would emerge in their own way. Mullen was at hand to "reassure, discuss and understand what's going on." The key word here is reassure.

In 2010, the US government inked a $60 billion arms deal with Saudi Arabia. The kit includes UH-60 Blackhawk and MH-6 Little Bird helicopters, very useful in counter-insurgency. When the Peninsula's political temperature rises, those helicopters will be the "first signs of peace and established government" in the region. At the Fifth Fleet base, Vice Admiral Mark Fox kept the EA-6B Prowlers powered up for emergency action. The deployment is essential for US war aims in West Asia and in the Gulf region—mainly as a deterrent against Iran through the patrolling of the oil lanes, especially the Straits of Hormuz. There is no way that the US or the Saudis would allow al-Khalifa to fall and a party like al-Wefaq, however popular, to come to power. Such an outcome would strengthen what Washington and Riyadh see as the revisionist bloc, led by Iran.

As it happened, US intervention was not needed. The Arab NATO took care of the problem itself.

VII. The Arab NATO

The Iranian Revolution of 1979 threw the United States, the Atlantic powers and the Gulf Arabs into disarray. At one stroke, the United States lost its gendarme of the oil lands—the Shah had been a reliable ally, with Kissinger calling him a "tough, mean guy" (this was opposed to the Saudis, whom Kissinger thought of as "the most feckless and gutless of the Arabs"). The Shah's replacement, the Ayatollah Khomeini and his clerics, disdained the Americans for their support of the Savak regime, and had no love for the Gulf Arabs either. Nevertheless, their general tenor was that they wanted to consolidate their "Islamic Revolution in One Country." Export of their brand of Islamism and *vilayat-e faqih* was not in the cards. The Islamic Republic had many problems within the country, and most pressing for the myopic regime was to set up their moral surveillance networks even though the most pressing for the people was the economic situation. Angered by the hostage crisis, Carter nudged Saddam Hussein, the Iraqi strongman, to open an all-out war against his Iranian neighbors. That war, the Iran-Iraq war, bled the two countries from 1980 to 1988 with one and a half million dead and untold amounts of the treasury wasted. The Reagan administration handed Saddam Hussein the cutting-edge dual-use military and civilian technology, including chemicals that would be used to make the weapons against the Iranian Basij-e Mostaz'afin, the great mobilization of the oppressed whose human waves were cut down by Iraqi chemical weapons. In 1986, the UN Security Council proposed to censure Iraq for its use of chemical weapons, illegal since the 1925 Geneva Protocol; the United States was alone in its vote against the statement. Reagan's National Security Council staffer Geoffrey Kemp recalled the sentiment toward Saddam, the mercenary for the United States and the Gulf Arabs, "We knew he was an S. O. B., but he was our S. O. B."

The Gulf Arabs feared less the "Shi'a Revival," with all its sectarian implications, and more the revolutionary egalitarian rhetoric from Tehran. Khomeini's pledge to take from the "privileged few" (*mustakbarin*) and give to the "under-privileged masses" (*mustaz afin*) threatened the foundations of the Gulf Arab emirates. They also feared retribution for setting Saddam on the Iranians. In October 1980, Iranian President Hojatolislam Ali Khamenei warned, "We are determined to send Saddam to hell. His collaborations' turn will come later. I am referring to the shaykhs in the Gulf region whose governments have supported unbelief against Islam."

On May 25, 1981, the emissaries of Bahrain, Kuwait, Oman, Qatar, Saudi Arabia and the United Arab Emirates (UAE) formed the Cooperation Council of the Arab Gulf States, known more generally as the Gulf Cooperation Council, the GCC, or as I would have it, the Arab NATO. The agenda was broad, including economic relations and a monetary union, but the concerns were narrow: military cooperation and collaboration against Iranian revisionism. The GCC's creation was welcomed in the Atlantic world (UK Prime Minister Margaret Thatcher wrote to Reagan on September 1981, pointing out that there "may be some genuine substance behind the newly developing Gulf Cooperation Council which could, in time, evolve along the lines of ASEAN," the Association of South East Asian States, more an economic than a military organization).

When the Bahraini authorities uncovered a coup attempt by the Islamic Front for the Liberation of Bahrain in December 1981, pressure on the military front escalated. The Bahrainis claimed that the Islamic Front was based in Tehran, although the group contained mainly Bahrainis, with some Kuwaitis, Saudis and Omanis. In February 1982, GCC Secretary General Abdullah Bisharah said, "What happened in Bahrain was not directed against one part of the body but against the whole body," an enigmatic way of saying that this was not just a coup against Bahrain, but against the Gulf Arab dispensation. Saudi Interior Minister Prince Nayef chided Iran for its "sabotage activities," and noted pointedly, "They have unfortunately become the terrorists of the Gulf." The Bahrain incident gave the GCC the opportunity it needed to set aside the minor parts of its agenda, and move to the main course.

By March 1982, the GCC formed a joint military force ("neither NATO nor the Red Army," said Bisharah). A series of hasty summit meetings across 1982 cemented the alliance, with a Defense Pact agreed upon in November. In deference to Iran's strength at that time, the GCC did not move to a formal mutual defense pact. That would have been a *casus belli* that they wished to avoid. In early 1983, the GCC held its first military exercises in the UAE, which over the years got more and more sophisticated, as the GCC states have used their petro-dollars to buy more and more high tech weaponry and training from the Atlantic states. Between the Saudi Eurofighter Typhoons and the UAE's F-16s, the GCC is close to demonstrable air superiority over the Iranians. But the real power will not come from any maddening war against Iran (the Iraqis already showed that this was going to be bloody and senseless affair). The real military build-up was for domestic repression. The GCC very quickly set up the capacity to exchange intelligence and to mutually train each other using the best riot control equipment on the market. Article 1 of the security control document of the GCC, after all, elides "opponents of regimes" with "criminals." On February 23, 1982, Prince Nayef supported the formation of a "Gulf internal security force to defend Gulf security and to be called the Gulf Rapid Deployment Force." Two years later, the GCC created the Peninsula (*Jazeera*) Shield Force, based in Saudi Arabia at King Khalid Military City and ready to deploy in the region when called upon.

The GCC's conundrum was made more complex when the Bush administration hastened to war against Afghanistan in 2001 and Iraq in 2003. What the Bush adventures did was deliver a gift to Iran, removing in two blows Iran's enemies on its two main borders (the Taliban to the east and Saddam Hussein to the west). In both cases, the new regime had a soft spot for Iran—in Afghanistan, apart from the old Iranian friend Ismail Khan of Herat there are a number of Afghans in government now who took refuge in Iran during the Civil War in the 1990s and the Taliban rule thereafter; in Iraq, the governing Islamic Dawa Party and its ally the Supreme Islamic Iraqi Council have long-standing ties with the Iranian government, as does the more radical Sadr Movement. The removal of Iran's enemies from its borders has now emboldened the regime, and thereby threatened the Gulf Arabs. Their scramble to bring the GCC's military arm to life once more has to be seen in the context of the revival of Iranian influence.

As the temperature continued to rise in Bahrain in 2011, the Saudis itched to act. The demonstrators refused to leave the Pearl Square Roundabout, in whose center was a three hundred foot sculpture of six arches holding a pearl. Each arch represented a *dhow*, the sail of a ship, and each of these represented one of the six members of the GCC. It was erected in 1982 to commemorate the first GCC summit held in the emirate, and an image of it came onto the half dinar coin of the realm. The GCC had to clear out the menace of instability that gathered at the monument to the GCC's emergence. It was an ironic moment.

A clear way forward appeared to the Saudi court when events in Libya and Syria took a turn for the worse. In Bahrain's Pearl Square, the protestors chanted *silmiyya, silmiyya*, peaceful, peaceful. To enter with military force against this cry would look very poorly on the Gulf Arab emirates. But the evolution of the conflict in Libya and Syria sent a chill through the Arab Spring. No longer the resolute protestors of Tunisia and Egypt, now the guns had come out, and even if the conflict was asymmetrical, no longer could the opposition claim to be peaceful. The heavy hand of State repression that followed in Libya and Syria opened the door for the Gulf Arab emirates. Now it was a question of handling the opportunity.

VIII. The Arab Spring

The social crisis engendered by the inflation of food prices triggered long-felt grievances against the national security state and the institutions of neoliberal economic policy. Places where a political culture had been incubated by brave activists and by workers' movements, such as Tunisia and Egypt, had the fastest dynamic forward. Grizzled leaders withdrew, and despite the attempts by the US and its Gulf allies to manage the transition, the people continue to move their agenda. Tahrir Square is rarely quiet. When the process toward freedom stalls, the Square fills up again. The contradictions of governance shall slow down some of the momentum, but not by much. The revolutionary destiny in these countries has been unleashed.

Elsewhere, the calculations of the powerful tried to derail the emergence of the Arab Spring. The early victims were Bahrain and Yemen. They could not be permitted to have their breakthrough. Too much was at stake. Legitimacy for the Gulf regimes would have been questioned, and this was not permissible as far as the US and its European allies were concerned. Addiction to oil produces a symbiotic relationship with the Gulf monarchies. Pretensions of liberty have to be set aside when it comes to Riyadh and Doha. The GCC was allowed to act to put down these expressions of democracy.

Cover for the action of the Arab NATO was provided by the convulsions in Libya, where the dynamic of the Arab Spring was to turn into the Winter of Arab discontent. Libya's Qaddafi was easily disposable. Protests against him that began in earnest in the 1990s had not been taken seriously outside Libya, and indeed when Qaddafi had previously cracked down (as he did in 1996) there was barely any forceful criticism of his regime. Over the past ten years, Qaddafi's strong-arms have faced less sanction than they have been used for the War on Terror. When the protests broke out in March and when these morphed into armed rebellion against Qaddafi, they provided the best fog for the conversion of the previously peaceful Arab Spring into a military conflict. The Libyan revolt was not conjured up by magicians who rule the Atlantic states, and nor can it be reduced to their machinations. But to ignore the guiles of the Atlantic states and the Gulf emirs is to blind oneself to the operations of the counter-revolution in the midst of what is the most important political development thus far in the twenty-first century.

Part 2. Libyan Winter.

I. The Bang That Ends Qaddafi's Rule

"Like me, you now await your cross with dread.
Whenever night falls, the echoes of a
phonograph record bring you back.
You traitor. Yes. The worst of all is to have
betrayed."
—Muhammad Farhat al-Shaltami,
"Indictment," July 26, 1969 (tr. Elliot Cola).

The WikiLeaks cache of US State Department documents from Embassy Tunisia revealed some rather sordid details about the life of Ben Ali and his family. One such cable, from 2008, noted, "President Ben Ali's extended family is often cited as the nexus of Tunisian corruption. Often referred to as a quasi-mafia, an oblique mention of 'the Family' is enough to indicate which family you mean. Seemingly half of the Tunisian business community can claim a Ben Ali connection through marriage, and many of these relations are reported to have made the most of their lineage. Ben Ali's wife, Leila Ben Ali, and her extended

family—the Trabelsis—provoke the greatest ire from
Tunisians. Along with the numerous allegations of
Trabelsi corruption are often barbs about their lack
of education, low social status, and conspicuous consumption." Revelations such as these provoked the
final disgust with Ben Ali. He lost legitimacy. There
was nothing left.

Across the border, in Tripoli, Libya, Muammar
al-Qaddafi once more opted for the erratic. He went
on Libyan State Television on January 16, and then
offered his statement of support for Ben Ali (oddly
calling WikiLeaks Kleenex), "Even you, my Tunisian brothers. You may be reading this Kleenex and
empty talk on the Internet. This Internet, which any
demented person, any drunk can get drunk and write
in; do you believe it? The Internet is like a vacuum
cleaner. It can suck anything. Any useless person: any
liar, any drunkard, anyone under the influence; anyone high on drugs: can talk on the Internet. And you
read what he writes and you believe it. This is talk
which is for free. Shall we become the victims of Facebook and Kleenex and YouTube? Shall we become
victims to tools they created so that they can laugh at
our moods?" Ben Ali had already left his post. Qaddafi perhaps feared that the contagion would spread
into Libya, and to an extent it did. But the fate that
would befall Qaddafi was not spread by WikiLeaks
or Facebook or even the dreaded YouTube (where I
watched his January 16 speech). It would come from
older movements, with deeper roots and grievances.

Around January 16, Qaddafi remained a loyal
soldier in the US-led War on Terror and in the promotion of neoliberal consumerism (apart from his general

"uncle-like" antipathy to information technology). In this way, Qaddafi resembled Ben Ali and Mubarak, which is perhaps what provoked his television address. In early February 2011, the IMF said of Libya that it has followed its "ambitious reform agenda" and the Fund encouraged Libya's "strong macroeconomic performance and the progress on enhancing the role of the private sector." These are all things that were said of Tunisia (praised by the IMF for its "wide-ranging structural reforms" and "prudent macroeconomic management" in September 2010) and Egypt (praised by the IMF for its five years of "reforms and prudent macroeconomic policies," in April 2010): neoliberal consumerism set aside the social costs to the population, the human sector that was not sound and did not benefit from prudent state policies. The pain of the IMF-led policies pushed the needle of distress beyond the bearable. Combined with the lack of democracy and the harshness of the security state, it is no wonder that the contagion spread as rapidly as it did.

Libya, however, did not suffer the sharp rise in grain prices, nor the overarching distress afforded by the global credit crunch that began in 2007. The centrally planned economy cushioned the macroeconomic indicators from the kind of free-fall that took place in Tunisia and Egypt. There were no bread riots in late 2010, nor was the protest in February linked directly to economic matters. Other issues took center stage in Libya, mainly anger at the suppression of genuine democratic opportunities for the population.

Rumors of a demonstration on February 17, 2011 hastened the hand of the Qaddafi regime. Two days before, the police arrested human rights lawyer Fathi

Terbil Salwa and the novelist Idris al-Mesmari. They, along with other lawyers such as Salwa al-Dighaili, made up the leadership of the February 17 Movement, formed to commemorate the date of the 2006 police firing in Benghazi at a demonstration which killed ten, and to build the movement for civil liberties that grew out of it. In 2006, the police opened fire at a crowd that assembled before the Italian consulate in Benghazi to protest against the Italian minister Roberto Calderoli, who had worn a t-shirt that depicted an offensive and Islamophobic cartoon published by the Danish newspaper *Jyllands-Posten*. Not only was this demonstration against the tide of Islamophobia sweeping through Europe, but it was also against the old colonial power, Italy, whose minister seemed to relish being hateful. That the police opened fire to defend the consulate of the old colonial power sent a chill through Benghazi, where there were deep roots of anger against the Qaddafi regime.

What was so remarkable about the 2006 protest and the movement that built on it was its catholic reach: the original protestors were largely political Islamists as well as pious Muslims and those who defended them were middle-class professionals and intellectuals (Terbil, al-Dighaili and al-Mesmari, for instance). The police firing revived deep-seated anger at the way Qaddafi's regime has treated the eastern part of the country (the old Ottoman *vilayat* of Cyrenaica), and it underscored the basic military state character of the Qaddafi regime, easy to turn to guns when other means lay at its disposal.

A few hundred people gathered outside the police headquarters to protest the arrest of Terbil and al-Mismari. The police broke up the crowd, and the Qaddafi regime sent the interior minister Abdullah Senussi and Sa'adi Qaddafi to take charge of the city. Sa'adi, who gives off the impression of being lost, fancies himself as a peace-maker and tried to walk the streets of Benghazi to that end. His charms were lost on the city. It was a failed mission. Enthused protestors gathered at the Maydan al-Shajara, where they fought off the police attempt to break up their resolve. News of the Benghazi revolt spread to other towns, and in Al Bayda' and Az Zintan the protestors burned down the traffic police headquarters and the police station respectively. The revolt, in earnest, tried to match the state repression with its own violence. There was no other way to go. Qaddafi's Libya would not tolerate a Gandhi. It had to be fought with force of arms.

On February 17, the Days of Rage protest was larger than it would have been had Qaddafi's regime not made the arrests two days before hand. Those arrests provided the best advertisement for the protests. Rumors spread that Qaddafi's regime, like Mubarak's before him, released thirty prisoners, armed them, and sent them to shoot at the protestors. Fourteen people died that day, with some additional killed in sporadic fighting in Al Bayda', Az Zintan and Darnah. The numbers were not huge, but they are of course considerable (ten here, thirteen there). Undaunted, the next day, the protestors in Al Bayda' captured a military base. In a sign of what was to come, the rebels executed "fifty African mercenaries and two Libyan conspirators" (according to *al-Jazeera*). In Derna, the rebels burnt down a police station, where prisoners died in their cells. Focus remained on the institutions of repression, the police and the military.

On February 20, a forty-eight year old executive at the state oil company, Mahdi Ziu, filled his truck with propane tanks and drove into the gates of Benghazi's *katiba*, the barracks that housed the main force of the regime. Protestors rushed in, and took the barracks.

By February 21, the city was in the hands of the rebels. Qaddafi's envoys (Sa'adi Qaddafi and Abdullah Senussi) fled back to Tripoli. The hasty speed of the fall of Benghazi showed the brittleness of the regime. Its base of support in the city was negligible, and its command over the repressive apparatus minimal. Those that remained with Qaddafi, such as the troops in the Elfedeel Bu Omar compound, were besieged and, as news reports put it, "butchered by angry mobs."

UN High Commissioner for Human Rights Navi Pillay denounced the behavior of the Libyan government. More condemnation would come soon. On February 22, the former British Foreign Minister David Owen called for "military intervention" and on February 23, Luxemburg's Foreign Minister Jean Asselborn called the situation "genocide." The words genocide and military intervention were chilling. They represented a push from the Atlantic powers to transform the rebellion into a massacre, and to insert themselves into North Africa and its Spring. Events on the ground did not suggest that things were so bleak for the rebels. The rebel's advance continued, and by the end of February the rebels had seized Libyan Air Force planes and Libyan navy ships. For which reason, on February 27, Abdul Hafiz Ghoga, a senior lawyer and human rights campaigner, announced in Benghazi, "We are completely against foreign intervention. The rest of Libya will be liberated by the people and Qaddafi's security forces will be eliminated by the people of Libya."

Ghoga's assertion was to be of no consequence by March 1, when the leadership of the newly created National Transitional Council of Libya (NTC) joined with the Atlantic powers, and the Gulf Arab emirs, to call for foreign intervention. The French, British and Americans hastened to put through a confusing resolution in the United Nations on March 17 (UN Resolution 1973). Aerial bombardment by NATO began on March 19. In no time, Qaddafi's military prowess was degraded. It took a few months for the NATO aerial and naval power to fully wipe out Qaddafi's regime, and for the rebels on the ground to make the most of the air cover to assert themselves over the Libyan landscape. On August 22, the rebel forces took Tripoli. Qaddafi disappeared. On October 20, Qaddafi was killed in Sirte, his hometown.

The future of Libya remained an open question. Would the Libyan rebels set aside the many sectarian (religious and tribal) affiliations that bedeviled them, and combine to properly fight off the Qaddafi regime? If it succeeded, what kind of Libya would these rebels create? During the military campaign, the rebels refused to succumb to a unified military command, which is what NATO preferred and so did NATO's generals, such as the CIA asset General Khalifa Belqasim Hifter. The rebels wanted to fight in a military coalition. This meant that with the fall of Tripoli, the rebel command remained diffuse. There was no civil war as such, but there was no unity either. There was a government, but no state with the authority to enforce its laws on the population. Each city (Misrata, Zintan, Dernah) has its own military authority, with little coordination amongst them and very little respect for the central government. There is still every indication that the neoliberal clique that authored the NTC remain in control over the main arteries of accumulation in Libya, notably the oil ministry and the central bank. It is these people, as journalist Patrick Cockburn comments, that "speak the best English" and are "prepared to go before [the United States] Congress to give fulsome gratitude for America's actions." Or as the *Middle East Report* editorial of March 23 warned, these are the people who "are apt to be the most willing to give favorable terms to Western oil firms for invigorated exploration and exploitation of the country's hydrocarbon deposits." Libya remains in political paralysis. It is not clear what kind of political dispensation will form. What is clear is that the new Libya has opened itself to the neoliberal reformers in a way that they found difficult even under a pliant Qaddafi. The rebels from below, who spent the most blood in the conflict, are not the immediate beneficiaries of the revolution, but they are not quiet. They retain their guns. They have their imaginations for a new Libya. What comes is to be seen. But how did we get here?

The "humanitarian intervention" from the Atlantic states and the Gulf Arabs attempted to wrest the dynamic from the rebellion from below, and from the Arab Spring in general. That it has not been able to succeed fully is a testament to the deep springs of suspicion about imperialism that linger across West Asia and North Africa, and to the faith of the people in their wanting control of their own lives. In November 1942, when Field Marshall Erwin Rommel's Afrika Korps was defeated by the Allies in Benghazi, Tobruk and then El Alamein, British Prime Minister Winston Churchill cautioned, "Now this is not the end. It is not even the beginning of the end. But it is, perhaps, the end of the beginning."

Before we get to the end of beginning, it makes sense to unravel the Libyan labyrinth, to understand how we got to February 15, 2011, then to the Atlantic involvement in this war and to what this says for the future of imperialism and the doctrine of humanitarian intervention.

II. Qaddafi's Revolution

In 1969, Colonel Muammar al-Qaddafi (age 27) surprised the aged King Idris, then in Turkey for medical treatment, with his attack on the Benghazi radio station on September 1, and with the subsequent *coup d'etat* against the monarchy. Inspired by the Free Officers of Egypt, Qaddafi and his fellow Colonels forced-marched the fragile Libyan State and even more fragile Libyan society into a new dispensation. Devastated by Italian colonialism and World War 2, the new Libya under Idris could aspire to little. In 1959, *Time* enumerated the particulars, with emphasis on the one resource that Qaddafi capitalized upon, "Free Libya's legacy from its past includes rich Roman ruins, live German land mines, and a fierce resentment among

Libya's predominantly Arab 1,130,000 population against all things foreign." Qaddafi drank deeply in the well of that patriotism and anti-colonialism, covering his coup in the mantle of 'Umar al-Mukhtar, whose face would then adorn the Libyan ten dinar bill and whose struggle against the Italians was made immortal for the worldwide audience by Anthony Quinn in the 1981 film (financed by Qaddafi's government), *The Lion of the Desert*.

As World War 2 slipped into the horizon, discussions in the Atlantic world threatened to divide Libya along its three Ottoman provinces: Tripolitania to the Italians, Cyrenaica to the British and Fezzan to the French (the Bevin-Sfora Plan of May 10, 1949). Fortunately for the Libyans, the Haitians voted against this plan in the United Nations and tipped the balance toward independence. But with King Idris on the throne, Libya enjoyed a constrained freedom. When the Italians established themselves in Libya in 1927, Idris and his *sanusi* circle escaped to British-controlled Egypt, where they became the clients of London (a fact begrudgingly noted in Evans Pritchard's informative *The Sanusi of Cyrenaica*, 1947). In 1951, when Libya was formed, Idris took up the mantel, but essentially retired to his honey-colored palace in wondrous Tobruk. Tripoli was a backwater for him. He preferred Cyrenaica. Idris' flag for the new Libya borrowed from Cyrenaica's emblems (with the star and the crescent), not Tripolitania's totems (a palm tree, a star and three half moons). Popular anger against the Idris realm grew in the west, and eventually in the east. Idris had to seek protection from the *HMS Bermuda* (in July 1958) and then the British 10th

Armored Division (on October 29, 1959, when they protected him from a general uprising and played, as a British government official wrote at the time, "a vital role in keeping King Idris alive and on the throne").

A pliant Idris signed off on an essential twenty-year Anglo-Libyan treaty in 1953, which by many appearances seemed to have been drafted in Prince Charles Street by the over-educated bureaucrats of the Foreign & Commonwealth Office. It allowed the British to maintain bases in eastern Libya (at Tobruk and El Adem), and the next year, it allowed the United States to lease the Wheelus Air Base just outside Tripoli (the cost was modest, $7 million and 24,000 tons of wheat as a down-payment and an annual rent of $4 million). It was from the Wheelus base that the US flew sorties across the Mediterranean, with the F-101 and F-102 aircraft screaming near the Gulf of Sidra. The troops stationed at these bases kept to themselves. "Most American servicemen are apathetic to service in Libya," wrote the anthropologist Louis Dupree in 1958, "and almost never leave the air base. Others, when they do leave, make asses of themselves."

The United States was interested in the southern coastline of the Mediterranean, what the Romans had called *mare nostrum*, our lake. In 1885, the Italian writer Emilio Lupi put the case for the lake plainly, "Even if the coast of Tripoli were a desert, even if it would not support one peasant or one Italian business firm, we still need to take to avoid it being suffocated in *mare nostrum*." The French had Morocco, the Italians must have Tripolitania. Seven decades later, US President Dwight Eisenhower welcomed Libyan

Prime Minister Mustafa Ben Halim to Washington, and told him that Libya "would, as far as the United States was concerned, be in the Middle East what the Philippines were to the United States in the Far East." Libya would be "firmly in our camp," he said, a tone set by the US Ambassador to Libya, John Tappin, who was eager to form a "southern tier" of North African states. Ben Halim had come to the Americans with a dowry in hand: he had signed a treaty with President Habib Bourguiba of Tunisia, and they were eager to forge an alliance that might include Algeria in a pro-Western bloc (if only the French could be persuaded to leave their neighbor alone). To be fair to Ben Halim, he was a vigorous supporter of the Algerian freedom fighter Ahmed Ben Bella. The fantasy of the Maghrebian bourgeoisie is evident here, that somehow their bent knee might convince the benevolent Americans to provide them with flag independence in order for them to turn over their sovereignty toward NATO's Mediterranean.

Such fealty to the old and new colonial powers unsettled the Libyan people. No wonder they protested so frequently. It was this patriotic sentiment that made Rajab Buhwaish's anti-colonial anthem *Ma Bi Marad* (I Have No Illness) so central to the imagination of the Idris-era intellectuals. Buhwaish, who was from the same tribe as the rebel hero 'Umar al-Mukhtar, had provided the best dirge of Italian atrocities, with the cautious lament, "I have no illness but endless grief." It provided the young Qaddafi with the poetry to offer his own jeremiad, "The sky over Arab Libya is being polluted by foreign planes." An early act of the new regime after 1969 was to jettison the foreign bases and to reclaim sovereignty for the new country. It won Qaddafi a great deal of popular respect. Wheelus became a Libyan military air base (Okba Ben Nafi Air Base), and when Tripoli expanded to embrace it, the regime turned it into the civilian Mitiga International Airport.

Libya had the misfortune of being a distant outpost of the Ottoman Empire and the Italian colonial adventures. It wanted for basic social development. When Qaddafi came to power, the main export was scrap metal. Libya's deserts were a dumping ground for the detritus from Operation Compass, the allied attack on the Italian and German positions between December 1940 and February 1941. That part of the war is celebrated in the Rock Hudson film, *Tobruk* (1967), where Hudson, playing a Canadian soldier points out, "A dead martyr is just another corpse." It gives you a flavor of the violence during the war, and the destruction. I remember being driven along the Mediterranean road as a child, looking in wonder at the half tracks and tanks littering the roadside. It was these ruins that provided the main export for Libya. Libya's second main export was esparto grass or *halfa* (needle grass) used to make high quality paper. Idris' regime ignored the economic question. They were satisfied with the rents collected from the imperial powers (and occasionally caviled to have these increased) and with the surplus that came from the hard working peasants (there was nothing like the inventiveness of King Mohammed V of Morocco, whose Operation Plow in 1957 at least attempted to modernize the agricultural sector). "Libya was just a tray of sand in 1951," recalled Abdul Hamid Bakoush, a close friend of King Idris. "It had an income of £3 million a year, and that came from Britain and the United States in rent for the bases on Libyan territory." Rents made up for economic development.

Esso (Standard Oil) discovered oil in the Zelten oil fields in Cyrenaica in June 1959. Hints of the possibility of oil underfoot had been around since the 1940s, and in 1955 Idris' regime passed a Petroleum Law that allowed the Seven Sisters to drill in parts of the country. Oil was mainly found in the northeastern and north-central sections, from As Sarie to Mabruk. By 1961, Standard Oil began to export Libya's oil. This was to soon become the major export of the country. Libya's oil was in demand because of its proximity to Europe and because it was sweet oil (which makes it easier and cheaper to process). By the time Idris was deposed, the country exported three million barrels of oil per day. Scandalously, the government received the lowest rent per barrel in the world. Idris was not known to be personally ostentatious, but his circle could not help themselves. Sayyid Abdallah Abed Al Senussi, called the Black Prince, was famous for his bribe-taking, and also famous for building projects that would allow him to recycle the oil profits into his pocket (one such was a road that began nowhere and led into the Sebha Oasis, later slated to be the home of an alleged chemical weapons plant). The Black Prince modestly named his company SASCO, the Sayyid Abdallah Senussi Company. The routine corruption of Idris' circle and their obsequiousness to their imperial friends are two of the reasons why there was barely any opposition to Qaddafi's coup. "The Idris regime was certainly one of the most corrupt in the area and probably one of the most corrupt in the world," confessed the US State Department's James Akins, "It was overthrown with surprising ease and there was almost no resistance."

Qaddafi's revolution was his regime's to tarnish. The Libyan people were with him in 1969. They would have been with his revolution in 2011 if it had delivered on its promise. But much had changed since then, even though in the first decades of the new regime so much was delivered to the population. That was perhaps part of the problem: the social goods were *delivered*. The social basis of Libya was not decentralized and its politics was not democratized. Nevertheless, only a mind unable to appreciate the slow movement of history would see nothing to celebrate in the 1969 revolution and what it was able to deliver to the Libyans at least in its first decade, if not in the first two decades. Take a look at the latest *Human Development Index* developed by the United Nations Development Programme (November 2010, updated June 2011). The Human Development Index (HDI) is a measure that looks at education, life expectancy, literacy and the general standard of living. In terms of HDI, Libya comes in 55th out of 170 countries, the highest from the African continent and behind only three other Arab countries (all very small oil and natural gas-rich states: Qatar, Bahrain and Kuwait). The HDI in Libya is higher than in Saudi Arabia. That the HDI does not count political opportunities is significant. It was the measure that most disturbed sections of Libyan society.

Qaddafi's regime pushed forward a series of radical developments to transform Libyan society. Over the first decade of the Qaddafi regime, the state took charge of the oil fields (1972) and raised the rents charged to multinational firms (Standard Oil, but also later Nelson Bunker Hunt's Titan Resources). That money was then diverted toward social welfare, mainly an increase in housing and health care. "I recall the new leadership was greeted with something like euphoria in 1969, especially by the young, some of whom I was teaching," remembers Graham Brown. "The new authority, calling itself The Revolutionary Command Council initiated a socialist programme — first nationalizing the oil companies, fixing a minimum wage, extending the welfare and health systems and slashing the obscene rents being charged by property owners. A limit was imposed on the rents that landlords could charge, fixing maximum rents at about one third of the pre-revolutionary level. Tripoli until then had been the most expensive city in the Middle East. Many large properties were taken over and let to the people at low rents. The vast sprawling shanty town just outside Tripoli was torn down and replaced by new workers' housing projects." When Qaddafi took power, the literacy rate in Libya was a miserable twenty percent. The consequence of the transfer payments lifted the rate to ninety percent by 1980.

Libya has often been described as a large desert with two towns on either end, as bookends for the sand: Tripoli in the west and Benghazi in the east. They are divided by about six hundred and fifty kilometers of roadway. But in the middle and into the south lay vast desert stretches where the Bedouin and the peasantry worked the land in miraculous ways to grow crops and to raise livestock. Qaddafi and his officers came from the small villages and small towns, modest men who had none of the pretentions of the monarchy. Aware of the hardships in the countryside, Qaddafi's regime allowed farmers to settle on confiscated Italian and Sanusi land, and the government provided them with low interest loans to buy farm equipment and inputs. "Land could be purchased interest free," writes historian Dirk Vandewalle in his *A History of Modern Libya*. "Until the farm became self-sufficient the farmer was eligible for a government salary."

During the second decade of the new regime, from 1978 to 1988, the state continued with the gist of these policies. The regime constrained private enterprise and encouraged workers to take control of about two hundred firms. Redistribution of land on the Jefara plain west of Tripoli was the rural cognate. The state stepped in to manage all macro-economic functions, at the same time as the Central Bank redistributed wealth by putting a ceiling on bank account holdings. It was a straightforward redistribution of wealth conducted as a currency exchange.

Qaddafi's populism was hemmed in by his regime's lack of appreciation for the administrative costs of this mammoth centralization of redistribution. After his coup, sections of the educated professionals fled the country, offering their services to the Gulf Arab emirs (so that Ben Halim became an advisor to Crown Prince Fahd bin Abdul Aziz) or to the financial and business world that centered around Beirut. As the state's administrative apparatus fumbled, Qaddafi attacked the overwrought bureaucrats. "They became even more inefficient," Vandewalle notes, "making Qadhafi's harangues against them a self-fulfilling prophecy that would lead to their evisceration after the mid-1970s." Qaddafi would continue to centralize social and economic functions around a state apparatus that was no longer capable of carrying these many functions. It was a mirror to what was happening on the political scene, where Qaddafi was even less disposed to democratic decentralization.

Qaddafi was never keen on the full agenda of socialism. He liked the abstract idea of redistribution, but like most authoritarian populists he had not considered the mechanisms to transfer authority and decision-making to localities who might then harness their newly provided wealth for the betterment of their towns and villages. Instead, Qaddafi turned over the fruits of social wealth to the people at the same time as his regime centralized the mechanism for the redistribution of those fruits. The gargantuan state was not capable of being efficient, and this led to serious problems of incentive in the population and to alienation from its mechanisms. Rather than address these administrative problems, Qaddafi relied upon the oil revenue to pacify the population. That he and his circle did not steal from the oil profits is commendable, and it is the reason why social projects made an impact on the lives of the people. By the 1980s, Libya could boast of very high human development indicators: in literacy and health, in the main. It was the oil that prolonged his revolution and allowed his central state to appear benevolent even as it monopolized decision-making in the country.

Qaddafi's own idea of democracy was centered around him, his clan (the Qadhadhfa) and his "men of the tent" (*rijal al-cheima*), his military associates and childhood friends. To be fair, Qaddafi's was not a personality cult of the kind produced by Saddam Hussein after 1978. The democratic set-up, which he called the *Jamahiriya* (State of the Masses), exceeded what King Idris allowed. The failure to engage with a real democratic experience rankled on Qaddafi himself, and he would return over the course of the following forty-two years several times with new ideas for it. In 1978, he created the Revolution Committee Movement (*harakat al-lajnati ath-thawra*) and then in 1988 he went to the General People's Conference to promise more civil and political liberties. The Revolution Committee Movement was not a real development. Like Mao's Cultural Revolution and Red Guards, it sought to undermine the official institutions by creating a parallel structure dominated by Qaddafi, who claimed to have no official position in the government. This abeyance of authority ("I am not the leader") was dangerous because it weakened the established systems, which turned to Qaddafi for his almost regal assent or views. The Revolution Committee Movement was filled with Qaddafi's cronies, such as Khalifa Khanaish, Khawaildi Hamidi, Mustafa Kharroubi, Abu Bakr Yunis, the leadership of the security services (chillingly named the Leader's Information Office, *Maktab Ma'lumat al'Qai'd*) and Abdessalam Jalloud (who was hastily removed for being too radical). There was no sense of the failure of the process of democracy, of the "state of the masses," of a rhetorical façade that stood in for the whims of the men of the tent. Qaddafi conducted the remarkable feat of centralization of power in the name of de-centralization.

Over time the limited democratic spaces strained against both the rhetoric of the regime and the aspirations of the people. In 2009, Qaddafi's son, Saif al-Islam Qaddafi delivered a speech at his alma mater, the London School of Economics. "In theory, Libya is the most democratic state in the world," he said, chuckling. When the audience laughed with him, he smiled and laughed along, saying, "In theory, in theory." Even the Qaddafi inner circle recognized that although the theory of the *Jamahiriya* or state of the masses is of interest, the practice has been anything but. By 2000, only ten percent of the eligible citizenry came to the Congress meetings, and over seventy percent did not believe that they could influence political decisions (as shown by surveys collected in Amal Obeidi's *Political Culture in Libya*). This is a serious indictment. That Qaddafi's regime had a strong stomach for authoritarianism is illuminated by his active support for Charles Taylor in his war against the people of Liberia.

In his *Green Book*, Qaddafi offered an alternative to the *Jamahiriya* idea of democracy. "The natural law for any society is tradition (custom) or religion." The State of the Masses claimed to organize community power absent the social baggage of tribe and faith. But such a move would be idealistic, and it would threaten the new regime with the loss of sections of the population to a brewing counter-revolution (whose main agents were the deposed royals and their imperial allies). There was little time to build up a new social fabric, so the Qaddafi regime for reasons of instinct or opportunity seized upon those provided for them. Qaddafi relied upon well-trod capillaries of power, the hierarchies of tribe, faith and army. Unwilling to opt for a radical democratization of the society, Qaddafi pursued a tense dance from the 1970s to 2011, offering carrots to his allies and sticks to his potential enemies, reining in the leadership of these traditional hierarchies, and then offering them patronage when it suited him. The mercurial style that Qaddafi adopted was not about his personality alone, but also a leader's natural response to a system that relied upon power brokers whose own loyalty was purchased through elements who did not have any ideological commitment to the system.

By the 1980s, the web woven by the Qaddafi regime began to unravel. The war in Chad wore down the military, and it ate into the exchequer. The return to eastern Libya of the Afghan Arabs *jihadis* by the late 1980s and the Algerian Civil War in 1991 brewed the stew of extremist political Islam in the towns of Dernah and Benghazi. The tribal leadership caviled at the regime, as it floundered. Old social classes pushed against the regime at the same time as the new social classes (the educated middle class professionals), made by the transfer payments of the national development regime set-up by Qaddafi, began to turn on it: they wanted more political power. The new dilemma seemed to be beyond Qaddafi, whose own health (two strokes) and poor capacity to delegate authority led to an unfinished battle between those who would be called the "reformers" (led by Saif al-Islam Qaddafi) and the national development "hard-liners" (putatively led by Mutassim Qaddafi). It is fitting that the leaders of the two wings are sons of Qaddafi—it tells us a great deal about the involution of his regime.

Geography of Identity.

Qaddafi's new regime purportedly attempted to overthrow the supremacy of the tribes. In fact, it strengthened his own tribe, the Qadhadhfa, and gained the trust of other significant tribes of the western and southwestern parts of the country, such as the Maghraha (of Misrata) and the Warfallah (from Sirte to Fezzan). These tribes are vast kinship groups, spread over considerable territory. A million or so of the Warfallah do not march in evolutionary lockstep. What Qaddafi's regime was able to enjoin was the support of the tribal elders, who by one way or another would procure the sympathy of their tribal structures for the regime for as long as that loyalty remained. The "tribal chiefs represent a sort of moral and social support," noted Hasni Abidi (director of CERMAM, Centre d'études et de recherché sur le monde arabe et méditerranéen). They are a "refuge, given the total absence of Libyan political institutions." What Qaddafi's regime was able to do was to create the illusion of the loyal tribes, and when fractures opened up with their leadership, the regime enforced allegiance. The ultimate tribe of the regime, the army, would be at hand to make it so.

The Revolution, in one sense, was also a revolution against the Sa'adi tribes of the East, those who had dominated the regime of King Idris. The King was an eminence of the Sansussi order, which was born in 1843 at the hand of the Algerian scholar Sayyid Muhammed bin Ali al-Sansusi in Al Bayda', in eastern Libya. The Sansussis built their strength around the *zawiyas*, the residential settlements of their order that happened to be built on the crossroads of trade routes. About a third of the country's population gave their allegiance to the order. It was powerful. Qaddafi saw it as the fifth column, and was not disposed to being generous. The Sa'adi confederation of the East was left out of the spoils of the new dispensation. By the 1980s, Benghazi looked a little worn compared to Tripoli. The returns of the oil rent and the social wage pledged by the new revolutionary regime offered only parsimonious help to the impoverished East. It meant that the Eastern part of Libya became a hive of conspiracy against the regime.

UN Commissioner Adrian Pelt recounts that when the Libyans deliberated over their 1951 Constitution, the longest debate was over whether the country should have a unitary or federal system. The Tripolitanians wanted a unitary system, and the Cyrenaicans wanted a federal system. The East was jealous of the privileges it had enjoyed under the Idris regime. It wanted to preserve these through political autonomy from Tripoli, now ruled by the men of the small towns (such as Qaddafi's own Sirte). It was a sore issue. Idris, who was ambivalent in the debate, did not throw his weight into it and the Libyan constitution settled eventually for a unitary system. It provided the legal basis for the policies that created the idea of Libya. Even as Qaddafi's prejudices offered parsimonious help to the impoverished East, his state-building policies ensured the creation of a Libyan national sensibility. In the 1960s there was no real Libyan cultural identity, with accents and food differing from one town to the next, so much so that identification between them was minimal. The regime's new education system drew talent from across the deserts, and enabled young people to move from one locality to another. The oil industry and the Great Man Made River (depicted on the twenty dinar note) pulled the new mobile middle class professionals, the oil workers, and the construction workers from one end of the country to another. It was the state bureaucracy and the military that finished the process, cementing the basis for Libyan personhood, now formulated around a culture polished by the authoritarian populist state.

Even as a Libyan identity flourished, neglect of the tribes of the East and of the communities of the Jebel Nafusa, the mountains of the Northwest, continued. Across North Africa, the Amazigh peoples (derogatorily known as the Berber) strive for autonomy and dignity. From the Kabyles of northern Algeria to the Riffians of northern Morocco and to the Tuareg of the Sahara, the Amazigh peoples or the Imazighen have struggled against the national liberation states, with little success. In Morocco, King Mohammed VI, in fear of the Imazighen revolts, hastened to allow Tamazight as an official state language. Qaddafi has been routinely hostile to any attempt by the Imazighen to comport themselves in their language, much like the Turkish policy of banning the Kurdish language and their identity (or the French, who, in the name of Enlightenment, banned the Tahitians from speaking their own language). Over the past decade, the Libyan state vacillated over the idea of recognizing the existence of the Amazigh peoples. In August 2007, the government allowed the World Amazigh Congress to be held in Tripoli. A year later, Qaddafi went to Jadu, in the Nafusa mountains, to meet with Amazigh leaders. "You can call yourselves whatever you want inside your homes," Qaddafi is reported to have told them, "Berbers, children of Satan, whatever—but you are only Libyans when you leave your homes." The idea of Libya as an Arab country was firmly in the imagination of the Qaddafi regime. It was a normal tendency of modern nationalism to deny the fractures within a nation-state, and to pretend that minority rights and cultural expression are the first gesture toward secession. The denial of those rights, history shows us, are more likely to spur secession than the recognition of them in the first place.

In 1993, Qaddafi survived an assassination attempt in the town of Bani Walid, in the Misrata district. Qaddafi went to the elders of the Warfallah tribe, those who dominate the region, and told them that they must both deliver the culprits and then collectively condemn the plot. They refused to do so. Qaddafi's alliance with the Warfallah frayed. It is in such instances that it becomes clear how Qaddafi lost the loyalty of the *natural* leaders. During the rebellion in 2011, substantial numbers of the Imazighen and the Warfallah turned their backs on Qaddafi and provided the basis for the final push against Tripoli. Sociologist Mohammed Bamyeh investigated twenty-eight of the tribal declarations issued by the tribal leaders between February 23 and March 9, 2011; he found that "the vast majority highlighted national unity or national salvation rather than tribal interests. These declarations also demonstrate that Libya's tribes are not homogenous entities, but rather are composed of diverse members with varying social and economic backgrounds. This reality reflects the nature of Libyan society as a whole, which has a 90% urban population and in which inter-marriages across tribal lines are common." Qaddafi's *natural* leaders could not control the desires and ambitions of their populations.

The Green Flag.

A nationalist in the Nasser vein, Qaddafi nonetheless was never keen on secularism. His *Green Book* dismissed Capitalism and Communism in favor of a "Third Universal Theory," to return the Arab world to the fundamentals of Islam in both politics and economics. His new constitution was founded on Islamic principles (article 2), and his new state attempted to do with Islam what it had done with the economy and with politics: nationalize Islam. The *waqf*, the religious trusts, were grasped by the state, which then brought the clergy to heel as well as promoted *ijtihad*, personal interpretation of the Koran, and a religious experience without the dominance of the *ulema*. Once more Qaddafi would dance between his absorption of Islam into his own Third Universal Theory and a more conventional, even *salafi* understanding of Islam (in 1973, for instance, he told the people of Zuwara that the *Sharia* should be the legal code of Libya). Expulsion of the Italian residents in Libya followed as much from Qaddafi's Islamic injunctions as from Nasserite nationalism, and so too Qaddafi's fellowship with Islamic revolution from Chad to the Philippines (the instrument for his ambitions was the 1972 created *al-Failaka al-Islamiya*, the Islamic League).

Political Islam's representatives began to dig deep roots, mainly in eastern Libya. It built up networks outside the mosques whose *ulema* had been largely nationalized. The first pass at political activity took place not inside Libya, but in exile in Sudan. There Dr. Muhammed Yusuf al-Muqarayif, formerly Libya's ambassador to India, created the National Salvation Front for Libya (*Inqat*) in 1981. Its most spectacular action was an assault on Qaddafi's residential compound, Bab al-Aziziyah, in Tripoli. The attack failed, and two thousand or so people were captured as a result of its failure. It would be a few years later before another dramatic episode reminded Qaddafi of the viability of this strand of political Islam as a dangerous foe. Further attacks came from *Inqat* and the Islamic Liberation Front. More repression followed, including the hanging of two students at the al-Fateh University in 1984 and the execution of nine members of *Jihad* on Libyan State Television on February 17, 1987. The emergence of the group *Jihad* was a premonition of what was to come: the small bands of dedicated fighters prepared to die for their cause.

Clashes at Tripoli University (January 8, 1989) and in Tripoli's mosques (January 20, 1989) threatened Qaddafi's monopoly over Islam. In 1989, fears of unrest led the regime to cancel a soccer match between Libya and Algeria. "Qaddafi is the Enemy of God," chanted the restive crowd, angry at being denied their pleasures, confident in the security of numbers. Qaddafi's response would become scripted, blaming the Islamists for being "hashish smokers and charlatan groups" (on February 24, 2011, Qaddafi would say that the rebels of Az Zawiya had taken "hallucinogenic drugs in their coffee with milk, like Nescafé"). Many hardened Islamists had fled Libya in the 1980s, joining up through the Maktab al-Khidamat, the Afghan Services Bureau run by Osama Bin Laden's mentor, Abdullah Azzam, as part of the Afghan Arab force to fight in Afghanistan. It was safer to conduct their *jihad* in far off Afghanistan than in Libya, where the regime remained powerful and dangerous.

With the Afghan war winding down by the end of the 1980s, the Afghan Arabs returned home. In Algeria, they came in large numbers as hardened warriors and formed the Islamic Salvation Front (FIS). Angered by the direction of Algerian society, frustrated by the US-led attack on Iraq in 1991 and stymied by the regime's cancellation of elections that they might have won, the forces of political Islam turned to the armed struggle. The Algerian Civil War cost almost two million lives and the destruction of the social wealth of the country. Nonetheless, it provided an opening for the Libyan Afghan Arabs, many of whom joined the Libyan Islamic Fighting Group (LIFG, the *al-Jama'a al-Islamiyyah al-Muqatilah fi-Libya*, founded in Pakistan in 1990). The LIFG drew from the experience of the Islamists in Egypt and Algeria to form small cells, *anqud*, and its ideologues (such as Sami al-Sa'idi, also known as Abu al-Mundhir) promoted this idea through making a distinction between *jihad* as a collective obligation for all Muslims (*fard kifaya*) and as an individual obligation (*fard 'ain*). By favoring the latter, they allowed these small cells to live amongst their less radical fellows and plot spectacular acts of violence to shift the social conditions to suit them. LIFG moved from Pakistan to Sudan and then to Algeria, conducting their leap (*al-wathba*) into North Africa.

The first major action by the LIFG was in Benghazi in 1995, and then in Derna and in the Jebel el-Akhdar (the Green Mountains). They tried to assassinate Qaddafi at least a few times, once in February 1996 in Sirt and once again in May 1998 near Sidi Khalifa, east of Benghazi. A major confrontation with the regime's guns in Wadi al-Injil (Bible Valley) in March 1996 cut down most of their fighters. Their military commander, Fathy bin Sulayman (also known as Abu Abd al-Rahman al-Hattah) was killed in September 1997. The guerrilla phase of the LIFG's combat ended at an Istanbul meeting in 1998. Mustafa Qunayfid, their leader, shifted the Libyan Afghan Arabs to fight in Chechnya. After 2003, they would go to join the insurgency in Iraq.

The East had sent a disproportionate number of its young to fight in Iraq. They did not go strictly for the purposes of *jihad*, or because they had fealty to *al-Qaeda*. A US embassy official snuck away from his Tripoli minder in 2008 and reported that the young men who went to Iraq did so because they could not effectively protest against Qaddafi. Iraq stood in for Libya. The official went to Dernah. Upon his return to Tripoli, he filed this memorandum for his superiors, "Frustration at the inability of eastern Libyans to effectively challenge Qadhafi's regime, together with a concerted ideological campaign by returned Libyan fighters from earlier conflicts, have played important roles in Derna's development as a wellspring of Libyan foreign fighters in Iraq. Other factors include a dearth of social outlets for young people, local pride in Derna's history as a locus of fierce opposition to occupation, economic disenfranchisement among the town's young men. Depictions on satellite television of events in Iraq and Palestine fuel the widespread view that resistance to coalition forces is justified and necessary. One Libyan interlocutor likened young men in Derna to Bruce Willis' character in the action picture *Die Hard*, who stubbornly refused to die quietly. For them, resistance against coalition forces in Iraq is an important act of 'jihad' and a last act of defiance against the Qadhafi regime."

It was out of the LIFG struggles that on June 29, 1996 a protest by LIFG members at the Abu Selim Prison in Tripoli took place. The regime killed 1,233 prisoners. Qaddafi's henchman (and brother-in-law), Abdullah Senussi, who would be sent to Benghazi in February 2011, was the interior minister then as well. The lawyer who would take up the case of the Abu Selim prison, Abdul Hafiz Ghoga became the spokesperson of the 2011 National Transitional Council of Libya, and one of his council members (and another lawyer) Fateh Terbil would hold a weekly vigil for justice for the dead.

A frazzled Qaddafi began to assert views about Islam that were not new to him, but which had been provoked by the emergence of the LIFG and the Algerian Civil War next door. During George H. W. Bush's telephone call with Mubarak on January 21, 1991, the US president said, "I've been disappointed in Qadhafi. He's been making some crazy statements." Mubarak's response is censored. Bush responded, "I think he is just grandstanding." In fact, he was doing more. He was trying to turn the ideological tide to his favor, complaining that in the context of the US bombing in Iraq that "Islam became the target of the West." In 1994, he reaffirmed his ban on alcohol, introduced the Islamic calendar and against UN sanctions dispatched pious Libyans to the *hajj* on state aircraft. He was the "shield of Islam," as one Libyan put it at that time.

Frayed Uniforms.

In 1978, the Libyan armed forces entered Chad after two decades of low intensity political and military conflict over a strip of land that divides the two countries (the Aouzou Strip). Debates over old colonial treaties and historical claims rested on a region believed to be home to large uranium deposits. Proxies for powers far from Tripoli and N'Djamena, the two countries went into a bloody conflict that lasted for ten years. Supplied by the Soviets and the East Germans, Qaddafi's Islamic Legionnaires at first simply provided resources to the Chadean rebels, but over the course of the decade were drawn into the war. The French intervened twice, and with superior air power beat back Qaddafi and his allies. By 1987, the Libyans had lost their own Chadean allies and remained vulnerable in Chad's northern deserts. The newly emboldened army of Chad, the FANT, assembled their fighting forces onto Toyota trucks armed with MILAN anti-tank guided missiles. This was the Toyota War of 1987, and it resembled in many particulars the use of such trucks in Libya itself in 2011. The Libyan army was routed, and it lost the Aouzou Strip, and if the Organization of African States had not intervened, it might have been threatened within Libya itself. The French intervened against Qaddafi, and the United States provided intelligence support to the FANT. It was a preview of 2011.

The Libyan army lost about eight thousand of its troops, about eight times what was lost by Chad's army. By some accounts, the Libyan armed forces lost a third of its infantry and considerable amounts of armor. Morale was at a very low level. The better sections of the Revolutionary Command Council, particularly the smart and capable members of the Free Officers, were either cashiered or brought to heel. If they had been allowed to flourish, Libya's military might not have run out of ideas or produced a disjuncture between the ordinary soldier and the officer class (increasingly the sullen children of an emergent favored section). It was never to recover its verve.

In 1986, the United States bombed Tripoli and Benghazi in retaliation for the Libyan bombing of a Berlin nightclub. Operation El Dorado Canyon comprised an aerial attack on Qaddafi's compound (where Qaddafi claimed his adopted daughter Hanna had been killed. In 2011, it was demonstrated that Hanna had actually survived the attack, and is now a doctor). It was a brief boost for Libyan nationalism, as the armed forces at the very least pledged their *bay'a*, their loyalty to Qaddafi. The defeat in the Toyota War reduced their confidence. The 1992 UN sanctions further sharpened the edge for the armed forces. The UN sanctions, Dirk Vandewalle argues, led to "mounting discontent and increasing privation in Libya, reflected in unpaid salaries, decreased subsidies, cuts in army perks and a shortage of basic goods." It was these cuts in army perks that counted strongly against Qaddafi.

Canny enough to recognize the problems in the military, Qaddafi recalled his best units to the western part of the country. The elite corps, including the 32nd Reinforced (later Khamis) Brigade, was brought to defend Tripoli. Its members were thought to be carefully recruited for their loyalty and trained to defeat anything weaker than the kind of sustained warfare that the US aerial power is capable of unleashing (as it did for a brief burst in those twelve minutes of the April 15, 1986 raid and then later in the demonstration effect of the 1991 war over Iraq). It was already a sign of weakness. The Libyan army was the regime's own Trojan Horse.

III. Revolution within the Revolution

"Libyans want to eat McDonald's
hamburgers, not uranium."
—Saif al-Islam al-Qaddafi, 2005.

United Nations sanctions came into effect in 1992. They had a huge impact on the Libyan exchequer. Between 1992 and 1998, the treasury lost about $24 billion, with infrastructure plans curtailed, no foreign investment for the ailing oil extraction devices, a $15 billion loss in oil income and a two hundred percent increase in the price of foodstuffs. The country was simply not prepared to withstand the pressure. Qaddafi's regime had failed to build up its economic reserves and to strengthen infrastructure during the previous decade. Unimaginative use of the oil surplus hastened the economic stagnation.

The Libyan people rallied around Qaddafi after the April 1986 attack. Anti-Americanism, easy enough with Reagan at the helm in Washington, provided cover for what Qaddafi called the "revolution within the revolution." This was the Libyan phrase to describe the entry of neoliberalism, or what Qaddafi called "popular capitalism." In 1987, anemic import substitution polices came to a close and "reforms" in agriculture and industry flooded out of the IMF manuals. By September 1988, the government abolished the import and export quotas, allowing retail trade in the new *souqs* to flourish in the cities. UN sanctions in 1992 threw the reforms into turmoil, and it allowed the old Qaddafi to emerge out of the sarcophagus that he had become. Cracks in the ruling elite at times slowed and at times speeded up the reforms. Qaddafi would enter the debate on one side, then another, speaking out of both sides of his mouth. It was clear that two main problems needed to be treated before the medicine of neoliberalism could be allowed to work: the Qaddafi regime had to make its peace with the United States to lift the UN sanctions, and to help it deal with what it saw as the virus of political Islam. Once the United States' allergic reaction to Libya could be sorted out, Qaddafi bet, the problems of Libya's economic and political vitality could be solved.

Moussa Koussa Travels Light.

> "We never would have guessed ten years ago
> that we would be sitting in Tripoli, being wel-
> comed by a son of Muammar al-Qadhafi."
> —Senator Joseph Lieberman,
> August 2009.

Moussa Koussa was one of Qaddafi's close allies, a man of the tent. His loyalty knew no bounds. In 1980, he was sent to be ambassador to London. There he told

The Times that "stray dogs" had to be killed. This was a reference to the Libyan dissidents. He was expelled from London. In 1996, it was the unit commanded by Moussa Koussa that fired into the LIFG in Abu Salim prison. But he was not Qaddafi's butcher. Polished by his time at Michigan State University, and well-regarded by Tripoli's diplomatic corps as an urbane man, Moussa Koussa was picked to travel from Atlantic capital to Atlantic capital to settle all the scores and bring Libya out of the diplomatic deep freeze.

The key were the cases of the Lockerbie bombing (Pan Am Flight 103), and that of the French aircraft (UTA Flight 772) bombed over Niger. Moussa Koussa could promise millions of dollars from Libya's oil money. The negotiations went back and forth. The promise of money and a return to the oil fields of Libya was too much for the Atlantic world to refuse. By April 1999, the UN sanctions were suspended, and in 2003 they were lifted. To add to the pot of blood money, Qaddafi decided to announce that Libya would "disclose and dismantle all weapons of mass destruction." This was on December 19, 2003, after the United States armed forces had chased Saddam Hussein from power on the pretext of weapons of mass destruction. The US was equally angry at Iran and North Korea, but it could not act militarily. Their nuclear card prevented a repeat of the Iraq adventure. That Qaddafi threw the card on the table revealed his obsequious intentions. Commercial links were restored the next year, when a US Congressional team (led by Congressman Tom Lantos) came to Libya. Lantos' team returned to the US with good news about Libya. In 2006, the US State Department decided to remove Libya from its list of state sponsors of terrorism. In October 2008, the Libyans promised to turn over $1.5 billion in a trust fund as compensation for the various bombings. President George W. Bush signed Executive Order 13477 which voided all outstanding claims against Libya. A US Ambassador arrived in Tripoli, in the wake of US oil companies (who have faster jets).

Moussa Koussa had done a remarkable job.

In 1999, Moussa Koussa opened conversations with various *jihadi* groups based in Europe. He wanted to defang their anger. At the same time, Qaddafi's regime put the screws on the hardened *jihadis* inside Libya, and tried to gain the favor of the US since both the American and Libyan regimes shared a fear of *jihadis*. After 9/11, Qaddafi was one of the first world leaders to offer his condolences for the "horrifying and destructive" attacks, as he urged Libyans to donate blood for the survivors in the United States. In October 2002, Foreign Minister Mohammed Abderrahman Chalgam admitted that his government closely consulted with the US on counterterrorism, and a few months later, Qaddafi's heir apparent Saif al-Islam warmly spoke of Libya's support for the Bush War on Terror. If you went to Qaddafi's website at this time, you would have read this remarkable statement from the old Colonel, "The phenomenon of terrorism is not a matter of concern to the US alone. It is the concern of the whole world. The US cannot combat it alone. It is not logical, reasonable or productive to entrust the task to the US alone." It needed Qaddafi, who was in sheer terror of groups such as the Libyan Islamic Fighting Group.

Qaddafi played a double game with the *jihadis*. On the one side, by about 2005, the regime had opened a dialogue with the LIFG. In January 2007, Saif al-Islam met with Noman Benotman, a former leader of the LIFG, and with the Qatar-based Sheikh Ali al-Sallabi. The head of LIFG, Abu Layth al-Libi, refused to meet with the Qaddafi regime. He had other fish to fry. In November, al-Qaeda's leadership in the borderlands of Afghanistan and Pakistan announced that the LIFG had joined al-Qaeda (Abu Layth al-Libi was with Ayman al-Zawahiri when the announcement was made). That was chilling to the regime, whose paranoia over the LIFG had intensified as the Atlantic powers made their own dramatic declarations about al-Qaeda in the Maghreb (the AQIM, despite the swagger of its leadership, has become a kind of trans-Saharan gang, involved in the kidnapping and smuggling businesses, drawing from the Taureg insurgency against the government of Mali and from the remnants of the Algerian civil war). It must have chilled Qaddafi much more to find that Ibn Sheikh al-Libi's funeral service in May 2009 was attended by thousands in his town of Ajdabia (al-Libi was arrested in Pakistan in 2001, and he died in Libyan custody, apparently with a wink and a nod from Egypt's Omar Suleiman). "The enemy of yesterday is the friend of today," Saif al-Islam said in March 2010 at a ceremony of national reconciliation with the *jihadis*. It was more theatre than real-life, but it was sufficient for Libyan State Television.

The *jihadis* had not been completely pacified, but their lingering presence allowed Qaddafi to pirouette his regime's antipathy to the United States into an alliance. It was enough to keep their water on a slow boil—so as to show the United States of their presence, and to therefore become a more credible ally in the War on Terror. General William Ward, head of the US military's African Command (AFRICOM), did not need to be persuaded. In a memorandum from 2009, General Ward wrote, "Libya is a top partner in combating transnational terrorism."

The settlement of the claims against Libya was not a neutral process, geared only to break the sanctions regime. Alongside the payment of the money came a remarkable shift in the ideological framework of the Qaddafi regime. By the middle of the first decade of the twenty-first century, little of Qaddafi's worldview would have been recognizable to the young officer of 1969. Qaddafi's interpreter of world events, Dr. Ahmed Fituri (the Secretary for the Americas in the Ministry of Foreign Affairs) had begun to write summaries of new books for the leader. It tells you something about a person if you know what they are reading. Qaddafi enjoyed the work of *Newsweek*'s international editor, Fareed Zakaria (his *The Future of Freedom* and *The Post-American World*), of Thomas Friedman (*The World is Flat*), of George Soros (*The Age of Fallibility*) and importantly, the *Foreign Affairs* essays of Secretary of State Condoleezza Rice (he kept a scrapbook of pictures and writings of Rice in his compound, in which one finds the bizarre statement, "I admire and am very proud of the way she leans back and gives orders to the Arab leaders…. Leezza, Leezza, Leezza. I love her very much. I admire her and I'm proud of her because she's a black woman of African origin"). When Obama won the 2008 election,

Qaddafi wrote a personal letter to him (November 9, 2008) in which he drew his own conclusion about the election, "The main point is that Blacks shall not have an inferiority complex and imitate the Yankees." The presence of Rice and Obama in the leadership of the Atlantic states seemed to allow Qaddafi to make that journey from revolutionary nationalism to obedience to the imperial capitals. As African Americans, Rice and Obama provided cover for American repression, allowing the ersatz nationalist to take his place happily beside them.

Personalities did not spur the transformation. It was rooted in the need to remove the sanctions, and to maintain the older animosities in the new era. The Qaddafi regime's distrust of the Iranians and the Saudis manifested itself in an attempt to join with the US anti-Iranianism, and to tar the Saudis with the thick brush of Wahhabism. When Congressman Tom Lantos visited Tripoli in 2006 (his second visit), he sat down with Moussa Koussa, who warned him, "Iran and Iraq used to balance each other out. Now, there is no balance." Moussa Koussa was "sure that the Iranians are enriching uranium and making a bomb," which was honey to Lantos' belligerent ears. Meeting with Military Intelligence chief Abdullah Senussi, Lantos heard how the Libyans expected the US to provide Saudi Arabia with its "judgment day" after 9/11, since most of the hijackers were Saudis, not to attack Afghanistan and Iraq. In November 2006, Ibrahim Dridi, Director of the Americas Office at the General People's Committee met with the US embassy personnel to alert them about the Libyan anxiety about "Chinese hegemony over the continent." Charge d'Affaires

Ethan Goldrich, bewildered by this turn of events, wrote to Washington, "We find it fascinating that the Libyans have identified a fear of Chinese hegemony as a potential source of common interest with us."

Other elements in the foreign affairs bureaucracy in Tripoli did not see the convergence with the United States and its Atlantic partners as such a boon. By 2009, Ahmed Ibrahim, the director of the Green Book Center and a former high official in the People's Congress, told a conference in Tripoli that this convergence with the United States was "a great sin," and that the Qaddafi regime should snub the US Ambassador, who he called a "rotten dog." But Ibrahim did not have the ear of the government. Behind his back, the pro-Western "reformers" in Libya called Ibrahim *al-Bahim*. *Bahimah*, the feminine of *bahim*, refers to a beast, with the street meaning being dullard. Ibrahim was known as The Donkey, largely because he tried unsuccessfully to ban the teaching of foreign languages (mainly English) in the 1980s. Such old-school revolutionaries had been sidelined by the late 1990s, even as they retained a small public following among those who had faith in the 1969 revolution's promise. At no point did Qaddafi bulldoze the statue in Bab al-Azziziya of a US warplane being crushed by a fist (a sculpture to commemorate the 1986 bombing of Libya). Such images remained part of the diet of state propaganda, even as the official current moved in a direction that pleased the Atlantic capitals.

It was this lingering faith in the revolution that allowed Qaddafi to awaken the demons of nationalism when it suited him, largely as a bargaining chip for greater economic or political benefits on the world stage. He would do this routinely as we shall see below when he tried to get better terms from the oil companies, eager to get their drills into the Libyan sands. There was an element of naivety in the Qaddafi foreign ministry. As Roland Bruce St. John put it in the *International Journal of Middle East Studies*, the Libyan foreign affairs bureaucrats addressed "diplomatic problems of overwhelming complexity with naïve, simplistic solutions." They are "increasingly frustrated as polices are greeted outside Libya with widespread disbelief or lack of interest and largely rejected." Nevertheless, on occasion, the old-school bureaucrats were able to push Qaddafi in a worthwhile direction. The most important such maneuver was Qaddafi's attempt to block the idea of a Mediterranean Union mooted by France's Sarkozy. France wanted to use its financial aid to the southern tier of the Mediterranean to yoke the countries into a new Union whose agenda would be matters such as immigration from Africa into Europe and providing a platform for Israel to be a full member. This Mediterranean Union would circumvent the African Union and the Arab League. Qaddafi called a mini summit of the Arab League in Tripoli to denounce the Union. In his speech on June 10, 2008, Qaddafi said that the countries of North Africa are "not hungry to this extent; we're not dogs that they can wave a bone in front of and we'll run after it." There was also the threat toward the creation of an African currency, to circumvent the use of the French franc on the continent for inter-country transactions. Much the same kind of virulence was reserved for the Italians, for when Qaddafi visited Berlusconi and the Italian parliament, he wore a picture of the great

Libyan hero Omar al-Mukhtar, on his lapel. It is a picture of the hero as dignified captive, surrounded by preening Italian army and civilian leaders as they prepared to execute the Libyan hero.

Qaddafi's residual anti-colonialism came out in his tussles with the Europeans. The Europeans were also eager for Libyan oil. Britain's Tony Blair and France's Sarkozy went to kiss Qaddafi's ring and pledge finance for oil concessions. It is the reason why the British government freed Abdelbaset al-Megrahi, the convicted Lockerbie bomber, in August 2009. It is also the reason why Berlusconi bowed down before Omar al-Mukhtar's son in 2008 and handed over $5 billion as an apology for Italian colonialism. In his characteristic bluntness, Berlusconi said that he apologized so that Italy would get "less illegal immigrants and more oil." Qaddafi remained wary of the Europeans, who needed his oil but seemed to despise his person. He saw the United States as somehow changed after 9/11, and hoped to build up relations with the United States as a counter to the pressures his regime seemed to get from the European capitals. No wonder that in August 2009, Qaddafi's testosterone-laden son, Mutassim, told US Senators John McCain, Joseph Lieberman and Susan Collins that the Libyans could easily buy arms from Russia or China, "but we want to get it from you as a symbol of faith from the United States." Qaddafi's anti-colonial ideology was like a gopher, breaking the surface erratically and just as fitfully hastening to bury itself deep into the ground. Qaddafi was willing to give up the main insurance policy of rogue states, his nuclear arsenal. This is an illumination of Qaddafi's bizarre belief in the benevolence of the United States. He was eager to forge some kind of *entente* despite the press of imperialism on the Global South.

External Security Organization Director Moussa Koussa, once ejected from London for his intemperate views, now "shared his views frequently and openly with his US contacts in the Central Intelligence Agency and the Department of State," as he put it to General William Ward in May 2009. CIA papers found in a cache of Libyan government documents in an abandoned Tripoli building show that Sir Mark Allen, the former head of counterterrorism in Britain's MI6 carefully nurtured a relationship with Moussa Koussa. A fax from 2003 shows that the British had arrested LIFG head Emir Abu Munthir in Hong Kong for passport violations. "We are also aware that your service had been co-operating with the British to effect Abu Munthir's removal to Tripoli," the fax notes, "and that you had an aircraft available for this purpose in the Maldives." The British were willing to help the US and Libya with the "extraordinary rendition" of Abu Munthir. Moussa Koussa was a crucial point man. It would not be a huge surprise that when the UN placed sanctions on senior members of the Qaddafi regime in March 2011 (UN Resolution 1973, appendix), Moussa Koussa's name did not appear there. It was also not an enormous surprise that Moussa Koussa fled to Tunisia in late March, and by March 30 arrived on a private Swiss jet at Farnborough Airport, in Britain. The flight was organized by MI6. Moussa Koussa was the highest profile defector during the 2011 battle to eject Qaddafi. Qaddafi had become for both Britain and Moussa Koussa a "stray dog."

Kuwait on the Mediterranean.

Once Moussa Koussa had successfully spread the oil largess to erase the UN sanctions and to placate the United States, the question of "reform" returned to the political elites of Libya. It was there that the main debate would flourish from the late 1990s to 2011. The basis of the disagreement was over how to deal with the newly emboldened oil companies, how to encourage foreign investment into the country, what to do with the massive "cradle to grave" social subsidy and how to negotiate the economically stagnant but socially necessary state sector. The debate broke along lines familiar in many post-colonial states that had been through the epoch of national construction of an economy (through import substitution or other means) and that had by the 1990s been pressured by structural forces (and by more overt forces, such as the IMF) to globalize. The "reformers" followed the script of the IMF, and the "hardliners" settled into an obduracy regarding the old ways (and so appeared unimaginative in this new climate). Their debates sharpened after the credit crunch of 2007, when oil prices oscillated and plans for privatization floundered as the ability to continue to pay out the social wages declined. It was in this maw that Qaddafi would lose very large sections of the population that had hitherto supported him for one reason or another. The regime's hegemony collapsed long before 2011. When the rebels took up arms, they had only to break the fear of the security state. For them, Qaddafi's "dissolution must follow as surely as that of any mummy carefully preserved in a hermetically sealed coffin, whenever it is brought into contact with the open air" (Marx on the

Qing dynasty). The rebels did not have to gain the support of the masses who held fast to Qaddafi, for such masses, by 2011, did not exist in large numbers. That was the task of the 2011 uprising.

On August 20, 2008, Saif al-Islam Qaddafi gave the keynote address at the third annual Libya Youth Forum. The two previous forums, in Sirte in 2006 and Benghazi in 2007, had provided Saif al-Islam with a platform to urge on reforms of the regime built by his father and his clique. The first two speeches were forthright, but timid. At the third meeting, held in a remote desert town on the Awbari Lakes, Saif al-Islam set aside his prepared remarks and spoke, nervously, from the heart. He praised his father, but said that Qaddafi had built a regime in a historically unique set of circumstances. It was not reproducible. Things had to change. Saif al-Islam called for total privatization of all aspects of life. "The state will not own anything," he reported, and "everything should be done by the private sector." As if this heresy were not enough, Saif al-Islam announced that genuine political reform was needed, including "what is perhaps called a constitution—let's say a people's pact similar to the social pact or a pact of the mass of the people." Aware of Qaddafi's predilection to promise political reform each year, Saif al-Islam pointed out, "we want to have an administrative, legal and constitutional system once and for all, rather than change every year." It was a biting criticism of his father's vacillation.

To conduct the neoliberal reforms that he envisioned Saif al-Islam brought in Libyans from the Diaspora and Libyan technocrats who hastened to break with the residual policies of the 1969 revolution. The people who would become essential to Saif al-Islam's program were Mahmoud Jibril, Tarek Ben Halim and Shukri Ghanem. All of them had been educated in the Atlantic world, and most of them spent much of their career overseas. Ben Halim, son of the last prime minister of Idris' reign, was a senior partner at Goldman Sachs, and Jibril had his own consulting business in Beirut, Cairo and Doha. They are figures of renown in their own circles, and had come to Libya on the say-so of Saif al-Islam because they were committed to the transformation of the rump of the revolutionary social wage set-up into a neoliberal system. What they wanted was to build a Kuwait in the Mediterranean.

By 2006, a leading figure in the Economics Ministry in Libya, Taher Sarkez, had begun to talk openly about the need to attract foreign investment capital, create free trade zones and enhance the fledgling stock market. In other words, to import into Libya the full spectrum of neoliberal economic policies: open doors to finance capital, a place for finance to run its casino activities and an industrial sector premised upon an absence of regulations. People like Rajab Shiglabu (Libyan Foreign Investment Board) and Ali Abd al-Aziz al-Isawi (Export Promotion Board) sought to break Libya out of its predicament, the Dutch Disease (a country that exports pricey raw materials, such as oil, develops a strong currency, a deterrent to exports of other goods since it makes those exports more expensive outside the country). The classic approach to deal with this Dutch Disease is to raise tariffs and subsidize manufacturing. Such an approach did not sit well with the neoliberal clique, who preferred to inoculate Libya from the petro-dollars by keeping more of it overseas, and by using what money was available to build up export-oriented infrastructure.

Ghanem, who had been trained at Tufts University, was an old hand in the Libyan oil bureaucracy. He had been at OPEC as Libya's representative, he worked in the Ministry of Economics and in the National Oil Corporation (NOC), being elevated to lead the NOC in 2006. Ghanem was the Prime Minister of Libya from 2003 to 2006, when Qaddafi had to bring him back to run NOC. Once back at the NOC, Ghanem calmed down the pressures brought on the multinational oil firms by the Libyan government to pay higher hidden costs and to pay money into a terrorism compensation fund.

Over the course of the next three years, as the reform agenda went back and forth, Qaddafi frequently turned to Ghanem. He wanted him back as Prime Minister, to replace the technocrat al-Baghdadi Ali al-Mahmudi (who had chanced to embroil himself in a series of scandals that showed poor management rather than corruption, and that showed him to be a poor standard bearer for the reform agenda). Ghanem, on the other hand, was capable and ideologically given over to the world of reform. He had the fortune of being well-regarded in the international oil world (not long after he was tasked to head the NOC the 27th Oil and Money Conference in London voted him "Petroleum Executive of the Year" for 2006; over the years the winners include executives from Chevron, Mobil, Royal Dutch Shell and Arab oilmen such as Abdullah S. Jum'ah of ARAMCO and Abdelrahman bin Hamad al-Attiya of Qatar). An open embrace of the multinational oil companies followed, with Ghanem thought of among oil executive and even oil engineers as the hope for turning Libya into a Gulf-like oil regime. Ghanem launched private Libyan oil companies (al-Sharara, Libyan Company for Distribution of Petroleum Products and al-Rahila) to take up the room previously dominated by the public sector firm, Braiga Company. The oil ministry was well on its way to resembling the oil sector in Qatar or Saudi Arabia.

Ghanem did crucial work in the most lucrative of Libya's sectors. But far more important reform work was taking place at the National Economic Development Board, headed by Mahmoud Jibril. Before he was coaxed by Saif al-Islam to return to Libya in 2007, Jibril ran a successful consultancy firm that trained Arab management leaders from Morocco to Jordan, and he operated an asset management business (whose clients included the second wife of the emir of Qatar, Sheikha Mozah bint Nasser al-Missned). He remained at this job till early 2011, when he joined the rebellion and quickly became its most important leader (after Qaddafi's regime fell, Jibril became the first Prime Minister). In May 2009, Jibril met with the US Ambassador Gene Cretz, whose staff produced a fascinating summary of the conversation, "The NEDB's role…is to 'pave the way' for private sector development, and to create a strategic partnership between private companies and the government. There is a still a 'gap of distrust' dividing the two. As to whether Libya has a Master Plan that includes all the 11,000 [privatization] projects, Jibril admitted that in the past two years, Libya had started executing projects without such a plan. However, the NEDB has been working with experts from Ernst and Young, the Oxford Group, and lately with five consultants from UNDP to advise the prime minister on the best sequencing and pacing of the projects in order to decrease poverty and unemployment. With a PhD in strategic planning from the University of Pittsburgh, Jibril is a serious interlocutor who 'gets' the US perspective. He is also not shy about sharing his views of US foreign policy, for example, opining that the US spoiled a golden opportunity to capitalize on its 'soft power' (McDonald's, etc.) after the fall of the Soviet Union in 1989 by putting 'boots on the ground' in the Middle East. At the same time, his organization has a daunting task to tackle, in terms of rationalizing 11,000 development projects in the chaotic Libyan government bureaucracy and also, to train Libyans to work in new sectors outside of the hydrocarbons industry. Jibril has stated American companies and universities are welcome to join him in this endeavor and we should take him up on his offer."

Apart from Ernst & Young and the Oxford Group, another consultancy firm that made its trip to Qaddafi's Libya was McKinsey & Company. They came to work with the Libyan Central Bank's project director Tarek Ben Halim to create a friendly financial environment inside Libya for foreign banks. The property rights law no. 9 of 1992 allowed for private property, but its foundation had to be strengthened. Ben Halim (son of Idris' Prime Minister) came back to Libya from Goldman Sachs, and was deeply aware of the mechanisms for such reforms. A market for finance needed to be constituted, but it could only flourish if the Central Bank ceased to be a political instrument and allowed itself to ride the tide of the market (in other words, to give up any political oversight to the powerful waves generated by monopoly banks).

The changes desired by the reform section mentored by Saif al-Islam would certainly slice away at the social subsidies provided by the regime using the oil money. This worried another strand of the regime, and they weighed in on Qaddafi. They wanted the old fox to take a firm stand against the reformers. This was wishful thinking. At best, Qaddafi gave a couple of speeches that recycled the old rhetoric. In 2006, Qaddafi warned, "Oil companies are controlled by foreigners who have made millions from them — now Libyans must take their place to profit from this money." Oil nationalization (1972) had made a positive impact on the people's lives, but those days were long gone. Oil money now slipped through the net into the Atlantic banks, where the accounts of the oil companies, Libya's Sovereign Wealth fund and the private accounts of the Libyan regime's elites grew substantially. Qaddafi's fulminations would only result in some modest nationalist window-dressing: oil companies had to adopt Arabic names (Total became Mabruk, Repsol became Akakoss, ENI became Mellita and Veba became al-Hurruj). Behind the names, the old game continued. If the social wages would not be properly funded, other results awaited the Libyan people. The Governor of the Libyan Central Bank, Farhat Bengadara longed for the kind of "shock therapy" that had been conducted under the auspices of Jeffery Sachs in Eastern Europe. This was classic neoliberal thought at work.

By early 2008, the tremors in the ruling elites of Libya came to a head. The neoliberal reformers wanted much more, but they were being stymied. Ben Halim resigned when he found himself unable to move the banking system fully into neoliberalism. Jibril threatened to resign at least three times, but he was brought back into the fold with promises from Saif al-Islam. In his 2008 speech to the Youth Forum, Saif al-Islam himself proposed that he would retire from politics. These men responded to a formidable section of the Old Guard who had not fully bought into the reform agenda. People like Housing Minister Abu Zayd Umar Dorda held fast to the ideals of the 1969 revolution, or else they worried that their own leeching of the social wealth for private gain would be supplanted by the new methods that would benefit the reform section.

Qaddafi proposed a unique solution in 2008. He wanted to abolish all the ministries and turn over governance to a new structure (to be developed in working groups by Mahmoud Jibril). This was a boon to the reformers. To tie the hands of the Old Guard Qaddafi offered a massive transfer payment scheme, to turn over oil revenues to individuals. This was a populist feint, since it would allow Qaddafi to suggest that he remained a man of the people at the same time as he would liquidate not only the institutional apparatus of his state, but would also make it impossible to congregate the oil wealth for social spending (such as for health and education, which would now have to be purchased on an individual basis). It was privatization that looked like populism. It is here that Qaddafi remarkably began to say that it was time to return Libya to the "natural state of things," that is to say to the dynamic from 1951 onward, interrupted by the 1969 revolution. The past forty years had to be set aside, and Libya needed to pick up on its arrested historical development.

The Old Guard returned to the fray, threatening a rise in inflation if Qaddafi simply turned over the oil money to every individual Libyan. They were, however, not willing to take up the cudgel on behalf of a better system. Forty years of accommodation to the Qaddafi regime had made them ideologically unprepared to fight for any alternative. They had become defensive and worn-down. As early as 2000, the Basic People's Congress had complained about the first generation of reforms. The Congress did not appreciate the privatization of state-owned enterprises and the creation of free trade enclaves. Their periodical, *al-Zahf al-Akhdar*, fulminated against foreign firms and the tourism sector. A section within them was also angry at Qaddafi's political concessions to scale back the UN sanctions and to earn favors in European capitals. The Congress tried to hold the tempo of reforms down. Their actions irritated the IMF, whose 2006 report on Libya concluded, "Progress in developing a market economy has been slow and discontinuous."

By 2007, the neoliberals were able to push through a slate of what they considered the painless reforms: easy import of consumer goods, privatization of banks, easing of currency regulations, and the creation of a new legal framework for commerce. In addition, the neoliberal reformers and business community proposed a few other easy reforms: customs exemptions, tax holidays, vouchers for education and health care. These sailed through. The Old Guard's worries were vindicated by 2009, when the Libyan

National Information Board estimated that in the third quarter of 2008 prices were almost ten percent higher than they were in the third quarter of 2007. Social unrest in the cities over the rise in food prices had dampened the enthusiasm of the neoliberal reformers. Facts on the ground did not support them. Qaddafi nonetheless went to the General People's Congress in March 2009 and once more proposed a "shock therapy" version of privatization and state evisceration. It was not popular on the ground.

Nothing came of this. Instead, Qaddafi took to fulminating against prominent businessmen (such as Husni Bey, head of HB Group, and Hassan Tattanaki, head of Challenger Ltd.). It was dangerous to accuse these men of corruption, particularly when it had become clear already that wealth had been siphoned off to high officials in the regime and into Qaddafi's own family. Neoliberalism metastasized into Libya, carrying forward its normal forms of privatization and an end to social welfare, but manifesting itself in its local forms—it developed along the grain of the equations of power, here the disgorging of the "state of the masses" into the hierarchies of family. The Qaddafi clan dug in. It looked like corruption, but it was really neoliberalism's manifestation in the conditions it found in Libya in the early 2000s. The new state had gone into overdrive to demolish what it considered bad construction, painting *izaala* (removal) onto its walls. No homes of the elite were slated for destruction and seizure by some foundation or firm. It had become plain even in the Libyan media of the 2000s that the *Riqaba* committee, or the Committee for Oversight and Audit, had become a spoon for the skimming of the cream of business activity, with that cream ending up in private hands.

Qaddafi's son Sa'adi had created a Free Trade Area in Zuwara, using the regime's funds and pressure. Qaddafi's daughter Aisha had created a charity, Wa'atassemo Foundation, which seemed to be a front for her business activity rather than for aid purposes. The other sons, Mutassim and Mohammed (who dominated telecommunications), had come to armed blows over a Coca Cola bottling plant in 2006. All of this was miserable. But it was not corruption on a grand, legal scale such as would be familiar to the CEOs of the financial world or of the Gulf Arab emirs. A US State Department cable from 2006 quite gingerly pointed out, "Compared to the egregious pillaging of state coffers elsewhere in Africa, or the lavish spending of the Gulf Arabs, the Libyans don't see much to complain about in their leader's lifestyle, as long as he does a good job of making sure other people get a piece of the pie." When the *New York Times'* Anthony Shadid and Kareem Fahim went into the abandoned Qaddafi properties in August 2011, they reported that they seemed ordinary. "Given Colonel Qaddafi's noted flamboyance, the residence of Qaddafi himself was not quite as grand as people might have supposed. They lacked the faux grandeur of Saddam Hussein's marbled palaces. There are no columns that bear the colonel's initials, or fists cast to resemble his hands or river-fed moats with voracious carp."

Qaddafi's children had no such scruples. Aisha Qaddafi's lavish compound in the Noflein district in Tripoli was built during those neoliberal reform years of 2005–08. Her brother, Hannibal financed his lavish lifestyle from the funds in the national shipping company. He liked his Dom Perignon and his Gulfstream jet, and had a reputation (with his wife the Lebanese model Aline Skaf) of brutality toward their domestic help (in 2008 they were arrested in Geneva for "bodily harm, threatening behaviour and coercion" against domestic staff, and they were known to have burnt the Ethiopian nanny of their two children, Shweyga Mullah, after she apparently failed to keep them quiet). The vulgar expenditures of the children were kept relatively hidden from the population. When the House of Qaddafi decided to be excessively lavish, its members took a flight to London or Geneva and threw themselves a party. No wonder that the citizens of Libya, like those of France two hundred and twenty five years ago and those in Egypt in 1952, walked bewildered through the palaces of their rulers, converting them into museums of excess that needed to be seen to be mocked, not seen to be envied.

In 2008, as the reformers found their way blocked, a prominent Tripoli attorney Ibrahim el-Meyet, a friend of Shukri Ghanem, went to meet the Charges d'Affaires in the United States Embassy. He complained for Ghanem, and then laid out why the neoliberal reformers felt that no shock therapy-type change would come as long as Qaddafi remained in power, "Despite the rhetoric, el-Meyet said he and Ghanem believe that al-Qadhafi is not genuinely ready 'in his heart and in his bones' to implement change, for two reasons. First, real change would entail undoing economic fiefdoms of regime loyalists whose profitability derives from political connections and who would be unable to successfully compete in an economy characterized by transparency and rule of law. Second, genuine reform would be a tacit admission that the Jamahiriya system, of which al-Qadhafi himself was the author, had failed. Al-Qadhafi perceives himself as 'a superman of history' and is not able to admit fault or weakness. Cosmetic attempts at economic reform are acceptable and help advance al-Qadhafi's goal of reingratiating Libya with the West, but the shared assessment of Ghanem and el-Meyet is that meaningful economic and political reform will not occur while al-Qadhafi is alive." This is not Qaddafi's own view of why he would not fully support the reforms. It also lays too much on the shoulders of Qaddafi alone, and not on the Old Guard's bloc and that of the public sector workers who fought against the reformers from the early part of the twenty-first century. Nonetheless, it says a great deal about the reformers themselves, who believed that Qaddafi had to go for their agenda to go even further.

If Saif al-Islam was not the son of Qaddafi he might well have thrown in his lot with the neoliberal reformers in the rebellion of 2011, many of whom formed the nucleus of the leadership of the Transitional National Council (Jibril first among them). Instead family ties and the intoxication of power must have led Saif al-Islam to remain by his father's side. But there is also an ideological reason why Saif al-Islam would have been loyal to his father, and denigrated the rebels. In September 2007, Saif al-Islam wrote a dissertation at the London School of Economics on "The Role of Civil Society in the Democratisation of Global Decision Making: From "soft" power to collective decision-making" (the work was advised by a leading neoliberal globalization theorist David Held). Saif al-Islam argued for the need to give NGOs voting rights at the level of international decision making, where otherwise the United States and its Atlantic allies hold sway. The "essential nature" of NGOs, he argued, is to be "independent critics and advocates of the marginal and vulnerable." To allow NGOs to temper the ambitions of the North is far more "*realistic*," Saif al-Islam argued, than to hope to transform international relations. That kind of realism led to his faith in the reforms and in February 20 speech for the harshest armed violence against the protests in Tripoli and Benghazi. "Civil society," in the language of neoliberalism, is restricted to the work of establishment NGOs that are loath to revise settled power equations. The ragged on the streets are not part of the "civil society"; they are Unreason afoot.

Saif al-Islam's mother Safia Farkash reportedly told an acquaintance at a dinner party in late 2007 that she was worried that her son's reforms had "exacerbated resentment of the Qaddafi family and other elites who had profited disproportionately from recent initiatives to open Libya's economy." The average Libyan, she worried, found their livelihood damaged by inflation, and found themselves now living beside a small section whose own confidence seemed to be on the rise. It was not the social conditions of life that breed resentment, but the perception of a relative distinction between the frustrations of the many and the casual temper of the few. She was perceptive. This is what Alexis de Tocqueville had written in his 1856 *L'ancien régime*, "It is not always by going from bad to worse that a society falls into revolution. It happens most often that a people, which has supported without complaint, as if they were not felt, the most oppressive laws, violently throws them off as soon as their weight is lightened. The social order destroyed by a revolution is almost always better than that which immediately preceded it, and experience shows that the most dangerous moment for a bad government is generally that in which it sets about reform." Saif al-Islam and the neoliberal reformers set in motion the collapse of the regime. They awakened a new sentiment that bubbled into protests. It would explode in February 2011.

IV. Libya's Million Mutinies

The rebellion in Benghazi began on February 15, 2011. For the first few days the protests were peaceful and the police fired on them. The number of dead by February 19 was about one hundred and four (according to Human Rights Watch). These numbers are approximations, because the proper forensic work was not possible absent entry into morgues. Human rights activist Fateh Terbil said on that day, "Our numbers show that more than two hundred people have been killed." "It feels like a warzone," he pointed out. Human Rights Watch's Tom Porteous told AFP on February 19, "We are very concerned that under the communications blackout that has fallen on Libya since yesterday a human rights catastrophe is unfolding."

The violence did escalate, but it was not as one-sided as it appeared at first hand. On February 21, the Libyan air force attacked Benghazi. The former Libyan Ambassador to India, Ali Abd al-Aziz al-Isawi said that the fighter jets were used to attack civilians. Others on the ground said that they targeted the military barracks and ammunition dumps. There was no attempt to verify the claims. Part of this was the lack of media access in the country (a problem magnified in Syria) and part of it is the fog of war. The Cairo-based Arab Organization for Human Rights asked for an international investigation of the war crimes. The UN's commissioner for human rights Navi Pillay denounced the Libyan regime on February 18, but she said nothing about the police station burned down by the rebels in Dernah or the execution of fifty "African mercenaries and Libyan conspirators" in Al Bayda'. That last quote was from an article in *The Guardian* (authored by Ian Black and Owen Bowcott, February 19). The full quote is from *al-Jazeera*:

> Amer Saad, a political activist from Derna, told *al-Jazeera*: "The protesters in al-Bayda' have been able to seize control of the military airbase in the city and have executed 50 African mercenaries and two Libyan conspirators. Even in Derna today, a number of conspirators were executed. They were locked up in the holding cells of a police station because they resisted, and some died burning inside the building. This will be the end of every oppressor who stands with Gaddafi. Gaddafi is over, that's it, he has no presence here any more. The eastern regions of Libya are now free regions. If he wants to reclaim it, he will need to bomb us with nuclear or chemical bombs. This is his only

option. The people have stood and said they will not go back."

This press report made no impact on the UN headquarters, because two days later, on February 21, the UN News Center reported that UN Secretary-General Ban Ki-moon was "outraged *at press reports* that the Libyan authorities have been firing at demonstrators from war planes and helicopters." The conventional narrative in the Atlantic world was that Qaddafi's regime had begun a full-bore attack on the unarmed civilian protestors. In no time at all, which is to say by February 23, word would leak out of London and Paris that the Atlantic states were worried about a potential massacre. Qaddafi, meanwhile, said on February 22 that he had "not yet ordered the use of force," and that "when I do, everything will burn." It is without question that when Qaddafi did give his orders to his Generals they probably mimicked those of the Serbian General Ratko Mladic, whose orders to his troops regarding a Bosnian city are chilling, "Shell them till they are on the edge of madness" (Qaddafi and Mladic are heirs to the words of William Henry Drayton, who advised his settler troops in their war against the Cherokees, "Cut up every Indian cornfield, and burn every Indian town"). But such orders had not yet been given in February, according to Qaddafi. A week later the US State Department's spokesperson Mark Toner warned that Qaddafi was given to "overblown rhetoric." But this rhetoric would have it uses if Qaddafi needed to go. It would be sufficient when necessary to turn that rhetoric against Qaddafi. Such speeches were tinder for the fires of imperialism.

The details of the ground-war are essential at this point. They tell us how swiftly the rebels were able to take over Benghazi, Tobruk, Misrata, Az Zawiya and even the Tripoli working-class neighborhood of Tajoura and the Mitiga International Airport ("a serious blow to the regime," wrote *The Guardian*'s Ian Black on February 26). The Warfallah tribal elders declared on February 23 that they no longer supported the regime. Defections from the Libyan government came first in drips and then in a flood. On February 17, Youssef Sawani, Saif al-Islam's close aide and head of the Qaddafi Foundation, resigned and joined the rebellion. This was an embarrassment, but it was not decisive. That was to follow. Mustafa Abdel-Jalil, Qaddafi's interior minister, resigned on February 21. He would become the head of the rebellion's political arm, the National Transitional Council when it was formed on February 27 by himself and 'Abd al-Fattah Younis. Major General al-Fattah Younis had been the Minister of the Interior in Qaddafi's cabinet, and was sent to Benghazi on February 18 to relieve the loyalists besieged in the Katiba military compound. Major General al-Fattah Younis defected with his troops. He would become the military leader of the rebellion.

As Abdel-Jalil and al-Fattah Younis formed the core of the NTC, the defections of entire military battalions and of individual air-force pilots would begin apace. In Benghazi and Tobruk considerable sections of the armed detachments gave themselves over to the rebellion. The naval base and airport in Benghazi went to the rebellion. Soldiers from Az Zawiya joined them. In Misrata, the Qaddafi troops shot at a crowd with rocket-propelled grenades, and the protestors fired back with an anti-aircraft gun. The cadets at an air force school joined the protests, took over the airbase in Misrata and disabled the jets. On February 24, the BBC reported, "In the eastern city of Benghazi, residents have been queuing to be issued with guns looted from the army and police in order to join what they are calling the battle for Tripoli. A number of military units in the east say they have unified their command in support of the protesters." BBC's Jon Leyne, reporting from eastern Libya, said that Qaddafi was likely ready less than ten days after the outbreak of the rebellion to make his final stand in Tripoli. The tide was with the rebels.

It was at this stage of the conflict that the United Nations Security Council passed Resolution 1970 (February 26). The resolution came to the Council from the Atlantic powers (France, Germany, the United Kingdom and the United States). The resolution called for an end to the hostilities, an asset freeze and travel ban on members of the Qaddafi regime, and an embargo on arms sales to Libya (which was interpreted to mean, no arms to either side in the conflict). There was a general understanding that the situation on the ground in Libya had devolved into an asymmetrical civil war, with the Libyan army (with air support) far stronger than the rebel army. There was no discussion about the defections to the rebels, and its gains. The language of a potential civilian massacre in any of the cities had not been raised. The statement by Nigeria's U. Joy Ogwu was typical. She expressed her concern about the "inflammatory rhetoric and loss of life occurring in Libya," and hoped that the sanctions would "provide for the protection of civilians and respect for international humanitarian and human rights law." The Council focused on the killing of the protestors in the cities and the refugee crisis that had inflicted the Tunisian-Libyan border.

The Libyan Ambassador to the United Nations, Abdel Rahman Shalgham, a leading figure in the Qaddafi regime for his entire career, defected to the rebels. He pushed the Council hard to create a no-fly zone and to ask the International Criminal Court (ICC) to investigate Qaddafi and his regime for war crimes. It took a great deal to persuade China, India and Russia to go along with the ICC involvement. But no-one was willing to go for a "no-fly zone," and the Russians in particular pushed in a clause against any foreign intervention. The Council did not hear from anyone loyal to the Qaddafi regime, even though on paper that regime continued to be the recognized government.

On the ground, meanwhile, the rebels, despite the bloodshed and without foreign assistance, seemed to be making headway. This was not Egypt and Tunisia, where the armies stood down and refused to fire on the protestors. Here the army had broken into two, one part remaining loyal to the Qaddafi regime, and the other giving itself over to the rebellion. Qaddafi still controlled the air, but even that seemed to be a momentary advantage. On February 21, two Libyan Air Force Dassault Mirage F-1 jets flew to Malta, and the pilots requested political asylum. This was a turn for the Air Force. A week later, on February 28, the rebels of Misrata shot down a Libyan Air Force jet. On March 2, when Libyan Air Force jets targeted the weapons dump at Ajdabiya, the rebels shot down one aircraft. Three days later, the rebels in Ras Lanuf shot down a fighter jet. On March 13, Colonel Ali Atiyya announced his defection at the Mitiga International Airport in Tripoli.

These high-level military defections continued. On March 1, Brigadier Musa'ed Ghaidan al-Mansouri (head of the al-Wahat Security Directorate), Brigadier Hassan Ibrahim al-Qarawi and Brigadier Dawood Issa al-Qafi defected to the rebellion. Troops joined them. On February 26, ten thousand troops in the east went to the rebellion. Meanwhile, in Az Zawiya the rebels held off the Qaddafi forces on March 1, they took Ghadames and Nalut on March 2, and battled Qaddafi's forces in Bin Jawad on March 5. As they advanced forward, Qaddafi's air force began to be an impediment. When the rebels moved toward Sirte on March 6, the Libyan Air Force fired on them, and they retreated to Ras Lanuf. By March 11, Ras Lanuf and Az Zawiya went back and forth between Qaddafi's troops and the rebels. Brega and Ras Lanuf are not heavily populated towns. They were not of supreme consequence to the fight. More important was Ajdabiya, the gateway to Benghazi.

On March 15, the rebels used their own air force to destroy two of Qaddafi's warships and they hit a third off the coast of Ajdabiya and Benghazi (as reported by *al-Jazeera*). It meant that the rebels had developed air power, strengthened the next day with the defection of two more fighter jets into Benghazi and two more battalions from Sirte, who took over its airport. In Misrata, the rebels defeated Qaddafi's forces on March 16, and took command of several of his tanks.

Nevertheless, by mid-March the Qaddafi forces had pushed the rebels out of the central towns and appeared to be advancing to Benghazi, and to Misrata. It is at this point that the calls began to intensify for either a "no-fly" zone or some kind of intervention to prevent a massacre. Britain's David Cameron had called for a "no-fly" zone on February 28, and the Arab League sharpened the call on March 12. The NTC asked the United Nations for a "no-fly" zone on March 2, the day after the military leader Major General al-Fattah Younis called for foreign intervention. As morale began to turn in the rebel's camp, the leadership sought salvation elsewhere.

Was a massacre impending? Qaddafi's troops had previously tried to take Az Zawiya (March 1) and Misrata (March 6), and in both cases the rebels held off the attacks. There is no question that blood was going to be shed, but that is not itself the definition of a massacre or of genocide. When Qaddafi took back Az Zawiya on March 7, credible reports suggested that the "minimum" loss of life was about eight people. Thirty-three people died on March 5 at Az Zawiya, with twenty-five being rebels and eight being Qaddafi soldiers. When Qaddafi's army shelled Misrata on March 6, twenty-one rebels were killed. These are the costs of war, not the outcome of genocide. Revolutions are fought. They cannot be given. The rebels seemed prepared. Protests in Tripoli amongst the working-class neighborhoods of Feshloom, Gurgi and Tajoura gave extra strength to the rebellion. These neighborhoods were in permanent siege. Martyrs lay on autopsy tables at Tripoli Central Hospital. The workers were not pusillanimous. They seized the moment. There would be blood. No revolution comes in a straight line. The workers knew nasty from their everyday lives. No-one would expect that real revolutionary change would come absent violence.

The conflict began on February 15. Six days later, the Libyan Deputy Permanent Representative to the UN, Ibrahim Dabbashi, having defected from the regime, said, "The regime of Qaddafi has already started the genocide against the Libyan people." What was the evidence for the genocide, which technically is the "intent to destroy, in whole or in part, a national, ethnic, racial or religious group" (Convention on the Prevention and Punishment of the Crime of Genocide, UN, 1948)? Where was the "intent to destroy" and where was the evidence that this had "already started"? Not to fix onto definitions, let us assume that Dabbashi did not mean "genocide," but simply what he had also said in the same press conference, that what was occurring were "crimes against humanity and crimes of war." The standard for these is no doubt lower. The Rome Statute (1998) that established the International Criminal Court (ICC) notes that "crimes against humanity" refers to "odious offenses" that are not "sporadic events, but are part either of a government policy…or of a wide practice of atrocities tolerated or condoned by a government." For these crimes, still, one would have to ascertain them in terms of quantity (how many dead?) and quality (how did they die?). Dabbashi, like many of the high level diplomatic defectors of the Libyan service, touted very high figures. Most of them seem to have based their numbers on a report from *al-Arabiyya*, based in Dubai and owned by a Saudi company,

Middle East Broadcasting Center, and Lebanon's Hariri Group (these are largely pro-Western and pro-Saudi business interests). On its Twitter feed, *al-Arabiyya* reported that 50,000 had already been wounded and 10,000 massacred by the Libyan government. The source for this story was Sayed al-Shanuka, the Libyan member of the ICC who had defected from the regime. This was on February 23, a week after the conflict began.

That number swept the media sphere. *Al-Jazeera*, based in Qatar, ran the story, as did the BBC and the US media. No-one seemed to ask where these deaths had taken place. France's Sarkozy and Britain's Cameron warned Qaddafi that they would act if this kind of killing continued. The word "genocide" defined the discussion. Even in the liberal-Left, commentators absorbed the idea that "genocide" had either happened (based on *al-Arabiyya* numbers) or was about to happen (the people here are Juan Cole and Gilbert Achcar). But already some credible organizations began to provide figures. On February 20, Human Rights Watch announced a figure of 233, with most of the dead in Benghazi proper. Benghazi was, by February 20, in rebel hands. One of the alarms rung by those who spoke of an impending massacre by late February was that the population of Misrata was going to be killed in large numbers. On April 10, Human Rights Watch released a report on the dead of Misrata, a major battlefield in the war. What they found for this city of four hundred thousand was that, according to Dr. Muhammad el-Fortia (of Misrata Hospital) who had the highest numbers, there were 949 wounded and 257 dead. Of these, surprisingly, the numbers of women dead were only 22, or three percent of the total. If the violence was indiscriminately or odiously unleashed on the population the percentage of women killed would surely have been higher. The discourse on genocide in Libya was either fanciful or based entirely on speculation. It simply did not happen. By the middle of June, the first credible figure appeared that showed that about ten thousand people had been killed. This was from Cherif Bassiouni of the UN, who led a UN Human Rights Council team to Tripoli. Bassiouni's panel found evidence of war crimes by Qaddafi's side, but also noted war crimes on the side of the rebels. This number comes not within days of the rebellion and the attacks by the army, and not in one site, but over the course of four months. It includes the violence from the Libyan army, the violence from the rebels and the violence of the NATO aerial assault. Much later, on December 18, 2011, the *New York Times'* C. J. Chivers and Eric Schmitt published a long investigation on the civilian casualties inflicted by the NATO bombardment. They found that the seven month air campaign came with "an unrecognized toll: scores of civilian casualties the alliance has long refused to acknowledge or investigate." That was long after the conflict had substantially ended. Bassiouni is a credible Egyptian diplomat, who has headed many panels to investigate human rights (such as in Afghanistan between 2004 and 2006), and has consulted with the US State Department. His figures seemed accurate to human rights specialists. Nevertheless, at no point did Bassiouni's panel call for an investigation of NATO's war crimes or of the attacks by the rebels on civilians (such as the so-called "African mercenaries"). The emphasis was on Qaddafi's human rights violations.

Even more startling evidence of the very poor investigation of the war crimes allegations comes at a Pentagon press conference on March 1. When asked about Qaddafi's aerial attacks on civilians, Defense Secretary Gates said, "We've seen the press reports, but we have no confirmation of that," and Admiral Mike Mullen added, "That's correct. We've seen no confirmation whatsoever." That the US military complex relies upon *press reports* to confirm the use of live fire seems remarkable—with the massive surveillance infrastructure in place it seems that the Pentagon would be able to make a reasonably more accurate assessment than *al-Jazeera* or BBC, or *al-Arabiyya*, upon whom they relied to base their assessment of armed conflict. Asked about the situation on the ground in Libya, Gates offered an "honest answer," which was that "we don't know in that respect, in terms of the number of casualties. In terms of the potential capabilities of the opposition, we're in the same realm of speculation, pretty much, as everybody else. I haven't seen anything that would give us a better read on the number of rebels that have been killed than you have. And I think it remains to be seen how effectively military leaders who have defected from Gadhafi's forces can organize the opposition in the country." Asked at this point if the rebels had asked for NATO air strikes, Gates answered, "no."

Around March 14, despite the talk of genocide, *al-Jazeera* reported that the rebels fought on. East of Brega they ambushed a Qaddafi column and took fourteen soldiers prisoner and killed twenty-five. The two major cities of the rebellion, Benghazi in the East and Misrata in the West, remained in rebel hands. On March 13, the rebels held off the Qaddafi attack on Misrata. The Qaddafi troops, according to *al-Jazeera*, had a break-down in discipline, and this cost them their superiority in firepower. The next day, Qaddafi's advance to Beng-hazi was blocked at Ajdabiya, held by the main rebel force under the command of Major General al-Fattah Younis. The Major General told *al-Jazeera* that he would defend Ajdabiya, and that the cities of the east were heavily armed, ready to take on Qaddafi's armies block by block. It had already become clear by March 14 that even if Qaddafi's armies took back towns, they were not capable of holding onto them. The rebellion seemed to have the initiative.

V. Intervention

By early March, the Libyan rebellion began to be hi-jacked by forces close to the Atlantic powers, whose interest in Libya is governed by oil and by power: it is my view that the Libyan rebellion gave the Atlantic powers, Qatar and Saudi Arabia an opportunity to at-tempt to seize control over an escalating dynamic that had spread across the Middle East and North Africa, which had already been called the Arab Spring. It threatened the US pillars of stability and the founda-tion of Saudi rule. This dynamic needed to be con-trolled, or at least, harnessed. Libya, which sits in the center of North Africa, with Egypt on one border and Tunisia on the other, provided the perfect space to hurry along the clock, to skip Summer and hasten to Winter. Apart from the obvious addiction to oil, the political issue came to the surface: to maintain the traditional order of things in the Arab world, with the main pillars of stability intact: Israel, Saudi Arabia, with the Gulf emirs, and the tentacles of the Atlantic world in the major capitals in the oil lands. No revision of that order was permitted. Libya opened the door to the counter-revolution.

Why did the Atlantic states want to remove Qaddafi? We shall have to wait for the leaks, the self-serving memoirs and the next major cache of WikiLeaks documents, this time perhaps from the Quai d'Orsay. By March, the French were in the lead at the United Nations. Initially it seemed that this was either a smokescreen or a wag the dog scenario. After all, during the Tunisian uprising, the French Foreign Minister Michele Alliot-Marie flew on a plane owned by Aziz Miled, a close associate of Belhassen Trabelsi, the brother-in-law of Ben Ali. When she returned to France, Alliot-Marie, or MAM as she is known, offered French assistance to help put down the rebellion. All this focused attention on the fact that Sarkozy was very close to Ben Ali, and in 2008 was made an honorary citizen of Tunis. Frédéric Mitterrand, Sarkozy's culture minister, went along the grain of MAM's offer of military assistance, in mid-January, "To say that Tunisia is a one-man dictatorship seems to me quite exaggerated." France had fumbled in Tunisia. MAM was fired, but her departure only heightened the stench of collusion between Sarkozy's circle and people like Aziz Miled, Belhassen Trabelsi and eventually, Ben Ali.

Libya would provide the smokescreen to cover over what the US embassy in Tunis described in 2005 as France's "tradition of cultivating close relations with ageing Arab world dictators." This was a classic case of transference. With cantonal election on the horizon in March it might have bolstered the fortunes of Sarkozy's anemic party (but it did not, as the far right and the socialists made considerable gains). As well, the French intelligentsia went out of its way to promote the war. Former Sarkozy Foreign Minister and legendary promoter of humanitarian intervention Bernard Kouchner threw himself at the English and French media to promote the war. He was helped along by *gauche caviar*, Bernard Henri-Levy (BHL), whom Tariq Ali called a "veritable Tintin." BHL phoned Sarkozy from his revolutionary safari in Benghazi, where he was also trying to steady the nerves of the neoliberal faction among the rebel leadership. The Élysée Palace needed fortitude of the BHL variety if it was to stay the course toward UN Resolution 1973 and the intervention. Sarkozy did not need much persuasion. Qaddafi had stymied his Mediterranean Union. He was an impediment to French interests in the region. The French led because the Libyan goose was ready to deliver a golden egg.

The Gaullist traditions of hesitancy over intervention were broken by the Kosovo war. No such tradition needed to be broken across the Channel in the United Kingdom or across the Atlantic in the United States. Oil is always a central preoccupation of the war planners among the cousins. The basic script for the US and the UK was set after the Iraqi coup of 1958 in a telegram sent by British Foreign Secretary

Selwyn Lloyd to his prime minister, the Conservative leader Harold Macmillan. If the British pre-emptively occupied Kuwait, Selwyn Lloyd wrote, it would get the oil into their hands quickly. There was a problem: "The effect on international opinion and the rest of the Arab world would not be good." Instead of this preferred, direct route, the best option was to set up a "Kuwait Switzerland where the British do not exercise physical control," but "we must also accept the need, if things to wrong, ruthlessly to intervene, whoever it is has caused the trouble." This ruthless intervention was necessary to protect the Gulf oil reserves and indeed the Arab oil lands, what the US State Department right after World War 2 called "a stupendous source of strategic power, and one of the great material prizes in world history." It would be silly to ignore the elephant in the room, namely oil.

If oil was one part of the equation, the other was the political necessity to exercise hegemony in the region, to maintain that stupendous source of strategic power. The US had come off very poorly with Obama's hesitancy in Egypt. Sending Wisner was the wrong move. So too was the dialogue with Tantawi over stability and Israel. The US needed to get back in the game as the Arab Spring seemed to spiral out of control. Libya was the impetus for a re-engagement on US terms.

On March 15, in the White House, President Obama's inner circle sat and made their plans. At the center of it were people who believed that George W. Bush's adventure in Iraq in 2003 destroyed the will among Northern states for humanitarian intervention. That will was to be reconstructed. Libya provided the opportunity. A senior administration official told *Time*'s Massimo Calabresi, "The effort to shoe-horn [the Libyan events] into an imminent genocide model is strained." Nevertheless, as early as February, the supporters of humanitarian intervention were "laying the predicate" for military force. Among those supporters were Samantha Power and Jeremy Weinstein (National Security Council), Susan Rice (UN Ambassador) and Hillary Clinton (Secretary of State). Obama had a harder time with his military commanders, who were loathe to enter another conflict on pragmatic grounds: they simply did not have the available troops if the conflict escalated. But Obama got their support, and on March 16 announced that if Qaddafi was not stopped "the words of the international community would be rendered hollow." This was the same argument used by George W. Bush against Saddam Hussein.

What really seems to have set the clock to intervention was the pressure from the Saudis and the other Gulf Arabs. They wanted to put down the Bahrain uprising and take control, in their own way, of events in Yemen. As well, the Saudi King hated Qaddafi. In 2003, at an Arab Summit, Qaddafi accused King Abdullah of "bringing the Americans to occupy Iraq." The following year, King Abdullah's people accused Qaddafi of trying to kill the King. In 2006 at another Arab Summit in Doha, Qatar, Qaddafi faced the King and said, "It has been six years, and you have been avoiding a confrontation with me. You are propelled by fibs toward the grave and you were made by Britain and protected by the US." The point about the British and the Americans is perhaps true, and it made for good television to watch Qaddafi erupt. The emir of Qatar, Sheikh Hamad bin Khalifa al-Thani, was embarrassed to see his senior potentate be scolded in this manner, and furious at Qaddafi. The memory of a monarch is longer than that of an elephant. It is also filled with petty slights that must be avenged. The monarch dreams that his enemies are flies to be swatted; when he wakes he razes cities. Any excuse to put that upstart from a minor tribe in his place was welcomed in the royal circles of Riyadh.

These are all speculations. It is of course the case that Libya's neoliberal reform agenda had been dented. Ghanem had sent his emissary, el-Meyet, to tell the Americans in 2008 that the agenda would not be able to move unless Qaddafi was out. The old man was willing to go along with the neoliberal reforms, but his regime was incapable of delivering it. It had to be knocked out. There were always conspiracies afoot, but these were not decisive. Three of the leaders of the February 17 Movement went to Paris on December 23, 2010 where they met other figures from the old anti-Qaddafi clique. Fathi Boukhris, Farj Charrani and Ali Ounes Mansouri sat down with Qaddafi's old aide-de-camp, Nuri Mesmari, who had defected to the Concorde-Lafayette hotel. What is essential to know about Mesmari, Qaddafi's shadow, is that he was a crucial figure among the neoliberal reformers, the point man who arranged state trips of foreign leaders and who pampered Qaddafi's children. It is said that Qaddafi insulted Mesmari at an Afro-Arab summit in Sirte on October 10, 2010, after which he decamped for Paris. It is also said that Qaddafi was angry with the entire clique by December 2010, and had asked Moussa Koussa for his passport. This can-

VIJAY PRASHAD

not be confirmed. What is clear is that by December Mesmari was singing to the DGSE and Sarkozy about the weaknesses of the Libyan state. Their man in Benghazi was Colonel Abdallah Gehani of the air defense corps. He was arrested by Qaddafi's regime in January 2011. The Atlantic states set aside Gehani by mid-March. He could not ascend to the leadership of the military side of the rebellion. The CIA already had its man in mind. He would soon be in place. We shall get to him below.

Cynics in Washington and Paris used Libya as a way to wash off the stain of Bush's Iraqi adventure from the carapace of the idea of humanitarian interventionism. This is cynical and inhumane. Out of such misplaced idealism comes enormous bloodshed for ordinary people.

Resolution 1973.

On March 19, the United Nations Security Council voted for Resolution 1973 to establish a "no-fly" zone over Libya. The violence against civilians and media personnel was cited as the reason for the new resolution (an earlier one, 1970, languished). The Council authorized a ban on all flights over Libya (except for humanitarian purposes), froze assets of a selection of the Libyan high command (including all of Qaddafi's family), and proposed to set up a Panel of Experts to look into the issue within the next year. Even as the members of the Council raised their paddles to indicate their "yes" votes, French mirage fighters powered up to begin their bombing runs and US ships loaded their cruise missiles to fire into Libyan targets. Their bombardments were intended to dismantle Libyan air defenses. This was the prelude to the establishment of a "no-fly" zone.

The ground for NATO's intervention was crafted after the genocide in Rwanda (1994), when an estimated million people were massacred over the course of a few months. This action happened in plain sight, with a United Nations team unable or unwilling to act to stem the violence. The sheer sin of the event pushed the UN toward a new doctrine, if not a new understanding of whether such genocides can easily be prevented (if the US and/or NATO had acted in Rwanda, what would they have bombed to prevent the genocide? How would they have bombed the hundreds of thousands of people who wielded *pangas* [machetes] to kill almost a million Tutsis. The tiny minority of *génocidaires* convinced the many to kill, Mahmood Mamdani shows us in *When the Victims Become Killers*. Aerial bombardment does not provide a simple solution to such a grave and difficult political problem). By 1999, President Bill Clinton declared, "If the world community has the power to stop it, we ought to stop genocide and ethnic cleansing." The International Commission on Intervention and State Sovereignty (2001) and then a UN Panel on these issue (2004) reported, "We endorse the emerging norm that there is a collective international responsibility to protect...in the event of genocide and other large-scale killing, ethnic cleansing or serious violations of international humanitarian law." The UN General Assembly at the 2005 World Summit suggested that the UN could authorize force "on a case-by-case basis, should peaceful means be inadequate." The final clause here is central, and it was not discussed at the Security Council in March.

No-one considered a peaceful path, even though the African Union had set up an Ad Hoc High Level Committee on Libya on March 10. It was sidelined, and in fact its team was prevented from going to Libya on March 19 as the French mirages took off to bomb the country. Humanitarian intervention (the alias for aerial bombardment) would come prior to and against any peaceful initiatives to stop the violence.

To create the "no-fly" zone, the Council allowed member states to act "nationally or through regional organizations" and to use "all necessary measures to protect civilians and civilian-populated areas." The problem with this confused mandate was at least two-fold. One: who would be able to execute the mandate? As Mahmood Mamdani astutely put the problem, the United Nations' resolution was "central to the process of justification, it is peripheral to the process of execu-tion." The UN had no real ability to take "all neces-sary measures," and nor would the African Union or the Arab League. Indeed, in the chamber, the Rus-sian and Chinese delegates caviled about "how and by whom the measures would be enforced and what the limits of engagement would be." The only power capable of such an action was the United States either alone or in collaboration with NATO, of which the US is a major part. In other words, the UN resolution was falsely universal, calling on "all member states" when it might as well have been decidedly particular, calling on NATO and the United States to act here as it had acted in Yugoslavia.

Once the war entered its critical stage in Septem-ber and October, the US military, the Obama White House and its assorted intellectuals began to promote the view that the US "led from behind." It was NATO that was in the lead, they suggested. This was a view put forward first by Ryan Lizza in *The New Yorker* for an essay entitled "The Consequentialist: How the Arab Spring Remade Obama's Foreign Policy." "Pursuing our interests and spreading our ideals," Lizza wrote, "requires stealth and modesty as well as military strength." As an Obama advisor told Lizza, "It's so at odds with the John Wayne expectation for what America is in the world." The US had learned its lessons about the perils of unilateral intervention. Obama had the soft touch against Bush's harder manner. But this is another illusion. When Roger Cohen of the *New York Times* tweeted about this, he received an immediate rebuke from the US Ambassador to NATO, Ivo Daalder, "That's not leading from behind. When you set the course, provide critical enablers and succeed, it's plain leading." The United States provided most of the surveillance, intelligence and reconnaissance capabilities, it conducted most of the refueling missions and it provided most of the aerial bombardment. Resolution 1973 was essentially an invitation for US power to be exercised from the skies of North Africa onto its ground.

The second problem with the Resolution was graver. It did not specify who would define the limits of "all necessary measures" and how long should these "measures" remain in force? The UN Resolution 1973 called upon the parties to facilitate dialogue and to seek the means for an "immediate establishment of a ceasefire." If NATO and/or the United States went into full-scale action that would embolden the rebellion to believe that under cover of the drones

and cruise missiles they would soon ride their Toy-
otas into Tripoli. There would be no stomach for a
ceasefire given the type of strategy NATO historically
utilizes. At the same time, Qaddafi would immediately
recognize that NATO's typical modus operandi was
to seek to isolate the regime's leader (as NATO did
with Slobodan Milosevic) by pushing for an ICC investigation on war crimes charges, to use aerial bombardment to degrade his armed force and to push the
rebels to make a full-scale charge to overthrow him.
Around the time of the Resolution, Sarkozy, Cameron
and Obama began to say that Qaddafi "has to go."
They wrote a joint opinion essay that appeared on
April 15 in various media outlets (including *The New
York Times*, where I read it). They laid out the full nature of their campaign against Qaddafi,

> So long as Gaddafi is in power, NATO and
> its coalition partners must maintain their op-
> erations so that civilians remain protected
> and the pressure on the regime builds. Then
> a genuine transition from dictatorship to an
> inclusive constitutional process can really be-
> gin, led by a new generation of leaders. For
> that transition to succeed, Colonel Gaddafi
> must go, and go for good.

If Qaddafi had to go "and go for good," there was
no room for any negotiation. There was no option for
a peaceful settlement. Assassination or war was the
only option. "To insist that Qaddafi both leave the
country and face trial in the International Criminal
Court is virtually to ensure that he will stay in Libya

to the bitter end and go down fighting," pointed out the International Crisis Group's North Africa director Hugh Roberts. "That would render a ceasefire all but impossible and so maximize the prospect of continued armed conflict." The entire idea that NATO was open to a peaceful path was a cynical smokescreen to camouflage NATO's singular agenda: to use its military might to give air-cover for the rebels to seize Tripoli, and, as far as the evidence suggest, to remain beholden to the NATO states for their fundamental assistance.

Given this, the NATO strategy would have no room for a "ceasefire." One of the principle planks of the confused resolution would never be met. That is why even Gilbert Achcar, who otherwise supported a "no-fly" zone wrote, "There are not enough safeguards in the wording of the resolution to bar its use for imperialist purposes." One senior diplomat told Pepe Escobar of *Asia Times* why his country could not support Resolution 1973, "We were arguing that Libya, Bahrain and Yemen were similar cases, and calling for a fact-finding mission. We maintain our official position that the resolution is not clear, and may be misinterpreted in a belligerent manner." Not long after the passage of Resolution 1973, US cruise missiles struck Libyan armed forces units and Qaddafi's home.

By March 20, it was clear that the United States and NATO had gone to war against Qaddafi himself.

The murkiness of the mission perplexed General Carter Ham of the US African Command (AFRICOM). Ham acknowledged that many of the rebels are themselves civilians who have taken up arms. Resolution 1973 did not call upon the member states to assist the rebels, only to protect civilians. It followed the Responsibility to Protect mandate of the UN. It was technically not permitted to enter the civil war on one side or another. There is no obligation to protect an armed rebellion, only unarmed civilians. By the first days of the NATO bombing, however, it was already clear that the "no-fly" zone would advantage the rebels and so violate the mandate. "We do not provide close air support for the opposition forces," General Ham notes, "We protect civilians." However, "It's a very problematic situation. Sometimes these are situations that brief better at the headquarters than in the cockpit of an aircraft." But this was disingenuous. The rebel spokesperson, and former *Good Morning Benghazi* presenter Ahmed Khalifa explained, "There is communication between the Transitional National Council and UN assembled forces," in other words NATO, "and we work on letting them know what areas need to be bombarded." This does not sound like the accidents of distance. It sounds more like collusion, with NATO taking a strong position on behalf of the rebels.

When Qaddafi's forces engaged the rebels, technically the NATO aircraft and cruise missiles were not permitted to interfere. The resolution had forbidden NATO from sending in ground forces. Technology had rendered the idea of "ground forces" redundant. The US brought its AC130 gunships and A10 Thunderbolt II aircraft into operation over the skies of Libya. These are not designed to help patrol the sky, but are capable of hovering in the sky and firing at ground troops and at heavy weaponry with its cannons (including a 40mm Bofors cannon) and machine guns. The AC130 is essentially "boots in the air," and its presence showed that the US arsenal (even under NATO command) was no longer patrolling the skies, but was actively engaged against Qaddafi's forces on the ground. A senior US military official told the *Washington Post* on March 22, "I would not dispute the fact that in some of our actions we are helping the rebels' cause, but that is not the intent." Things got murkier by May, when US Navy Admiral Samuel Locklear told Congressman Mike Turner that the NATO forces were trying to assassinate Qaddafi. There was no UN mandate for this, nor did the US political leaders authorize this publicly (although Obama did say that "Qaddafi has to go," a more modern version of "who will rid me of this meddlesome priest"). Locklear had much more measured language, but the gist was the same. As Turner reports it, Locklear told him, "The scope of civil protection was being interpreted to permit the removal of the chain of command of Qaddafi's military, which includes Qaddafi." In any form of English, this means assassination. This was after the April 30 NATO aerial attack on Qaddafi's compound that reportedly killed three of his grandchildren. Resolution 1973 was violated by the NATO actions then, even if NATO's intent was pure.

A hundred years ago, Italian planes inaugurated aerial bombardment over these very cities: Benghazi, Tripoli. The Futurist F.T. Marinetti flew on one *sortie*, finding the bombing runs to be "hygienic" and a good "moral education." The air force communiqué from November 6, 1911 considered the runs to "have a wonderful effect on the morale of the Arabs." The *Daily Chronicle* hesitated on the same day, "This was not war. It was butchery. Noncombatants, young and old, were slaughtered ruthlessly, without compunction and without shame." The Italians took cover behind international law. The Institute for International Law in Madrid found that "air warfare is allowed, but only on the condition that it does not expose the peaceful population to greater dangers than attacks on land or from the sea." Much the same kind of logic floated around in NATO's Brussels' headquarters prior to the UN vote and then afterwards.

In the camp of the Left, certainty was no longer an option. Qaddafi's threats against the weaker forces in the East were hard to ignore. Arrests, assassinations and artillery fire in the West were equally appalling. There was no easy lever to use against Qaddafi's power. Many who would otherwise stand surely against humanitarian intervention were now not so sure. Much the same kind of predicament stopped liberals and leftists when George H. W. Bush promised to destroy Saddam Hussein's regime (those of us who stood on vigils for the dead of Hallabja in 1987 will remember the debates). These are not manufactured discussions. They are real. No countervailing armed force of the Left was available to defend the rebels. No Vietnamese army, such as entered Cambodia in 1978–79 to crush the degenerate Khmer Rouge and save Cambodia from the maniacal policies of Pol Pot. No Cuban troops, such as came to the aid of the MPLA (who can forget the 1987–88 Cuito-Cuanavale siege and the eventual victory of the MPLA and the Cubans against the South Africans, a mortal blow for the apartheid regime). These are episodes of military intervention when the balance of forces favored the Left. Was the Resolution 1973 "no fly" zone intervention such a feat?

The events of late February are positioned as a false dilemma. Only two options are presented (massacre or intervention), when others presented themselves: the rebels had begun to take control of the dynamic, and would prevail, and the African Union had begun to assert itself as a peace-maker, and would perhaps have convinced Qaddafi to accept a ceasefire. In one case, the rebels might have won the military campaign on their own, albeit on a much longer timeframe (perhaps the Egyptians would have entered the campaign at some point to open a humanitarian corridor for the civilians of the East to flee to Egypt). In another, a peace agreement might have allowed Qaddafi to decamp with dignity and for a regime change to take place with many of the same faces from the NTC in the new government (alongside a few regime stalwarts, including Saif al-Islam). Those who posed this false dilemma had no faith in either the rebels or in the African Union. Their horizon of human action remains frozen in a colonial mindset: the natives are barbarians and the Europeans are the saviors.

Few had any illusions about the actions of the "coalition." Even the *guru* of liberal interventionism, Michael Walzer, believed that Libya was the "wrong intervention." Why the West sought to bomb Libya and not the Gulf States, or Darfur or indeed the Congo was plain to see. The answer to every question is the same: oil. In Bahrain, as we shall see, the Saudis and their Gulf Arab allies were given carte blanche to crush the dissent in the peninsula and preserve the monarchies that encircle the first amongst equals, the realm of King Abdullah and the oil barons. Yemen was on the brink. Deals were being struck. Senior figures in the military and in the political wing who had abandoned Ali Abdullah Saleh had been given assurances from their powerful backers. As long as the revolution did not go too far, and as long as the military could contain any move to radical democracy, all would be forgiven. The bogey of al-Qaeda took care of Washington, and that of radical republicanism took care of Saudi Arabia. The realm of care could not include Bahrain or Syria, the Congo or Sri Lanka. There would be no intervention in oil-rich Gabon, where Obama mourned the loss of the old-hand dictator Omar Bongo in 2009 with platitudes that should be reserved for genuine leaders of their people. It is mockery that greets the pious declarations of human rights when these rights are so stingily doled out to areas of the world that seem to matter more than others. The question that burned up the media in the Global South was why this was the "right intervention," and why not Syria, why not Bahrain, why not all the other important sites where the "international community" (namely the NATO powers) did not bother?

Secretary of State Hillary Clinton and US Ambassador to the UN Susan Rice did not have an easy time at the UN. South Africa, Nigeria, Brazil and India balked. The Chinese and Russians were not keen. It took the Arab League's assent to give Obama the lever to move South Africa's Jacob Zuma in a rushed phone call. India's Manjeev Singh Puri pointed out that his country could not support the resolution because it was "based on very little clear information, including a lack of certainty regarding who was going to enforce the measure…. Political efforts must be the priority in resolving the situation." Brazil's Maria Luiza Riberio Viotti also demurred, largely because Brazil "believed that the resolution contemplated measures that went beyond [the] call" for the protection of civilians. She worried that the actions taken might cause "more harm than good to the very same civilians we are committed to protecting," and that no military action alone "would succeed in ending the conflict." A senior diplomat from a country among the non-permanent members of the Security States told me that he feared that Resolution 1973 would create a political moral hazard: would a secessionist or rebel movement that was weak risk an armed uprising knowing it would be crushed so as to force a NATO intervention on its behalf? Such a suicidal rebellion, which might be emboldened by the example of 1973, might result in huge casualties, the opposite of the responsibility to protect.

No doubt my diplomatic source was correct. By early September, the Syrian Revolution General Commission, the umbrella bloc of activists opposed to the Asad regime, called on the "international community" to act. "Calling for outside intervention is a sensitive issue," said its spokesperson Ahmad al-Khatib. "That could be used by the regime to label its opponents as traitors. We are calling for international observers as a first step. If the regime refuses it will open the door on itself for other action, such as no-tank or no-fly zones." By early 2012, no such Libya-style military intervention was in the cards. On the surface, the once-bitten governments of China and Russia refused to give their assent to a tough resolution in the style of 1973. Beneath the bluster, other motivations made their impact felt. The Israelis worry greatly about their security in this new Arab Spring environment: the emergence of political Islam into Egyptian political life threatens security on that border, while the Lebanese continue to refuse to police a border while in a state of dormant war. Despite his own bluster, Bashar al-Asad has turned out to be a resolute border guard for Israel. The worry in the US State Department and in the Israeli government is that there is no alternative to Bashar's regime in Syria as far as this kind of border service is concerned. The US cannot be seen to make any moves in defense of Bashar, and they need not do so: the Chinese and Russian wall allows the US and Israel to benefit as free riders. No-one wants to see the precipitous fall of the Asad regime. This cynical analysis might give pause to the Syrian rebels, who have been willing to lose blood on the streets hoping for an intervention that will not come. Geo-politics does not dictate it.

Brazil, China, Germany, India and the Russian Federation abstained from the vote on Resolution 1973. Ten voted with the United Sates, France and the UK. There were no negative votes. It was hard enough to abstain.

China did not use its veto. Later, Foreign Ministry spokesperson Jiang Yu said that her government had been led by the Arab League's plea. They had not anticipated such widespread air strikes. Turkey, which did not play an active role at the UN, was also furious at the "all necessary measures" part of the resolution. Prime Minister Recep Tayyip Erdogan expressed the kind of indignation he had shown at Davos when sharing a panel with Israel's Peres in 2009,

"We have seen in the past that such operations are of no use and that on the contrary, they increase loss of life, transform into occupation and seriously harm the country's unity." Both China and Turkey suffer from regional divides (Tibet and the Kurds). Libya's East-West cardinal split is far more dramatic than anything that these countries face, but the principle is nonetheless unsettling. If a rebellion breaks out in Qamdo prefecture, would something like Resolution 1973 return to the Security Council?

The idea of the "no-fly" zone came to the Security Council from the defected Libyan representatives (February 21), from the National Transitional Council in Benghazi (March 2), from the United Kingdom and France (March 7) and from the Arab League (March 12). That the idea first came from the Libyans at the UN and then from the NTC before it came from the NATO states is important to note, but not significant in itself. Liberal intervention takes cover behind invitations. The US invaded the Philippines in 1898 only after being invited to join in the struggle against the Spanish by Emilio Aguinaldo. When the Spanish fled, the US decided to take over. This kind of imperial grammar moves from 1898 to the twenty-first century with ease. It is important to note, however, that there was no unanimity in the NTC. On February 27, Abdul Hafiz Ghoga, the NTC's spokesperson announced in Benghazi, "We are completely against foreign intervention. The rest of Libya will be liberated by the people and Qaddafi's security forces will be eliminated by the people of Libya." The strident calls from Benghazi for intervention come only after March 10, when France recognized the NTC.

The calls were heard in the NATO capitals when it was clear that the neoliberal reformer Mahmoud Jibril was the key political person in the NTC (he met with Sarkozy and Hillary Clinton in Paris on March 14) and that the military wing of the NTC was in firm hands (of whose, we shall see below). This new clique had banked on NATO air support. It wanted the NATO intervention to strengthen its own hand among the rebels, and to sideline the more patriotic and anti-imperialist among them. The NATO intervention was an essential part of the attempt to hijack the Libyan rebellion.

In the UN's Security Council "emergency room" there is a mural done by the Norwegian artist Per Krogh. Its panels showcase everyday life in Northern Europe. At its bottom center there is a phoenix, rising from the flames, around which stand people who might just be "Eastern" (the women here have their faces covered, and the men wear turbans). A field artillery gun points at these people. It is their fate. Under such illusions, the Security Council deliberates.

The Europeans and the US knew that they would not have been able to turn those guns as they wished in the case of Libya without cover from the Arab League, and from the African Union. The former was much more eager for intervention, and the latter hoped to effect some kind of political solution. Neither was willing to put all its efforts to stop NATO's entry into a rebellion that seemed to have its own dynamic. If the Arab League had said no to the intervention, or if the African Union had been more forceful in its disapproval (such as disregarding the UN and sending its team to Tripoli on March 17, 18,

19 or 20), then it would have been embarrassing for the Atlantic powers to have insisted on a resolution. Bernard Kouchner, the leading advocate for humanitarian intervention writing in *The Guardian* on March 24, provides us with an open statement of the importance of the Arab and African fig-leaf, "Fortunately, the UN, the African Union and the Arab League are here to provide us with a legal framework so that this momentary violence—under resolution 1973—may serve to achieve real peace, surely preferable to a pacifism that would allow civilians to be slaughtered." They did not provide a "legal framework." They provided political cover.

Saudi Arabia Delivers the Arab League.

On March 12, the Arab League voted to back the idea of a "no-fly" zone. At this Cairo meeting, only eleven of the twenty-two members of the League attended the vote. They were hornswoggled by the veteran Saudi diplomat, Ahmed bin Abdulaziz Qattan. Six of the eleven representatives present were members of the Gulf Cooperation Council, the GCC or Arab NATO. It is worth pointing out that four of the GCC members are also participants in NATO's Istanbul Cooperation Initiative, formed in 2004 to create "inter-operatibility" or military cooperation between NATO and these four states (Bahrain, Kuwait, Qatar and the United Arab Emirates). The Arab NATO is also an adjunct of NATO itself.

To gain a simple majority of those present in the Arab League meeting in March, the Saudis only needed three more votes. They got them. The only countries at the table who voted against the "no fly" zone were Algeria and Syria. Eleven countries were not present. It was hardly a quorum.

Youssef bin Alawi bin Abdullah, the Omani foreign minister, announced this news at a press conference. The GCC's leader Abdelrahman bin Hamad al-Attiya preened for the cameras, "Libya has lost its legitimacy." Amr Moussa, Secretary General of the Arab League, told *Der Spiegel*, "The United Nations, the Arab League, the African Union, the Europeans—everyone should participate." The Arab League had indeed provided the smokescreen for other motivations. This was the spur to get the vacillating members of the UN Security Council to push for a "no fly" zone. Mahmoud Jibril hastened to Paris to huddle with the NATO political leaders at a G-8 meeting on March 14. Obama worked the phones, using the Arab League's vote as the carrot. On March 17, the UN Security Council voted for the resolution.

The day before the Arab League vote, the Saudi regime, according to Toby Jones writing in *Foreign Policy*, "ordered security forces to blanket the kingdom's streets, choking off popular demonstrations and sending a clear signal that public displays would be met with a crackdown. Prince Saud al-Faisal, the kingdom's usually reserved foreign minister, warned that the regime would 'cut off any finger' raised against it in protest." Demonstrations in al-Hofuf and al-Qatif were fumigated.

Two days before the UN vote, the GCC sent a detachment of 1000 Saudi troops and 500 United Arab Emirates troops (along with a detachment of Jordanians) across the causeway that separates Saudi Arabia from Bahrain. They were part of the GCC's Peninsula

Shield. Their commander, Major-General Mutlaq bin Salem al-Azima said, "We have instructions from our top leadership that we are tools of peace and that we will never attack, but in the meantime, we will never allow anyone to attack us." These "tools of peace" set about doing what they had been trained to do, namely to beat the protestors and fire into crowds. Human Rights Watch documented the death of at least eighteen people, but cautioned that this number was perilously deflated (the Bahraini authorities refused admission to hospitals, and indeed arrested doctors and nurses who made unpleasant noises). Joe Stork, deputy director of HRW's Middle East section said in late March, "Bahraini security forces have frequently shown a reckless disregard for human life during crackdowns on protesters. Firing birdshot pellets at close range is not crowd control—it can be murder." A few weeks later, Stork noted, "Bahrain's ruling family intends to punish any and everyone who criticizes the government. The aim of this vicious full-scale crackdown seems to be to intimidate everyone into silence."

The White House released an anodyne statement, urging the GCC partners to "show restraint" but privately quite pleased with the outcome. Defense Secretary Gates had been in Manama on March 11, a few days before the Peninsula Shield entered the country. He offered the al-Khalifa family "reassurances of support" from the United States. That is what they wanted to hear. It was sufficient.

The Bahrain Centre for Human Rights remains in business a year after these events, documenting the harsh treatment of political prisoners and harassment of journalists and politicians. The opposition's paper, *al-Wasat*, was silenced (the regime arrested its founder, Karim Fakhrawi, on April 5, and he died in custody a week later; it main columnist Haidar al-Naimi was arrested at the same time). The struggle in Bahrain continues. Occasionally protestors appear on the site of the Pearl Monument (now destroyed by the authorities who did not want it or its name to memorialize the protests and the crackdown). Mohamed Ali Alhaiki, Ali Jawad al-Sheikh, Nabeel Rajab and so many more continued their futile vigil. They have faced the full flavor of repression from the Bahraini government. Rajab was arrested and beaten brutally in the early 2012, a sign of the ongoing protests and counter-revolution. In the context of this repression and the ban on international media entering Bahrain, and you might as well say the *janazah* for the protests.

Nada Alwadi, who covered the protests for *al-Wasat*, points out that the Bahraini activists know that the "United States is not in favor of any changes… the US posture has played a major role in marginalizing Bahrain in the eyes of the international media." In early January 2012, several thousand Bahrainis protested before the UN building, chanting, "Down, Down Khalifa," and holding signs urging the UN to "intervene to protect civilians." The protestors came from the al-Wefaq party and the more secular Saad Party. One of the issues before them was to protest an anodyne report released by a commission set up by the King to assess the protests and the crackdown. Strikingly, the commission was chaired by Cherif Bassiouni, the official who had previously led a UN Human Rights Council team to Tripoli. In Libya, Bassiouni was harsh against the regime; in Bahrain, he was forgiving to the Kingdom. Protected by the calumnies of power, the baffling crimes of the Bahraini regime are forgiven.

As the crackdown continued into the end of 2011, the Bahrani government took refuge in US forms of crowd control. They hired former Miami police department head John Timoney to come and train the Bahrain police. Timoney had cut his teeth at the New York Police Department, then made his name in Philadelphia controlling the people at the Republican National Convention (2000) and in Miami during the Free Trade Area of the Americas protest (2003). Journalist Jeremy Scahill wrote of Timoney's work in Miami, "No one should call what Timoney runs in Miami a police force. It's a paramilitary group. Thousands of soldiers, dressed in khaki uniforms with full black body armour and gas masks, marching in unison through the streets, banging batons against their shields, chanting, 'back…back…back.' There were armored personnel carriers and helicopters." A Commission of Inquiry in Miami found that the flagrant use of riot police in their outlandish gear stifled free speech since it scared public citizen action. Bahrain did not need to dig deep into its older traditions to crush dissent and affirm its autocracy; the Miami model from the cradle of liberty is sufficient.

That they had been able to get away with murder pleased the GCC members. At a meeting on March 20 at the UAE, Saudi Prince Turki al-Faisal told his peers that the Gulf NATO needed to take care of its own security. "Why not seek to turn the GCC into a grouping like the European Union? Why not have one unified Gulf army? Why not have a nuclear deterrent with which to face Iran—should international efforts fail to prevent Iran from developing nuclear weapons—or Israeli nuclear capabilities?" The deal on Libya allowed the GCC to act in Bahrain, which has now emboldened the Gulf Arabs to think of a nuclear shield. This is catastrophic for the region.

Once the air war began over Libya, the members of the Arab League knew they had been taken for a ride by both the NATO countries and the GCC. The debate inside the League appeared on the surface in a very bizarre fashion. It seemed as if the League's members did not know what a "no fly" zone entailed. Nawaf Salam of Lebanon, for instance, said that the resolution did not authorize the occupation of "even an inch" of Libyan territory. The League's Amr Moussa said that the NATO bombing "differs from the aim of imposing a no-fly zone." To *Der Spiegel*, Amr Moussa said he did not know "how nor who would impose the no-fly zone." If this meant that NATO would be able to define the assault on Libya, Amr Moussa said, "That remains to be seen." The Arab League's contortions seemed bizarre if one believed that they actually did not know what a "no fly" zone would look like. But this is not credible given the actual experience of a "no-fly" zone maintained during the 1990s over Iraq, an Arab League member state. The only adequate explanation, reaffirmed by a diplomat from an Arab state who concurred with this theory, is that once the air war began the League's members balked. Amr Moussa, who had pretensions for the Egyptian presidency, had to back off from full support of resolution 1973. He was dragooned to stand beside UN Secretary General Ban Ki-moon in

Cairo and recant (Ban's car was assaulted as he left the Arab League headquarters by protestors chanting "no-fly, no-fly").

Amr Moussa's bid to become Egypt's next president faltered, as he seemed to be outmaneuvered in the Arab League over Libya. One of the key players who whipped Amr Moussa into line was Qatar. At the Arab League, it was Qatar that pushed ahead of Saudi Arabia, pressing the GCC to line up for the "yes" vote. Qatar did not only provide the political support for the resolution. Once it passed, Qatar worked with NATO on the military end (recall that Qatar is a member of NATO's Istanbul Cooperation Initiative). Qatar's Mirage fighter jets and its C-17 Globemasters went into action in the air, while Qatari Special Forces hit the ground. Libyan rebels came to Qatar to train at the same time as Qatar became the base for the communications apparatus of the TNC (a television station, Libya Ahrar TV, and a radio station broadcast into Libya from an office in Doha's fabled Souq Waqif). Qatar also became a de facto headquarters of the Libyan Contact Group. The first meeting of the group was held in Doha on April 13. It was chaired jointly by the United Kingdom and Qatar. At this meeting, the Contact Group reiterated the rhetoric of peace, called on Qaddafi to go and then established it as the main channel of communication between those who were prosecuting the air war (and the trainings for the rebels) and the rebels themselves. In other words, the Contact Group and the Transitional National Council opened discussions about financing (a Temporary Financial Mechanism was set up), humanitarian assistance and "recovery" once the war was over. It was the central focal point for deals about the future of Libya, and Qatar's fingerprints were all over it. Qatar also sent its military chief, Abdelrahman bin Hamad al-Attiya to Cairo to discuss its Libyan strategy with the ruling Military Council on April 6. Egypt, by some accounts, had provided arms to the rebels. But it would not enter the conflict with its military. That might have made NATO irrelevant.

Retribution by the disgruntled Arab states against Qatar and the GCC's manipulation of the Arab League came in May. The lead candidate to take over the GCC from the retiring Amr Moussa was the GCC's former head Abdelrahman bin Hamad al-Attiya. Al-Attiya, a Qatari, had been an active player in getting the Arab League's support for the "no fly" zone. His country, Qatar, was a major booster of resolution. The Arab League would have taken al-Attiya without complaint had this bad feeling over 1973 resolution not prevented unanimity. At the last minute, the Egyptians threw in their venerable diplomat, Nabil Elaraby, who became the Arab League's Secretary General in May 2011. Al-Attiya had been set aside.

Africa's Dented Shield.

Gabon, Nigeria and South Africa voted for UN Resolution 1973. South Africa had intended to vote against it or to abstain, but a phone call from Obama to Jacob Zuma was the decisive factor. The vote from these three weakened the process that was ongoing in the African Union (AU), namely to create a framework to bring peace to the overheated Libyan conflict. On March 10, the African Union's Peace and

Security Council met in Addis Ababa, Ethiopia, and set up a High Level Ad Hoc Committee on Libya. They were to fly in to Tripoli and put pressure on Qaddafi. Qaddafi respected the African Union. After he felt let down by the Arab League in the 1980s, Qaddafi pivoted toward Africa. He had become the biggest backer of the African Union (including using Libyan state funds to build houses for all the African leaders for their 2001 summit in Lusaka). If anyone could influence Qaddafi, it was the African Union. By all indications, Qaddafi did not want to become an utter pariah, at least not in the eyes of those whom he sought out as his peers (the African leadership). That was the only possible lever.

The African Union Panel on Libya included heads of government (such as Amadou Toumani Touré of Mali) and foreign ministers (such as Henry Oryem Okello of Uganda). Touré was an interesting choice. In 1991, as head of the parachute commandos he overthrew the austerity dictatorship of Moussa Traoré (who governed Mali from 1968), but turned over the country to civilian rule. Not for nothing is he known as "The Soldier of Democracy." Ten years later, Touré returned to politics, and has since won two elections to lead his country. Okello studied and lived in Britain for a number of years before he returned to enter the family business (his father was president of Uganda in the 1980s). He was an active member in the Juba peace talks with the Lord's Resistance Army. Their credibility is as good as anyone else.

The other two members of the Panel are pale shadows of Touré and Okello. Mohamed Ould Abdel Aziz also conducted a coup in Mauritania. To his credit, he resigned his position, put on a suit to campaign and won the election to the presidency in 2009. But there was no real transition. Congo Brazzaville's Denis Sassou Nguesso has presided over his country and run it since 1979. Sassou Nguesso shares much with Qaddafi, including a putative radical past (he is the leader of the *Parti congolais du travail*, but is better known as a big spender to tender his own family's needs). He saw the writing on the wall in 1991, was ousted from power, engineered a civil war that lasted through the 1990s and returned to being head of government in 2002.

Their effective leader was Jacob Zuma of South Africa. When formed on March 10, the Panel had hoped to arrive in Tripoli before March 20. But they were prevented from their mission by Resolution 1973 and the immediate assault on the country. The UN declined to allow the African Union Panel to proceed, despite assurances from both Tripoli and Benghazi that they would entertain the mediation. It was a remarkable example of the UN stopping a peace envoy and preferring bombardment.

A month into the conflict, the UN allowed the African Union Panel to try its hand. The conflict appeared to be at a stalemate, so the NATO spokesperson Oana Lungescu said that the alliance has "always made it clear that there could be no purely military solution to the crisis." The African Union proposal was quite simple: an immediate ceasefire, unhindered delivery of humanitarian aid, protection of foreign nationals and a dialogue between Benghazi and Tripoli for a political settlement. Zuma's South Africa had voted for Resolution 1973, so he had credibility in

Benghazi. On April 10, Zuma saw Qaddafi but did not fly to Benghazi. It was a bizarre turn of events. An already demoralized African Union had to chalk up another defeat.

The African Union stumbled along. A preparatory meeting of the African Union panel met on June 26 but did not suggest anything new. They had their roadmap, but it required NATO to stand down. By the AU's meeting in Equatorial Guinea on June 30 the African Union's Libya panel's chair, Mauritania's President Mohamed Ould Abdel Aziz, had already gone on record that Qaddafi "can no longer lead Libya." But the African Union, unlike NATO and Benghazi, would not make Qaddafi's departure a *precondition* for negotiation. That was a recipe for no dialogue at all, as the International Crisis Group recognized in its June 6 report (*Making Sense of Libya*). The African Union did not count out Qaddafi's removal, but would only allow that as a possible outcome of the discussion between the two sides. No such discussion took place.

The International Crisis Group report upheld the African Union view that "a political breakthrough is by far the best way out of the costly situation created by the military impasse." Their position mirrored the basic peace platform of the African Union. It asked for a third party political intervention. The Atlantic powers could not be a third party. They have no credibility to be unbiased. The Crisis Group went elsewhere for its mediators, "A joint political initiative by the Arab League and the African Union — the former viewed more favorably by the opposition, the latter preferred by the regime — is one possibility to lead to such an agreement." Such political intervention could not occur, the Crisis Group argued, without "the leadership of the revolt and NATO rethinking their current stance."

The position of the Crisis Group and the African Union was shared by Brazil, Russia, India, China and South Africa (the BRICS states). At their summit in Sanya, China on April 14 the BRICS states essentially endorsed the African Union's stalled process. The BRICS had a vision that was far more robust than that of the Atlantic powers. It came out of the 1990s, when it appeared as if History had ended and Americanism was the sole approach to human affairs. During the 1990s, the countries of Africa, Asia and Latin America tried to develop a new set of institutions to push against the economic and political assertions of the Atlantic powers. As the Group of Seven (G7, 1974), these Atlantic powers corralled the Third World's initiatives inside the United Nations and gave priority to the G7's own favored institutions (the IMF, the World Bank, the General Agreement on Trade and Tariffs and of course NATO). The Non-Aligned Movement (NAM, 1961) formed the Group of Fifteen (G15, 1989), which narrowed into the India-Brazil-South Africa (IBSA, 2003) bloc, and finally to the BRICS (2006). The BRICS states had made their claim to planetary governance, with a platform that is far more multipolar and polycentric than that of the Atlantic powers. The African Union would act more as an agent of the BRICS than of Washington and Paris. Libya was a test case for the transfer of power from the G7 to the BRICS — or at least a demonstration effect of whether the BRICS (taken seriously for its surplus

capital during the credit crunch) would be acknowledged as a serious partner during a political crisis. As
it turned out, the G7 disregarded the BRICS. This was
the undoing of negotiations and a peaceful settlement.
The opinions of artillery held the day.

Before the March 17 vote in the UN, the BRICS
states had agreed in principle not to support another
"humanitarian intervention" by NATO. It turned out
that all the BRICS states were on the Security Council in 2011, with two of them (China and Russia) as
permanent members and the rest rotating through as
temporary members. If the bloc had held fast and if
the African Union members in the Council (Gabon,
Nigeria and South Africa) had abstained or voted
against the resolution it would have been embarrassing to the G7 — if Germany had still abstained that
would have been eight abstentions or no votes in a
Council of fifteen. Such a divided Council would not
have been able to go through with this resolution, and
with so much uncertainty it would have been acceptable for either China or Russia to veto it. But this did
not occur. South Africa voted with the G7.

The BRICS states came to Sanya for their second major summit. Between discussions on the credit
crunch and their mutual trade relations, the BRICS
states released a statement on the events in the Middle
East and North Africa. What they saw was a "shift
of power towards ordinary citizens," a fact that must
have certainly confounded one or two of the heads of
government who had to swallow hard while they accepted that phrase into the final communiqué. When
it came to Libya, the consensus was not so clear. The
Sanya Declaration was a bit stifled. Nonetheless, the

five states agreed that the military option should not be relied upon to bring peace to Libya — reconciliation between the population required a political platform, and guarantees that revenge would not be on the table and that the good of Libya would harness maximalist claims from either side. "All parties should resolve their differences through peaceful means and dialogue in which the UN and regional organizations should as appropriate play their role." The BRICS states called for an immediate ceasefire to assess the degradation of the civilian infrastructure, and to provide humanitarian aid. This was to be monitored by some combination of UN peacekeepers and the African Union peacekeepers, with every indication that if this plan would go through the BRICS countries might have provided some material and logistical support.

The regional organizations, the African Union in particular, had made its attempt. It had been set aside. The energetic UN envoy, the Jordanian politician Abdul Ilah al-Khatib (who once famously said of the Atlantic powers, "Only when there is a crisis do they realize that they have to do something"), went from capital to capital attempting to draw down the violence and produce some kind of pathway to peace. For the UN, the war had become a humanitarian catastrophe. Between February and July, about 630,000 civilians had fled the country (including 100,000 Libyans), and another 200,000 Libyans had been internally displaced. Al-Khatib's deputy told the UN Security Council in late July, "Both sides are willing to talk, but they are still emphasizing maximum demands at this point and patience is clearly required before detailed discussion can begin." It never did begin. The talking appeared to be a smokescreen. It proved that the UN could not operate in a field where it is crowded out by the opinions of artillery, notably the very loud guns of NATO.

Russia, who had neither exercised its veto in the UN nor used its muscle against Qaddafi, now invited Jacob Zuma to bring the BRICS case to the Russia-NATO Council meeting at Sochi, the Black Sea resort, on July 3. The main item on the agenda for the summit was for NATO to smooth Russia's ruffled feathers. The Council was created in 2002 to make sure that the increased tensions between the two did not detract from Russia's support of the War on Terror. NATO's gradual march eastward, attracting former Eastern bloc states into its agenda came just after NATO's air war in Yugoslavia (1999) and its war in Afghanistan (2001 onward). All this seemed to Moscow like encirclement. Bush's insistence upon missile defense, and the US push to bring NATO and several Eastern European as well as East Asian states into its missile defense plans rattled Moscow's justified paranoia. The war over South Ossetia in 2008 allowed Moscow to flex its muscles, but this did not dampen NATO's confidence; its ships entered the Black Sea to deliver aid to Georgia (Russia went technical here, pointing out that the number of NATO ships in the area violated the 1936 Montreux Convention).

Over the past decade, Russia has moved closer to the new formation that comes out of the Non-Aligned Movement, the G-15 and IBSA. China joined IBSA to block the new trade rules that would have gone through in Cancun (2003) and to formulate a common agenda at the Copenhagen (2009) meeting on climate.

These discussions and the creation of a common platform produced the BRICS formation. Russia, long
adrift somewhere between its own Cold War past and
Boris Yeltsin's subservience to the US, found a new
anchor with the locomotives of the Global South.

At Hainan, in April, the BRICS powers strongly
criticized the NATO war on Libya, and formulated
the principles that would appear in the African Union
High Level Ad Hoc Committee on Libya's June 15
statement to the UN. BRICS held out for a negoti-
ated settlement, and cautioned against the habits of
war. Ruhakana Rugunda, of Uganda, represented the
African Union at the UN meeting, where he pointedly noted, "It is unwise for certain players to be in-
toxicated with technological superiority and begin to
think they alone can alter the course of human history
towards freedom for the whole of mankind. Certainly,
no constellation of states should think that they can
recreate hegemony over Africa" (Rugunda was the
Ugandan representative to the UN, and has now been
moved to a domestic cabinet post). The African Union
told the UN that given its experience in Burundi, in
particular, it would be able to handle the negotiation
and the transition in Libya.

It was in this context that the Russians involved
themselves in the Libyan stalemate, sending unof-
ficial diplomats to Libya and pushing back in the
halls of NATO. At Sochi, Russian president Medvedev invited Zuma, who has been at the head of the
African Union's attempts in Libya, to join the delib-
erations. Zuma told the NATO chiefs that they had
overstepped the UN Resolutions (1970 and 1973),
and that the only way forward was negotiations. If

the NATO chiefs could pressure the Benghazi Transitional Council to back down from its maximalist position (Qaddafi must go immediately), Zuma suggested, the way could open for peace with honor. The NATO chiefs listened to Zuma tell them about the African Union's Framework Agreement on a Political Settlement, and watched Medvedev applaud the African Union for its work and offer his support to the Framework and the African Union's Roadmap. Russia and the African Union offered to lean on Qaddafi to abide by the terms of the Roadmap, and they wanted NATO to lean on the Transitional Council to do the same. There was even a suggestion that they would provide an exit for Qaddafi, moving him out of Libya to a post at the African Union or somewhere to smooth the transition to peace in Libya.

NATO left Sochi indifferent to Russian concerns over missile defense, with bland promises over progress at their next meeting in Chicago. On Libya, there was no progress, as there could be none. Libya is the first battleground of a new "cold war," this one not between the US and Russia, but between the G7 (and its military arm, NATO) and the BRICS (who have not much of a military arm). The G7 commands the skies and the rhetoric of freedom, but it does not have a sustainable economic base and no sense of a political process that does not come with aerial bombardment and its threats. NATO's sword would never grow cold.

The BRICS failed to build on the momentum after the credit crisis of 2007 forced the G7 to invite them to help save the world financial system. The BRICS states showed up, opened their checkbooks, but seemed to do so servilely. They did not insist on greater power in the secret rooms where the G7 makes its decision. When the search for a candidate to lead the IMF opened up in the summer of 2011, the BRICS states failed to coalesce around their candidate (a European once more leads the IMF). They also failed to foist their alternative to the deflationary strategies of the international financial organizations. All this took place despite the fact that the IMF announced that the United States will cease to be the world's largest economy by 2016 (that reign began in the late 1920s). In its place will come China, the anchor of the BRICS. Wen Jiabao, the Chinese premier, tried to reassert the BRICS position with "How China Plans to Reinforce the Global Recovery" (*Financial Times*, June 23). Wen called the bet. China is at ready, but not yet to take on the political challenges alone. It sought to work through the BRICS formation, but without a confrontational attitude. Neither China nor the BRICS in general are willing to stand up to the G7 in the international arena.

On the question of international politics, the BRICS have been a bother to the G7. If the BRICS were defeated in their quest to participate in the Libyan imbroglio, they have so far declined to allow the G7 to repeat their Libyan mission in Syria. The BRICS have refused to allow any strong UN resolution for that country. The grounds are that NATO misused Resolution 1973 on Libya, and it would do the same in Syria (the G7's case on Syria was made by the French representative to the UN Gérard Araud on June 13 in *O Estado de Sao Paulo*, to win over the Brazilians away from what the French see as South African obduracy). Since June, the BRICS states blocked a resolution in the Security Council. In early August, the Council condemned the "widespread violations of human rights and the use of force against civilians by the Syrian authorities," but refused to test the waters of sanctions or threats. On August 31, the *New York Times* editorial fulminated, "Russia and China, along with India, Brazil and South Africa, are blocking a United Nations Security Council resolution that could impose broad international sanctions on Damascus. Their complicity is shameful." What the *Times* did not recognize is that this blockage is a consequence of the shabby treatment of the "international community" by NATO over the Libyan war. What is shameful is the disregard the G7 showed to the world when others had good ideas to help stem the bloodletting in Libya. What is more important here is that the US and the Israelis do not want an intervention in Syria. What appears as the emergence of the BRICS on the world stage might simply be that their reticence to sign-off on a NATO intervention in Syria is along the grain of similar hesitations in Washington and Tel Aviv.

Peace was never the point. The conflict was always about the removal of Qaddafi, and his regime.

America's Libyans.

In early March, I got a message from an acquaintance who works in the many shadowy enclaves around Washington, DC. He gave me a name, Khalifa Hifter, and the name of a town, Vienna, Virginia. Make the connection, the friend said.

It did not take long to discover the story, one that was initially totally ignored and then later treated as if it were unspectacular (I wrote about him in *Coun-terPunch* and then talked about him during my debate with Juan Cole on *Democracy Now!*, on March 29, 2011. That evening, miraculously, my computer was hacked and the database destroyed). An ex-Colonel of the Libyan army, Khalifa Belqasim Hifter had ar-rived by at least March 14 (although I think earlier) in Benghazi to share the military command with Ma-jor General al-Fattah Younis (and Omar el-Hariri). There was always a whiff of mystery about al-Fattah Younis, Qaddafi's secretary of the interior till he de-fected in Benghazi on 22 February. Omar Mukhtar el-Hariri also has a complicated story. He was one of the original members who conducted the coup of 1969, a man not of the tent, but just outside it (he taught Qaddafi how to drive a car). Later el-Hariri reflected that the Free Officers had no clear idea what to do with the new Libya and made many mistakes. It is what turned him against Qaddafi. In 1975, el-Hariri attempted a coup against Qaddafi, but failed and re-mained in prison and in house arrest in Tobruk till 2011. When the uprising began, el-Hariri rose to be-come al-Fattah Younis' no. 2. Neither al-Fattah You-nis nor el-Hariri could be counted upon to be proper NATO allies. They had not been made "inter-operat-able." For that, the CIA had to insert Hifter back into the saddle.

Things on the political side were more reliable for the NATO command. The NTC was in the hands of two well known neoliberal reformers. One of them was Mahmoud Jibril, the lead neoliberal "reformer" in the Qaddafi regime who worked, as we saw, closely with Saif al-Islam on the privatization of Libya. The

other was Ali Abd al-Aziz al-Isawi who was Qaddafi's
Director General for the Ownership expansion program {privatization fund], and then later Secretary of
the Committee for Economy, Trade and Investment.
It helps that al-Isawi had a PhD in privatization from
the Academy of Economic Studies in Bucharest, Ro-
mania. By early March 2011, people like Jibril and
al-Isawi, who had resigned in February from his post
as Libya's ambassador to India, were in firm control
of the NTC.

As their figurehead, Jibril and al-Isawi had the
venerable former Justice Minister in the Qaddafi regime, Mustafa Abdel-Jalil (who resigned his post on
February 21 after he was sent to observe the events
in Benghazi by the Qaddafi regime). Trained at the
University of Libya, Abdel-Jalil was as comfortable
with his country's legal system as with *Sharia* law. A
religious conservative in many respects, Abdel-Jalil
was nonetheless a loyal regime man. When the UN
Human Rights Council and others made modest calls
for Abdel-Jalil to investigate extra-judicial killings in
Libya between 2007 and 2011, he demurred saying
that the Internal Security Agency Officers had state
immunity. Despite his loyalty to the regime's codes,
Abdel-Jalil showed an independent streak as a judge.
This is why he was adopted by Saif al-Islam to reform
Libya's justice system.

Jibril, al-Isawi and Abdel-Jalil are all Saif al-Islam Qaddafi's men, whose commitment to the reform
agenda unites them and whose laxity regarding the
power of imperialism makes them able to see NATO
as benevolent. Abdel-Jalil is no fool. In January 2010
he told the US Ambassador Gene Cretz that many

Libyans are "concerned" with the US government support for Libya and for the perception that the War on Terror was "against Muslims." Nevertheless, Abdel-Jalil, according to Cretz, "has given the green light to his staff to work with us." The political control of leadership faction of the NTC was firmly in the hands of the neoliberal reformers by early March of 2011. They were, in a sense, America's Libyans.

Hifter returned to take charge of the military wing. He made his name in Qaddafi's war against Chad in the 1980s. At some point in that conflict, Hifter turned against Qaddafi, joined the Libyan National Salvation Front, and operated his resistance out of Chad. The *New York Times* (May 1991) ran a short piece on Hifter's 1980s operation. "They were trained by American intelligence officials in sabotage and other guerrilla skills, officials said, at a base near Ndjamena, the Chadian capital. The plan to use exiles fit neatly into the Reagan administration's eagerness to topple Colonel Gaddafi." When the US-supported government of Chad, led by Hissène Habré fell in 1990, Hifter fled Chad for the United States. It is interesting that an ex-Colonel of the Libyan army was able to so easily gain entry into the United States. The US State Department said that Hifter and his men would have "access to normal resettlement assistance, including English-language and vocational training and, if necessary, financial and medical assistance." Also of interest is the fact that Hifter took up residence in Vienna, Virginia, less than seven miles away from Langley, Virginia, the headquarters of the CIA. In Vienna, Hifter formed the Libyan National Army.

In March 1996, Hifter's Army attempted an armed rebellion against Qaddafi in the eastern part of Libya. The *Washington Post* (March 26) noted that its reporters had heard of "unrest today in Jabal Akhdar Mountains of eastern Libya and said armed rebels may have joined escaped prisoners in an uprising against the government." The leader of the "contra-style group" was Hifter. Twenty-three rebels, soldiers and prisoners were reported to have died in this uprising and prison break. It is worth reporting that the Libyan Islamic Fighting Group also conducted an operation in the Wadi al-Injil (Bible Valley) in March 1996, perhaps coordinated with the Libyan National Army. Was it a coincidence that about four months later Abdullah Senussi's guards opened fire on the (mainly LIFG) prisoners at Abu Salim jail and killed 1200, the burr under the saddle of the Islamists and the human rights lawyers that would finally push them to their rebellion in 2011?

History called Hifter back fifteen years later. In March 2011, Hifter flew into Benghazi to take command of the defected troops, joining al-Fattah Younis whose troops had been routed from Ras Lanouf on March 12. They faced the advance of Qaddafi's forces toward Benghazi. It was in this context, with the uprising now firmly usurped by a neoliberal political leadership and a CIA-backed military leadership, that talk of a no-fly zone emerged.

In late March, the military wing went through its own power struggle. A new military spokesperson, Colonel Omar Ahmed Bani announced that Hifter, who had hitherto been no. 3 in the hierarchy but in command of the ground forces, would be the head of the rebel armed forces. A few days later, the NTC reversed Ahmed Bani's announcement and declared that al-Fattah Younis remained in command. Hifter had his base among the civilians who joined the rebels, while al-Fattah Younis was thought to be popular among the defected troops. Many in the NTC felt that Hifter had returned with a great deal of arrogant self-assurance, with the belief that his history and his links to the CIA earned him the right to be in charge. "We defined the military leadership before the arrival of Hifter from the United States," said Hafiz Ghogha, the vice president of the NTC. "We told Mr. Hifter that if he wants, he can work within the structure that we laid out." Apparently this was not enough for Hifter, whose minions went for more.

In late July, al-Fattah Younis and two of his aides were arrested in Benghazi on the grounds that he was working for Qaddafi (or so it is said, since the entire episode remains murky). He was killed very quickly, and his body was burned. The remains of the three dead were found outside Benghazi, disposed of crudely. Benghazi went into crisis, as large crowds gathered for al-Fattah Younis' funeral and his family remained angry at the events that led to his assassination. NTC chairman Abdel-Jalil said that the assassination was the result of a "conspiracy," and on grounds of incompetence he dissolved the NTC and asked Mahmoud Jibril to reform a new government with Jibril as Prime Minister. The war was coming to a close, with all signs showing that the rebels and NATO had the upper hand. al-Fattah Younis was dispatched mysteriously, Jibril was given sole charge of the NTC and the new government of Libya, and the military command rested with the CIA's Libyan,

Hifter. Jibril, who the US State Department felt was a "serious interlocutor who gets the US perspective" was poised to govern the new Libya. People like Mahmoud Jibril and Khalifa Hifter were more accountable to their patrons in Paris and Washington than to the people of Libya, whose blood was spilled on both sides for an outcome that is unlikely to benefit them.

IV. NATO's War

"One is left with the horrible feeling now
that war settles nothing; that to win a war is
as disastrous as to lose one."
—Dame Agatha Christie, 1890–1976.

Neoliberal revolutions are bland. For heroism they require the courage of ordinary people, like those rag-tag looking young people who jumped on Toyota trucks, grabbed any old guns and went off to the front lines to face the rump of the Qaddafi army. Some of them had been steeled in Qaddafi's prisons, others in his armed forces, and yet others by what they had seen from their fellows in Tunisia and Egypt. They had hopes that far exceeded anything that Qaddafi could satisfy. In 1969, they would have fought alongside him had the Idris regime put up any resistance. By 2011, they turned their guns against him. He had become their Idris.

Early in the combat, the *New Yorker*'s Jon Lee Anderson met some of the young Benghazi rebels. "In the early days of Qaddafi's counterattack," Anderson

writes, "youthful fighters were outraged that the enemy was firing real artillery at them. Many hundreds
have died." They came dressed to play the part of
the martyrs, while behind the scenes, the bourgeois
gladiators put on their pin-striped suits and tested out
their French and English. Some of these young people
found their courage and went into combat. But they
were not the main fighting force. That came from the
defected soldiers, the rebels from the mountains, the
rebels from the Islamists and from the working-class
who were willing to remove their guns from the oil-
cloths and risk their lives in combat.

Among the soldiers going to the frontlines came
the battle hardened fighters of the Libyan Islamic
Fighting Group and the other smaller offshoots of political Islam. After the February rising in Benghazi,
the old LIFG fighters and their political leadership
formed the Libyan Islamic Movement (*al-Harakat al-
Islamiya al-Libiya*). They entered the conflict in small
bands. For example, in late March, one of the rebel
frontline leaders Abdel-Hakim al-Hasidi said that he
had recruited about twenty-five men from the area
around Derna who were now in combat around Adjabiya. These fighters, al-Hasidi told *Il Sole 24 Ore* "are
patriots and good Muslims, not terrorists," but he
added that "members of al-Qaeda are also good Muslims and are fighting against the invader." Al-Hasidi
had fought in Afghanistan and was captured in Pe-
shawar, Pakistan in 2002, from where the US handed
him over to the Libyans. He was jailed in Libya and
released in 2008. Abu Sufian Ibrahim bin Qumu had
fought in Afghanistan in the late 1980s, been captured in Sudan and taken to Guantanamo, and then

released to the Libyan authorities in 2007. In 2005, the US government thought that Abu Sufian was a "probable member of Al Qaida and a member of the African Extremist Network." He was released in 2010 when Saif al-Islam brokered a deal to rehabilitate the Islamists. In 2011, Abu Sufian led a section of fighters from Darnah. Like al-Hasidi and Abu Sufian, Abdel Hakim Belhaj (also known as Abu Abdullah al-Sadiq) was a veteran of the Afghan war. Unlike al-Hasidi, Belhaj had been a fighter in the late 1980s and a major force in the LIFG in its return to North Africa. Broken by the Qaddafi regime, Belhaj and his cohort fled. He was arrested in Malaysia in 2003, tortured in Thailand and returned to the Libyan government in 2004. In Tripoli, Belhaj was tortured with the connivance of the CIA and MI6. Like Abu Sufian, he was released in 2010 by Saif al-Islam. When Tripoli fell to the rebels, Belhaj, the emir of the LIFG, took over the city's Military Council. Belhaj's deputy is Mahdi Herati, who came into the battlefield from his boat on the Gaza Flotilla that tried to break the Israeli blockade of the Hamas-controlled Gaza Strip. When news of Belhaj's elevation broke, the neoliberal reformers hastily tried to underplay his links and his role in Tripoli. Washington, Paris and London were chagrined. But among the rebels, Belhaj is a hero. He risked his neck on the front lines. NATO helped from the sky.

Men like Abu Sufian, al-Hasidi and Belhaj came from common stock. They were part of a Libyan Diaspora whose addresses were in the hills of Afghanistan and Pakistan, in the cities of Sudan and Yemen and in the rough country of the North Caucuses. Not for them the professional world of Beirut and Paris, London and Washington, DC. It was the more well-heeled Libyans who met in London to form the National Conference for the Libyan Opposition in 2005. Of the seven organizations that gathered into this Conference, the oldest and most established was the National Front for the Salvation of Libya (it was formed in Sudan in 1981, attempted to overthrow Qaddafi in the 1980s and then went into hibernation). The Libyan League for Human Rights, based in Geneva, was founded in 1993 by a series of important former regime liberals such as Soliman Bouchuiguir and the former Libyan Minister of Foreign Affairs in the 1970s Mansour Rashid el-Kikhia, killed in 1993. El-Kikhia was one of the most well-known dissidents of the Qaddafi regime until his mysterious death in Cairo. Another group, the Libyan Constitutional Union seems to have a singular purpose, to revive the constitution of the Idris era and perhaps to bring Prince Muhammed as-Senussi to the throne of his great uncle. The Union, based in Britain, is led by Sheikh Mohammed bin Ghalbon, who has nurtured a sentimental attachment with the royal family, including King Idris and Queen Fatima who lived in Cairo's Sultan Palace (in Dokki, across the Nile from Tahrir Square). The most recent organization to join the Conference was formed in London in 2002, the Libyan Tmazight Congress. The Conference collapsed in 2008.

The Conference from 2005 to 2008 set the template for the role of the Libyan Diaspora in the Benghazi-based National Transitional Council. When the NTC was formed in February 2011, it mimicked the kind of unity that was already there in the Conference. What united the thirty-one members of the

NTC was hatred of Qaddafi. That was the alpha and the omega of their movement. Constitutional liberals sat side-by-side with Constitutional monarchists, religious conservatives took their place beside social democrats. They had a very limited platform, mainly galvanized as an opposition. On March 19, the Council released a "Declaration of the founding of the Transitional National Council," whose purpose was to remove Qaddafi and restore order. Their "Vision of a Democratic Libya," released in late March, reaffirmed the basic planks of liberal democracy: a Constitution, elections, political pluralism, human rights, freedom of speech and so on. Its seventh of the eight points introduce some ideas about the economy, but these are vague. The nation's economy was to be used "for the benefit of the Libyan people by creating effective institutions in order to eradicate poverty and unemployment." These institutions will, in hedged neoliberal language, be the product of "genuine economic partnerships between a strong and productive public sector, a free private sector and a supportive and effective civil society, which overstands corruption and waste." But all this is very generic. To gain unity, the members of the NTC had to strike for the lowest common denominator of agreement. The NTC is not the National Liberation Front (FLN), entering Algiers in 1961 with a firm commitment to a specific program. Their eight principles are mainly about liberal democracy.

What the NTC has not projected is its neoliberal commitments. At its March 19 meeting, there were three points to the agenda. The first point was the war and the politics of the NTC with regard to

Qaddafi's continued hold on power. The second point was to designate that the Central Bank of Benghazi would be the authority for Libyan monetary policy (to run it the NTC chose one of its own Sadiq Amr el-Kabir, a venerable banker from the Arab Banking Corporation based in Manama, Bahrain). Hearing this news, Robert Wenzel of the *Economic Policy Journal* noted, "I have never before heard of a Central Bank being created in just a matter of weeks out of a popular uprising. This suggests we have a bit more than a rag tag bunch of rebels running around and that there are some pretty sophisticated influences." Not on the council itself, but in its penumbra was Dr. Ali Tarhouni, a student activist at the University of Benghazi in the 1970s and later in exile a professor of economics at the University of Washington in Seattle. Tarhouni would become the new Finance Minister. Tarhouni was the financial brains of the Council. The third point was the establishment of the Libyan Oil Company with power over all oil production and oil policy in the country (initially headquartered in Benghazi before they moved to its offices on Bashir Saadawi Street in Tripoli, Saadawi being the Misratan leader of the National Congress Party who fought for Libya's independence in the early 1950s). None of this was on the surface of the NTC's program. It was hidden in plain sight, lost behind the verbiage about Qaddafi's crimes—the glue that held the NTC and its troops together.

One of the crucial statements in the NTC's document received almost no comment when it was published, "The interests and rights of foreign nationals and companies will be protected." This pleased the multinational oil firms. No more erratic pronounce-ments from Qaddafi.

In late March, as the Council made these deci-sions, Mustafa Gheriani of the February 17 Move-ment told Jon Lee Anderson that they are "Western-educated intellectuals" who would lead the new state, not the "confused mobs or religious extremists." The latter were the working-class, whose blood had al-ready begun to lubricate the revolt against Qaddafi. The neoliberal reformers had not seen blood. Many of them were busy in the Atlantic capitals, pushing their agenda, making promises that would only be reveled after Tripoli had fallen to their minions. The gen-eral tenor was that "without NATO's support from above, the rebels on the ground would have stood no chance of success" (as the *Boston Globe* put it on Au-gust 23). The narrative that would soon emerge was that NATO delivered Libya to the neoliberal reform-ers. The Libyans who fought on the ground would be treated as abstract heroes, but they would not be seen as the actual inheritors of the new Libya. That was foreordained in the conduct of the conflict, and in how NATO would seek to deliver the spoils. Libya, which began to march to the tune of Tunisian and Egyptian drummers, found itself being torn in two directions: silenced by the war-drums of Qaddafi on one side and those of Jibril and his neoliberal team on the other. A caricature of Tahrir Square mocked the Libyan dreams of a new society.

Once NATO got into the act, its bombardments set the stage for the war. The war took place in sev-eral overlapping, but distinct stages. It was remark-ably well executed in military terms. Even though it seemed to take longer than it did, the collapse of the Qaddafi regime was swift.

Bombardment.

After March 19, Operation Odyssey Dawn conducted six weeks of sustained bombardment of Qaddafi's military and communications infrastructure. The Libyan Air Force and military bases were put out of commission, as were oil installations, power grids, television and radio stations and the homes and offices of the leadership. In mid-June, one of NATO's strikes killed some civilians in Tripoli. NATO's operation commander, the Canadian Lt. General Charles Bouchard noted, "NATO regrets the loss of innocent civilian lives and takes great care in conducting strikes against a regime determined to use violence against its own citizens." What was awkward about this apology is that it did not come to the heart of the NATO strategy. Its bombers routinely struck the major cities, targeting the oil installations and the bases. The massive firepower launched at Tripoli in particular seemed much less precision bombing (to take out some specific target) and more terror bombing (to break the morale of the civilian population). This was the philosophy of "shock and awe" or rapid dominance developed by Harlan Ullman and James Wade, with the basic premise that overwhelming force from the air would strike a society hard and "paralyze its will to carry on."

The US State Department's legal counsel, Harold Koh told the US Senate Foreign Relations Committee that the Libyan adventure "does not constitute a war" because there are no US ground troops in Libya, there is a limited risk of escalation, there is a limited means of military means and, remarkably, there are no US casualties. What you have instead are Drones and Cruise Missiles that strike at populations whose sorrows do not trigger any the legal terms that indicate warfare and suffering. We are back to the first aerial bombardment in world history, the Italian bombing of Tajura and Ain Zara in 1911. The first communiqué from the air force said what the NATO command would be more embarrassed to say, which is that the bombing had "a wonderful effect on the morale of the Arabs."

Denials about the ferocity of the bombardment and the civilian casualties had been casual during the conduct of the war. On August 8, NATO aircraft targeted the town of Majer, south of Zlitan city. At that time, evidence of sustained bombardment of civilian homes had begun to emerge. The next day the *New York Times* noted, "There was no evidence of weapons at the farmhouses, but there were no bodies there, either. Nor was there blood." Case closed. On December 18, 2011, when C. J. Chivers and Eric Schmitt of the *Times* went back over the story, they offered the following narrative:

> The attack began with a series of 500–pound laser-guided bombs, called GBU-12s, ordnance remnants suggest. The first house, owned by Ali Hamid Gafez, 61, was crowded with Mr. Gafez's relatives, who had been dislocated by the war, he and his neighbors said. The bomb destroyed the second floor and much of the first. Five women and seven children were killed; several more people

were wounded, including Mr. Gafez's wife, whose...lower left leg had to be amputated, the doctor who performed the procedure said. Minutes later, NATO aircraft attacked two buildings in a second compound, owned by brothers in the Jarud family. Four people were killed, the family said. Several minutes after the first strikes, as neighbors rushed to dig for victims, another bomb struck. The blast killed 18 civilians, both families said. The death toll has been a source of confusion. The Qaddafi government said 85 civilians died. That claim does not seem to be credible. With the Qaddafi propaganda machine now gone, an official list of dead, issued by the new government, includes 35 victims, among them the late-term fetus of a fatally wounded woman the Gafez family said went into labor as she died. The Zlitan hospital confirmed 34 deaths. Five doctors there also told of treating dozens of wounded people, including many women and children.

This is one incident. There are many others. When asked by Human Rights Watch to allow an investigation, the new Libyan authorities were clear. Fred Abrahams of HRW was quite mute in his allegations (he touted a figure of fifty civilians killed by NATO, hardly a credible number given the *New York Times* analysis). "We're not alleging unlawful attacks, let alone war crimes," said Abrahams. "We believe the onus is on NATO to investigate these cases thoroughly so they can identify and correct the mistakes."

NATO denied the "mistakes." Ibrahim Dabbashi, the Libyan representative to the UN, asserted that forty thousand people had died in the civil war, but that "Qaddafi was responsible for these deaths." If NATO or the rebels had killed anyone it was because Qaddafi had used them as human shields. "There is no need for a NATO investigation," Dabbashi noted, "Usually it is acceptable that there will be some civilian casualties because of some errors." Mistakes, errors: that is as far as memory is going to allow for the NATO bombardment. Humanitarian intervention cannot permit its preferred means to be tarnished. Given this attitude, we shall never know the scale of the civilian deaths as a result of the NATO bombardment, conducted to protect civilians.

The bombardment of Libya between March and August 2011 was a massive campaign, with twenty thousand sorties launched to erode the power-base of Qaddafi. No regime can last such an assault. It was remarkable that Qaddafi was able to hold off for as long as his regime did.

Serbian Model.

The NATO states followed their playbook from the later stages of the break-up of Yugoslavia. Early into the conflict, Paris, London and Washington shifted their allegiance to the NTC, the rump government that stood in for the 1990 declaration of Kosovo by its "parliament." The sustained bombardment degraded the forces and the morale of the government (the bombing of Tripoli from the first day of the NATO attacks standing in for the bombardment of Serbia). The entry of the International Criminal Court (ICC) to call for an investigation of the now isolated enemy (Qaddafi = Milosevic). The ICC's erratic and arrogant lead investigator Luis Moreno-Ocampo opened an investigation into Qaddafi and his family on March 3, long before the UN Resolution 1973 of March 17. He aggressively made statements as if *of fact* about alleged war crimes by the Qaddafi regime. For instance, Moreno-Ocampo stated that Qaddafi's regime was giving Viagra to its troops to promote mass rape of women. Moreno-Ocampo said this at the same time as the US Ambassador to the UN, Susan Rice, made these allegations. "The coalition is confronting an adversary doing reprehensible things," she told a closed-door meeting at the UN, but was reluctant to offer any specific details. Margot Wallstrom, the UN Special Representative on Sexual Violence in Conflict, was equally reticent to talk about specifics, but nonetheless was confident that reports of rapes had been "brutally silenced." It took Amnesty International's very experienced investigator, Donatella Rovera, three months to uncover that there was no fire for this smoke. It was a figment of the imperial imagination.

Moreno-Ocampo did not open any investigation into the NATO civilian bombings in Libya (as he has not in the earlier experiences in Afghanistan and Iraq). The August 8 bombing of Majer is a test case. Abubakr Ali, who watched the funeral of his family told a CNN reporter, "This was a civilian home. No army, no military, no Qaddafi forces. It's a family sleeping safely in their place. This is the protection of civilians," he added in disgust. A local official told the reporter, "NATO is waging wide-scale war on the people. They are destroying everything." Amnesty

International called for an investigation, but got no response from the ICC. On January 19, 2012, three human rights organizations released a comprehensive report on war crimes by NATO in Libya. The Arab Organisation for Human Rights, the Palestinian Centre for Human Rights and the International Legal Assistance Consortium studied the areas which NATO deemed as military targets and found that they were civilian areas. "We are not making judgments," said Raji Sourani of the Palestinian Centre for Human Rights. "That is not the mission mandate. But we have reason to think that there were some war crimes perpetrated." NATO dismissed the report, and the ICC did not bother with it. There would be no investigation of the war. The final nail in the coffin of the investigation was struck by UN Secretary General Ban Ki-moon late in 2011: "Security Council resolution 1973, I believe, was strictly enforced within the limit, within the mandate."

On a few occasions NATO targeted the radio and television stations in Tripoli, arguing that this was "to disrupt the broadcast of Gaddafi's murderous rhetoric." How NATO could see this as part of Resolution 1973 is unbelievable, and how this can pass by the foreign media as acceptable (the killing of journalists) beggars belief. The Coalition to Protect Journalists wrote a careful and correct letter to NATO command, "As an organization of journalists dedicated to the defense of press freedom around the world, we are concerned any time a media facility is the target of a military attack. Such attacks can only be justified under International Humanitarian Law if the media facility to being used for military purposed or to incite violence against the civilian population. For this reason, we believe it is essential for NATO to provide a more detailed explanation as to the basis for July 30 attack on Libyan broadcast facilities." No such explanation was forthcoming. There was no outrage on CNN or *al-Jazeera*. The "international media" showed its hand as an adjutant in NATO's war, calling into question its trustworthiness. Moreno-Ocampo yoked the ICC to the NATO strategy, and undermined the integrity of the ICC in the process.

Snake Oil.

It was essential to control the narrative about the war. Amnesty International's press releases did not bother the "international media." Meanwhile, *al-Jazeera*, which had played a cheerleaders role in Tunisia and Egypt, did the same in Libya. But this time, *al-Jazeera* did not have to distinguish itself too far from its paymasters, the Qatari royals who were the biggest boosters of the rebels. "*Al-Jazeera* was producing uncorroborated reports of hospitals being attacked, blood banks destroyed, women raped and the injured executed," reported Patrick Cockburn. He talked to Amnesty's Libya expert, Diana Eltahawy, who told him, "We spoke to women, without anybody else there, all across Libya, including Misrata and on the Tunisia-Libya border. None of them knew of anybody who had been raped. We also spoke to many doctors and psychologists with the same result." Investigation was irrelevant. What was important was the story. No wonder that the US State Department helped Jibril's NTC hire a series of Washington, DC public relations (lobby) firms, such as Patton Boggs

(Vincent Frillici, the former director of operations for NATO, ran the NTC's account at Patton). The fulminations at the mouth continued, despite the lack of evidence. The White House Middle East strategist, Dennis Ross brushed aside the briefing books to tell a group of foreign policy experts at the White House Roosevelt Room, "We were looking at 'Srebrenica on Steroids'—the real or imminent possibility that up to a 100,000 people could be massacred, and everyone would blame us for it." Such numbers and such fears would remain on the surface of news reports. It would eclipse news of rebel attacks on what they called "mercenaries" (but were often dark-skinned migrant workers or southern Libyans who were either fighters or else were simply hapless civilians), of NATO civilian deaths or of other such unsavory information.

When news came of the displacement of the entire population of the town of Tawergha, only twenty-five miles outside Misrata, as the war came to the close, it produced a little embarrassment and then silence. Tawergha once housed thirty thousand people. It is now empty. An unusual story in the *Wall Street Journal* (June 21) provided some context for the events. The rebels from Misrata who fashioned themselves as "the brigade for purging slaves, black skin" rode into Tawergha, a town that housed mainly dark-skinned Libyans. Ibrahim al-Halbous, commander of the rebel force, said of these townsfolk, "They should pack up. Tawergha no longer exists, only Misrata." The fate of ethnic cleansing had already taken place within Misrata, where the Ghoushi neighborhood saw its Tawerghan natives driven out. Ibrahim Yusuf bin Ghashir, an NTC member, told HRW in October, "We think it would be better to relocate them somewhere else — Tripoli, Benghazi, the south — give them housing and compensation for their losses in Tawergha." He was angry at the atrocities allegedly committed by some Tawerghans against the people of Misrata. Qaddafi did recruit amongst the darker-skinned Libyans and the Bedouin. What the rebels did in places such as Tawergha, on the other hand, was not to fight Qaddafi loyalists, but to deliver collective responsibility on an entire town. There has been no investigation of the Tawergha ethnic cleansing by the new Libyan government. This is soon to be a forgotten story.

The rebels had to be the White Knight, unsullied, as Qaddafi had to be the Dark Prince, repellent.

Along the Mediterranean Road.

By early April a pattern set in. The rebel forces drew Qaddafi's broken up armed columns into the east. The rebels followed the example of the Toyota War in Chad, likely learning their lessons from Hifter. They used retrofitted pick up trucks and land cruisers that are faster and easier to maneuver than Qaddafi's tanks and armed columns. One would have thought that after the Chad debacle, Qaddafi would have learned his lessons. But obviously he did not. In the Chad war, the French provided air cover, and here it was NATO's planes. If you do not fear an aerial attack, the pick-up truck is an adequate way to move swiftly into and out of engagements with the enemy. Qaddafi's forces moved toward the oil-processing facilities near the towns of Ras Lanuf, Brega and Bin Jawad. The rebels, like mosquitos, would dart toward them, and then retreat to Adjabiya. This meant that Qaddafi's forces had to keep coming along the roads, being drawn into open territory where they were being bombed from the air by NATO's aircraft and cruise missiles.

When it appeared clear that Qaddafi's forces were being boxed in, Saif al-Islam gave his amazing interview to the *New York Times* (August 3), offering the paper a window into the regime's thinking. The regime needed to peel away the body armor of the rebels, which meant that they needed to make a link with the political Islamists. Arguing that it was the Islamists who killed al-Fattah Younis, Saif al-Islam said, "They decided to get rid of those people—the ex-military people like Abdul Fattah and the liberals—to take control of the whole operation. In other words to take off the mask." Saif al-Islam, who had long fashioned himself as one of those liberals, now said that he was ready to sign an agreement with the Islamists to turn Libya into "Waziristan on the Mediterranean, an Islamic zone, like Mecca." The Islamists "are the real force on the ground." It was a move of great desperation. The Islamists disdained the Qaddafi regime. It wanted no pact with it. Saif al-Islam's interview was a sign of the weakness of the Qaddafi regime along the Mediterranean road.

If By Sea.
Qaddafi's troops oscillated along the Mediterranean road and garrisoned Tripoli, but they did not have access to the air or to the sea (the "no fly" zone morphed into a "no water" zone). The rebel forces outflanked Qaddafi's now degraded armed forces with a naval landing at Misrata, providing relief to the rebels in

that city. It is likely that at this stage the British SAS troops joined the rebels. The SAS had fought in Tobruk in 1941 and Benghazi in 1942. Rather than admit that official SAS troops had now returned to Libya, the British first said that these were "experienced military officers" who were former-SAS and were now in Misrata by on their own accord. After Tripoli fell, the British no longer made such a mess about them being former-SAS. These SAS troops with the Misrata rebels became the conduit to NATO command in Naples (under the supervision of the Canadian commander, Lt. General Charles Bouchard).

The sea landing was important but not essential. Arms had already been airdropped into the city, and so had supplies. But the maritime channel allowed much greater volume to enter the city. The sea landing demonstrated that Qaddafi had few options even in the western part of the country. It relieved the Misrata fighters from a long siege. Qaddafi's most wretched violence took place against this city. He had given orders to his commanders to turn the "blue sea red," and to treat the entire city as hostile territory. Qaddafi's main commander Youssef Ahmed Bashir Abu Hajar told his forces, "It is absolutely forbidden for supply cars, fuel and other services to enter the city of Misrata from all gates and checkpoints." Such collective punishment against Misrata mimics what the Misratans did to Tawergha.

Guns In the Mountains.
One of the most contentious moments in the UN Security Council debate over Resolution 1973 was on arms delivery. Resolution 1970 had declared an arms

embargo against both sides in the conflict. When the draft of 1973 returned to the Council, the US insisted on adding a crucial phrase: the Council authorized members to "take all necessary measures, *notwithstanding paragraph 9 of 1970*, to protect civilians and civilian populated areas." Paragraph 9 of the February 26 resolution established the arms embargo. The new resolution upheld the embargo, but then this curious, bureaucratic phrase with "notwithstanding" at its core seemed to circumvent the strict embargo. On March 26, White House spokesperson Jay Carney told the press that the resolution provided the US with "flexibility within that to take that action [supply military equipment] if we thought that were the right way to go." In other words, the arms embargo was flexible. The next day, US Defense Secretary Robert Gates told NBC's David Gregory that on the question of the arms supply, "No decision has been made about that at this point."

The French were less chary about arms delivery. They moved weaponry by air to Benghazi, and then to Misrata before they were parachuted into the Jebel Nafusa and into the southern part of Libya. The French justified their action by saying that their arms drops were in the same league as the use of NATO attack helicopters against Qaddafi troops in Misrata— to "unblock what has become a blocked situation," as Philippe Gelie of *Le Figaro* put it on June 28 (more colorful in French, *donner un coup de pouce afin de sortir d'une situation bloquée*). The Imazighen who got some of the arms in the Jebel Nafusa intensified their campaign in the mountains. Having gained control of the highlands, the Imazighen moved to link up with reb-

els in Az Zawiya, just west of Tripoli. When Az Zawiya fell, Qaddafi's regime lost access to its supplies.

This was a crucial blow. Evidence of the retribution set in early in the conflict. In Yafran, the
homes of those of the Mashaashia who supported
Qaddafi were "set upon and burned," as the *New York
Times* put it (August 9). "These occupants vanished
from the mountains, apparently having fled. Many
Amazigh residents say the Mashaashia are not welcome back."

Operation Mermaid Dawn.

By August 17–18, the NATO and rebel assault moved
toward Tripoli. The "target set became larger," a
NATO official admitted, and so NATO's aircraft and
cruise missiles could strike large troop detachments,
or simply their bases. An early plan for the war called
for the NATO strikes to become "unbearable." During
the final bombardment of Tripoli, by all accounts, the
strikes were a form of annihilation. The troops were
now concentrated and easy to strike. US satellite im-
agery showed where Qaddafi's troops were, and this
information was relayed to the rebels on the ground.
In other words, NATO provided logistical and communication support to the rebels in the final stage. As
well, Special Forces units from Qatar, France, Britain and the United States were on the ground with
the rebel units, helped call in air strikes and offering
leadership for some of the more difficult strikes. The
communications systems in Tripoli had been knocked
out. The city was a sitting duck.

Between August 18 and 20, NATO hammered
Tripoli with a bombardment that some describe as

apocalyptic. One of the more dramatic events of the weekend was the aerial attack on a tent-city outside Qaddafi's compound. *Forbes* notes, "The identities of the dead were unclear, but they were in all likelihood activists who had set up an impromptu tent city in solidarity with Qaddafi in defiance of the NATO bombing campaign." Such incidents are apparently legion. The Qaddafi regime, before it disappeared, claimed that the bombings in this period in Tripoli killed about 1,300 with 5,000 wounded. These figures will never be verifiable. They are gone in the dust of the fall of Tripoli.

The bases of the 32nd (or Khamis) Brigade were strewn with corpses, many of "deserters" killed by the troops as the bombs fell and others felled by the bombs themselves. Whatever happened to the defensive unit around Tripoli is mysterious. It is likely that they vanished into their kin networks. Or they might have been less disposed to the regime than supposed, and went into hiding, waiting to reappear as civilians. Or they were scared by the massive bombardment and simply decided to throw in the towel. There was no *al-tarbur al-khamis*, no special uprising to defend Qaddafi and his regime.

The bombing raids on August 20 weakened the city. At 8pm on August 21, just when the Ramadan fast was to break, the sirens went off in the mosques of Tripoli (the main one was at the Ben Nabi mosque on Sarim Street, in the city's center). This siren was the call for the underground rebels to seize the city. Rebel leader Fathi al-Baja said that over the past three months the NTC had worked to build up armed "sleeper cells" inside Tripoli. It was a daring move, and swift.

Inside Tripoli, sections of Qaddafi's security staff had already reached out to Benghazi and given over their allegiance to the new regime. People such as Mahmoud Ben Jumaa, a senior officer in Qaddafi's personal security team, worked closely with the Tripoli underground in his neighborhood of Fashloom. Ben Jumaa made contact with the neighborhood committee that included people like Abdel Basat al-Tubal, a brigadier general in the local police. In Souq al-Jouma'a, a nearby suburb, Hakim Boulsayn worked closely with another informer in the internal security service. In the industrial suburb of Tajoura, the local underground was also in touch with the security services, who shielded them from the crackdown in March.

Weapons had also come into the city from the sea over the previous days, as NATO vessels filled with weapons docked in Tripoli (according to the Benghazi military commander Colonel Fadlallah Haroun). An amphibian assault on the city came alongside renewed aerial bombardment. The 15,000 strong Tripoli Task Force (trained in Qatar, and helped along by Qatari Special Forces) pushed into the city. They were the spear. Tripoli fell to the rebels. They stormed into the Green Square, now the Martyrs Square.

Gunfire rent the air. It could have been both celebratory and accusatory, joy or anger. In some places, it meant that scores had to be settled. Rebels marched around taking out their anger on the "loyalists" or the "mercenaries." One rebel, Ahmed Bin Sabri showed *The Independent*'s Kim Sengupta the bodies of thirty men, hands tied behind their backs, bound and dumped on the side of the road. "Come and see," he said, "These are blacks, Africans, hired by Gaddafi, mercenaries." Racism combined with a visceral hatred for Qaddafi found its outlet on these dark-skinned soldiers and migrant workers. "Any Libyan with a black skin accused of fighting for the old regime may have a poor chance of survival," wrote Patrick Cockburn in late August. It was a pitiful start to the new order. Amnesty International found that the rebels had killed detainees at two camps in Tripoli. At one of them, Khilit al-Ferjan, about 160 detainees tried to escape. "As the detainees barged through the hanger gates, two other guards opened fire and threw five hand grenades at the group," wrote Amnesty in a report. Twenty-three detainees survived the attack. Much the same kind of blood-letting took place in the southern desert oasis of Ghadames, where the Tuareg were forced out because of their support for the Qaddafi regime. Some of them decamped to Mali, where they joined the National Movement for the Liberation of the Azawad and went to war against the Malian government in early January 2012.

The regime refused to fall fully immediately. The rebels said they had some of the Qaddafi family in custody, including Saif al-Islam. Then, remarkably, Saif al-Islam appeared in person for a press conference, said that the fight was still on and disappeared. A few days later, it appeared that Qaddafi's family, minus Saif al-Islam and the old Colonel had arrived in Algeria. Towns such as Bani Walid, Sirte and Sabha (in the south of the country) refused to give up. They held fast, under siege from the rebels. NATO bombed them at will. They were the *bouches inutiles*, the useless mouths that could be done away with. Qaddafi remained defiant, but scarce. He was already now irrelevant. NATO had fired him.

V. The Son et Lumiére at Sirte

On the dusty reaches out of Sirte on October 20, a convoy flees a battlefield. A NATO aircraft fires and strikes the cars. The wounded struggle to escape. Armed trucks, with armed fighters from Misrata, rush to the scene. They find the injured, and among them is the most significant prize: a bloodied Muammar Qaddafi stumbles, is captured, and then is thrown amongst the fighters. One can imagine their exhilaration. A cell-phone video camera traces the events of the next few minutes. A badly injured Qaddafi is pushed around, thrown on a car, driven around on its bonnet, and then the video gets blurry. The next images are of a dead Qaddafi. He took a bullet in the side of his head.

These images go onto Youtube almost instantly. They are on television, and in the newspapers. It was impossible not to see them.

One of the important ideological elements during the early days of the war in Libya was the framing of the arrest warrant for Qaddafi and his clique by the International Criminal Court's selectively zealous chief prosecutor Luis Moreno Ocampo. It was enough to have *press reports* of excessive violence for Moreno Ocampo and Ban Ki-Moon to use the language of genocide; no independent, forensic evaluation of the evidence was necessary. NATO sanctimoniously said that it would help the ICC prosecute the warrant (this despite the fact that the United States, NATO's powerhouse, is not a member of the ICC). This remark was echoed by the National Transitional Council, the rebels' political instrument in Benghazi.

Humanitarian intervention was justified on the basis of potential or alleged violations of the Geneva Conventions. It is disquieting that the intervention is to "end" with a violation of those very Conventions, notably the Third Geneva Convention (article 13 on the treatment of prisoners) and the Fourth Geneva Convention (article 27 again on the treatment of prisoners).

It would perhaps have been inconvenient to see Qaddafi in open court. He had long abandoned his revolutionary heritage (1969–1988), and had given himself over to the US-led War on Terror at least since 2003 (but in fact since the late 1990s). Qaddafi's prisons had been an important torture center in the archipelago of black sites utilized by the CIA, European intelligence and the Egyptian security state. What stories Qaddafi might have told if he were allowed to speak in open court? What stories Saddam Hussein might have told had he too been allowed to speak in an open court? As it happens, Hussein at least entered a courtroom, even as it was more kangaroo than judicial. No such courtroom for Qaddafi. Dead men tell no tales. They cannot stand trial. They cannot name the people who helped them stay in power. All secrets die with them.

A month later, on November 19, Saif al-Islam was detained in Ubari, in the south of Libya. He was flown to Zintan, where he was held in custody by the rebels. There was no transfer to any judicial authority. Three months later, in January 2012, Donatella Rovera of

Amnesty International, worried about this delay. "At the moment," she noted, "there is no central authority to speak of, so it's difficult to speak of an independent judiciary." City-based rebels acted for themselves. The Zintan rebels had plans for Saif al-Islam. They were not willing to hand him over to the ICC or to the new government. But Saif al-Islam is not the only person. Seventy thousand Qaddafi fighters sit in Libyan jails without recourse to any judicial procedure. This worried the UN's Human Rights office. Mona Rishmawi and Hanny Megally of the UN made several trips to Libya, pointing out the situation is a "recipe for abuse." The Qaddafi-era prisons remain, and only the nature of the prisoners has changed. The Islamists and liberals are now the jailers; the pro-Qaddafi fighters are enchained.

Libya's cities celebrated the fall of Qaddafi. But what are the people celebrating? Certainly there is jubilation at the removal from power of the Qaddafi of 1988–2011. That Qaddafi had alienated everyone. It is in the interests of NATO and the neoliberal clique to ensure that in this *auto-ða-fé* the national liberation anti-imperialist of 1969–1988 is liquidated, and that the neoliberal era is forgotten, to be reborn anew as if not tried before. That is going to be the trick: to navigate between the joy of large sections of the population who want to have a say in their society (which Qaddafi blocked, and Jibril would like to canalize) and a small section that wants to pursue the neoliberal agenda (which Qaddafi tried to facilitate but could not do so over the objections of his "men of the tent"). The new Libya will be born in the gap between the two interpretations.

The manner of Qaddafi's death is a synecdoche for the entire war. NATO's bombs stopped the convoy, and without them Qaddafi would probably have fled to his next redoubt. The rebellion might have succeeded without NATO. But with NATO, certain political options had to be foreclosed. NATO's member states are now in line to claim their reward. However, they are too polite in a liberal European way to actually state their claim publicly in a quid-pro-quo fashion. Hence, they say things like: this is a Libyan war, and Libya must decide what it must do. This is properly the space into which those sections in the new Libyan power structure that still value sovereignty must assert themselves. The window for that assertion is going to close soon, as the deals get inked that lock Libya's resources and autonomy into the agenda of the NATO states. One hopes for Libya that the original leaders of the February 2011 rebellion (Fathi Terbil Salwa, Idris al-Mesmari and Salwa al-Dighaili) will produce a revolution within the revolution, seizing the dynamic from NATO and its allies and reviving Libya's independent road. If they do, they might redeem the fallen promise of 1969.

VI. Aftermath

Right until the end of August, the war appeared to linger in a stalemate. The fighting was fierce, but no side seemed to make great ground. The NATO bombings, the arms drops and the use of the naval logistical route hastened the collapse of Qaddafi's regime. But before the end, those who had thrown their lot in with the rebels worried about the outcome. Early in the conflict, on March 2, Hillary Clinton warned that if the rebels did not prevail Libya might become a "giant Somalia." Before the "no-fly" zone came into effect, Mustafa Alani of the Gulf Research Center in the UAE told the *Los Angeles Times*, "People might not like it but the only other option is to allow a civil war to develop in Libya. You're going to create another Somalia." On March 30, Moussa Koussa, now defected to the Atlantic world and a featured speaker at the Libya Contact Group meeting in Doha, Qatar pleaded, "I ask everybody to avoid taking Libya into civil war. This would lead to so much blood and Libya would be a new Somalia." It was this fear of the Somalia outcome that led NATO and its adjutants to push for the opinions of artillery. They would smash Qaddafi fast and prevent a civil war from germinating any further. Moussa Koussa, who knew the ground realities as well as anyone else, feared that absent a hasty dispatch of Qaddafi this is precisely what would happen.

The leadership of the rebellion came from out of the bowels of the Qaddafi regime. But that has been so in most revolutions, since Louis-Marie, *vicomte* de Noailles and Armand, *duc* d'Aiguillon began the great orgy against feudal privileges in the 1789 Estates-General in France. George Washington, who once wore the uniform of the British army, asked de Noailles to accept the sword of Cornwallis when the British surrendered, this in honor of de Noailles and his brother-in-law the Marquis de Lafayette for their service in the American Revolution. From de Noailles we come to al-Jalil, Jibril and their inheritor Abdurrahim el-Keib. But there is a warning for al-Jalil, Jibril and el-Keib: de Noailles fled revolutionary France for the United States when the unstoppable revolution could no longer tolerate his background and his wealth. It is not clear what will happen to al-Jalil, Jibril and el-Keib, but what is already evident is that the rebels from below have no patience for signs of the continuation of the old regime into the new dispensation. They have other things in mind, other ways to conceive of their Libya.

Mortal Combat.

> "The 'humanitarian' intervention introduced
> to save lives believed to be threatened was
> in fact a political intervention introduced to
> bring about regime change."
> — Richard Haass, Council on Foreign Relations, "Libya Needs Boots on the Ground,"
> *Financial Times*, August 22, 2011.

Qaddafi's collapse has sent an important message to the other "rogue states." His major error was to give up his nuclear weapons agenda. The nuclear cover is now seen from Pyongyang to Tehran as the only adequate insurance policy against the agenda of NATO. Despite the averted cataclysm, few would not discount the blue chip standard of the nuclear shield. Particularly after Hillary Clinton noted that the military intervention in Ivory Coast in April 2011 "sends a strong signal to dictators and tyrants throughout the region and the world" that they "may not disregard the voices of their own people." A UN official said of those events, "The action in the Ivory Coast was given a psychological lift by the fact that it is happening against the backdrop of Libya, and supports Mr. Obama's narrative that intervention is justified in some cases." Despite political deadlock and a divided polity, it is for the "international community" (the G7) to translate the voice of the people, or to provide the narrative of justification for intervention. Interventionism is back, thanks to NATO's Libyan adventure.

On August 22, President Obama interrupted his Martha's Vineyard holiday to release a simple statement, "NATO has once more proven that it is the most capable alliance in the world and that its strength comes from both its firepower and the power of our democratic ideals." Not sure how those "democratic ideals" came into play over the skies of Libya, but certainly NATO's firepower showed it to be extremely capable. Once Qaddafi's regime fell in late August, NATO's Secretary General Anders Fogh Rasmussen began to crow about NATO's role. "NATO is needed and wanted more than ever," he said, "from Afghanistan to Kosovo, from the coast of Somalia to Libya. We are busier than before." To celebrate its Libyan glory, NATO's Sea Breeze 2011 naval exercise entered the Black Sea, close to the Sebastopol-based Russian Black Sea Fleet. The pressure on Russia, exercised earlier in Georgia and in the Black Sea, was once more to be increased. The idea of the Mediterranean as NATO's lake was at the forefront, so too was the idea that NATO was the most effective force to deal with political problems (notwithstanding the Afghan example).

Under cover of the Libyan war, Obama's administration released the Presidential Study Directive on

Mass Atrocities (PSD-10) that defines the prevention of mass atrocities as both "a core national security interest and a core moral responsibility of the United States." PSD-10 gives the US government *carte blanche* in authorizing an escalating series of actions against a country that on the basis of its analysis is endangering its civilians: sanctions can go to an embargo, and eventually to military intervention. The basic thrust of PSD-10 is that the United States is the only country with the muscle capable of enforcing the Responsibility to Protect doctrine, and so it must do its duty. The National Security Staff's Senior Director Samantha Power has pushed for the PSD-10, and the Libyan conflict allowed it to go through.

Not only would the United States and NATO be the *gendarmerie* of the planet, but they would also be able to blow life into hitherto suppressed peoples. "We can help the Arab Spring well and truly blossom," said NATO's Rasmussen after Tripoli's fall. This was a view repeated in many policy circles in the Atlantic world. In late August, former State Department counselor Philip Zelikow wrote in the *Financial Times* (August 22) that Qaddafi's fall "will renew a sense of momentum" to the Arab Spring. The Spring, for Zelikow and for Rasmussen, is not in the people who thronged the squares or took bullets in the frontlines. It is to be found elsewhere.

> Much of the drive in Arab Spring policymaking is currently coming from the Persian Gulf states, such as Saudi Arabia, the United Arab Emirates and Qatar. It is their hour. The Saudi government is playing a critical role

in the Arab diplomacy now isolating Syria. The UAE, with the Saudis, came up with the funds that allowed Egypt's interim rulers to hold off the conditional packages being offered by the international financial institutions. The Qatari government has played a vital role in the Libyan revolution.

Humanitarian intervention sweeps in from the skies. It helps save civilians, who are then given their freedom. Those who are so generous are then authorized to "help" with the reconstruction. This assistance seems a lot like the mandates of the post-World War 1 era. The intervening powers stay around, set up bases, offer technical support and send in their multinational corporations to take charge of raw material extraction. We are already far from the open racism of A. J. Balfour who warned in December 1918 that self-determination could not be applied "pedantically where it is really inapplicable…. You cannot transfer formulas more or less applicable to the populations of Europe to different races." Now we are all to enjoy the fruits of liberal democracy, with elections as the sweetest offering. Meanwhile, behind the electoral process, the technocrats who demonstrate their fealty to the international bond markets and the IMF will control the Central Bank and the Oil Company. From this perch they will try to turn over the Spring to the old circuits of power and property. They will try to continue the neoliberal reform agenda of Saif al-Islam, now without the impediment of the old guard. That section, beholden to the Revolution of 1969, has now exited power. It no longer has the basis to make its objections plain. In the neoliberal dispensation, such views have been rooted out by the removal of Qaddafi. All that will be allowed is marginal debate on aspects of governance that have nothing to do with the neoliberal agenda—on that agenda, I doubt very much that the new Libyan government will allow much debate.

It is a terrific irony that the neoliberal reformers could transform into the rebel leadership, while the Old Guard now seems identified with Qaddafi. In the last decade, it was this Old Guard that fought against Qaddafi's new allegiance to the neoliberal view. They are now scared, sullen, withdrawn. Some have fled Tripoli for the outer reaches of Libya or to neighboring Algeria. Others are incognito. They do not wish to be named. Politics is the poisoned chalice. They have drunk enough for many lifetimes. There seems to be no room in this new Libya for their old socialist visions. It is simply *jahiliyya* [ignorance] to the Islamists, and obstinacy to the neoliberals.

By November, when it was clear that the war was over, Jibril left his post as interim Prime Minister. He had completed his historical mission, which was to be the liaison between the National Transitional Council and NATO. Jibril was too closely linked to the neoliberal reformers to be capable of bridging the gap between the fighters and the neoliberals. Mustafa Abdel-Jalil remained in office as the chair of the NTC. He appointed Abdurrahim el-Keib to replace Jibril. El-Keib came to his post with little tarnish. He had left his native Tripoli for the United States where he trained as an engineer, taught at the University of Alabama, and went to work at the Petroleum Institute in the UAE. Being from Tripoli, having lived outside Libya for much of his life, all gave the oil engineer a great deal of credibility. He would be the new face that bridged the fragile new regime with its overseas brokers.

Petrol and Dollars.

On the day that Tripoli fell, the *New York Times* ran a story with the transparent headline, "The Scramble for Access to Libya's Oil Wealth Begins" (August 22). The use of the word "scramble" could not be accidental. It was the word used to describe the period after the Berlin Conference of 1884–85, when the Atlantic powers began a "scramble for Africa," having divided it up on a map in Germany. Three years later, Otto von Bismarck, the host of the conference said, "The map of Africa is in Europe." This was a prescient remark, for it made clear that the disputes over Africa were not about Africa itself but about inter-European (and US) rivalries. Much the same kind of activity emerged once the NTC consolidated itself, and created its National Oil Company. Oil executives streamed into the country, holding the elbows of diplomats whose aerial power had to be translated into commercial benefits. "We don't have a problem with Western countries like Italians, French, and UK companies," Abdeljalil Mayouf (of the Libyan oil firm, AGOCO) told Reuters. He didn't add the United States to the list. That was probably an oversight. The problems lay elsewhere. "But we may have some political issues with Russia, China and Brazil."

As Cameron and Sarkozy toured Tripoli in the company of the NTC leadership and BHL, the veritable Tintin, the NTC's spokesperson Jalal al-Gallala told the BBC that those outsiders who helped the reb-

els would get "special consideration" in all future con-
tracts. He specifically noted that the ones at the head of
the line included the French, the British and the Qatar-
is. The United States was again conspicuously absent.

The BRICS states that did not fully support the
Benghazi rebellion were going to be punished, and
the G7 states and their Arab allies would be reward-
ed. It was simple arithmetic morality: you help us, we
reward you. "We have lost Libya completely," said
Aram Shegunts, director general of the Russia-Libya
Business Council. Russia's Gazprom Neft and Tatneft are off the board. The Chinese, who previously
had seventy-five companies in Libya with thirty six
thousand staff and fifty projects worth $18 billion, are
silent. There is no word from Brazil's Petrobras and
Odebrecht. All their projects are on hold.

France's Total, Italy's ENI, Austria's OMV,
Britain's BP and Vitol, and the United States' Hess,
ConocoPhillips and Marathon jostled at the head of
the queue. Beside them were Qatar Petroleum and
BB Energy of Turkey and Jordan. During the war,
Qatar Petroleum came into the country with its ex-
perts and its own access to cash and oil. During the
fighting, Qatar helped get the oil port of Marsa el-
Harigh working, and overhaul a Liquefied Natural
Gas plant in Brega. They also worked to bring in oil
supplies via BB Energy. From having almost no in-
terests in Libya, Qatar is close to the head of the line.
"It's not a single country that's helping—the NTC is
working now with all its international partners," said
Aref Ali Nayed who is the Libyan ambassador to the
UAE. "The Libyan people are very proud people,
they will never forget their friends." Much the same

came from Finance's Ali Tarhouni, "We are indebted to the French, and I cannot find the right words to say it. If everything else is the same, of course we will remember our friends."

Libya's oil reserves are prized for their quantity (largest reserves in Africa) and quality (proximity to Europe and easy to process). Before the war, Libya produced 1.6 million barrels a day. As the *Times'* Clifford Krauss put it, "Colonel Qaddafi proved to be a problematic partner for international oil companies, frequently raising fees and taxes and making other demands. A new government with close ties to NATO may be an easier partner for Western nations to deal with. Some experts say that given a free hand, oil companies could find considerably more oil in Libya than they were able to locate under the restrictions placed by the Qaddafi government." In other words, in a few years, oil production from Libya might far exceed the 1.6 million barrels. BP had already begun to explore for oil in the Gulf of Sidra and other firms had conducted explorations in the deserts of the southeast. Estimates place Libya's oil reserves at 46.4 billion barrels (three percent of the world's oil reserves), and five trillion cubic feet of natural gas: but this might turn out to be an underestimate.

David Tafuri, partner at Patton Boggs, traveled to Benghazi in August to discuss how to move the US Treasury to help unfreeze the Libyan sovereign funds and other assets in Atlantic banks. Jibril and Ali Tarhouni had been to Washington in May to talk to the Treasury officials. They were pressured on a pledge to ensure that Libyan oil sales are conducted in dollars, not in Euros (and certainly not in the Gold Dinar that Qaddafi had been trying to concoct for the African continent, a revival of the Gold Dinar proposal that Malaysia's Dr. Mahathir put on the table in 2003). This new currency was frowned upon by the IMF. It is utterly off the table for the new Libya. It was one of the things that the neoliberals disdained. The Central Bank did make one change with the currency: in January 2012 it announced that Qaddafi-era banknotes were to be transferred for a new design.

By May, at the G7 meeting in Deauville, France, the ministers of the Atlantic world created the Deauville Partnership. This Partnership was a mechanism to tie in the countries of the G7 with the Middle East and North Africa, alongside the IMF. Atlantic aid and IMF support was premised upon certain responsible steps from the various West Asian and North African countries—strengthen governance, support private sector-led growth, target subsidies and transfer payments to "free up resources for investments in infrastructure and education and support for the neediest," and finally to "avoid measures that will have adverse long-term fiscal consequences or be difficult to unwind later." Tunisia and Egypt jumped on board, and soon were joined by Jordan, Kuwait, Morocco, Qatar, Saudi Arabia, Turkey and the United Arab Emirates. Libya joined soon after its National Transitional Council was recognized by the IMF as the legitimate government of Libya in September. As IMF chief Christine Lagarde put it in line with the Deauville Partnership requirements, "The new authorities will need to quickly restore oil production to generate revenues, stabilize the currency, reestablish a payment system, introduce sound public financial management, and start reforms to foster a more inclusive and sustainable growth for the benefit of all Libyan citizens." Full neoliberalism is on the march into Tripoli, called forward by the Libyan neoliberal "reformers" and their IMF-G7 ideological allies.

The point of view of petrol and dollars leads inexorably to a convergence with the ideology of the pillars of stability. Already murmurs can be heard amongst the neoliberal reformers that Israel's security must be paramount and that NATO military interests must not be scoffed at. Ahmed Shebani, whose father was in the last of Idris' cabinets, formed the Democratic Party of Libya in July as a political adjutant of the NTC. Shebani is a businessman who has long been one of the promoters of neoliberal reform in Libya. In an economic conference hosted by Saif al-Islam in Tripoli in March 2007, Shebani joined businessmen and human rights activists who wanted to put pressure on the regime to push their agenda. It was important to yoke the economic reforms to political ones, partly to maintain the wide coalition. "Do you think we can create social and economic prosperity without political reform," Shebani asked? The main thrust for political reform was to wrest control from the blocked Qaddafi regime to more pliable hands. It was not a surprise then to read Shebani tell *Haaretz* in the midst of the rebellion, "We are asking Israel to use its influence in the international community to end the tyrannical regime of Gadhafi and his family." Political reform would mean an entry into the system of brokerage that includes Israel and has the United States at its apex. It is why critics of the NTC fear that once Libya is pacified, the new government will welcome the US, or NATO, to settle into one or more bases in the country, to bring AFRICOM to Africa. None of this will happen in a hurry. If it were so, it would look bad. First Libya must settle into a modicum of independence. Then the *quid pro quo* will occur.

Perhaps it has already begun under the table. In early January 2012, journalist Franklin Lamb offered a chilling story from Tripoli. Oil has been flowing to the NATO countries, Lamb says, but with no recompense. A Central Bank official told Lamb this, and it was verified by another employee who told Lamb that she had not seen any money coming in as well. This outraged her because of the long lines outside local banks with account holders waiting hours for their savings. Why is there no money coming for the oil that has exited? "The reason is said to be that NATO countries are being shipped oil (also to gas and oil rich Qatar) free of charge," Lamb reports, "under a payback arrangement with NATO for its regime change services."

Rebels From Below.

In August, I heard from US Ambassador David Mack, who, as the second secretary at the US Embassy in Libya from 1969–72, had met Qaddafi a few times and was since 2005 the honorary chairman of the US–Libya Business Association. Mack, who was ambassador to the UAE in the 1980s, has a very sound grip of the Libyan dynamic. He spoke with fluency and compassion about events in Libya, and hoped for an outcome that best approximated the radical imagination sparked by the revolt. At one point in the discussion, however, Ambassador Mack faltered. He said that one of the problems in Libya is that the Libyan people have an unusual expectation of democracy: for them, democracy means housing, food, work and health. The Libyans will have to be schooled in what democracy really is, Ambassador Mack noted, which is to say, political democracy: elections and rule of law. The other matters, social and economic democracy, are simply not guarantees.

What Ambassador Mack says is not offensive, but realistic. This is what "democracy" has come to mean in the Atlantic world. When Obama, Sarkozy and Cameron speak of democracy for Libya, they mean the electoral sort. This is also what the neoliberal reformers mean by democracy.

Ambassador Mack is enough of an anthropologist to know that this is not what the average Libyan means when they talk of democracy. They mean much more, including a fundamental desire for dignity. This is why, for instance, the rebels of Misrata refused to allow Jibril to foist Albarrani Shkal, a former army general, on the town as Tripoli's head of security. Jibril was simply adhering to the seventy page plan drafted by his cousin 'Arif Nayid, that cautioned against the Iraqi experience ("Disbanded elements should be integrated into society and provided economic opportunities so as to discourage them from taking up arms, as happened in Iraq"). The people of Misrata did not understand this sort of logic. They were not willing to allow the "blood of the martyrs" to be sacrificed for expediency. The protestors believed that Shkal was the operations officers for the 32nd (Khamis) Brigade, and this history should not be ignored in his appointment. "We won't follow Shkal's orders, no," said Walid Tenasil. "Our message to the NTC is: just remember the blood. That is it."

That is it.

A modern state is defined by its monopoly over violence. The new Libyan regime tried to yoke the various city-based militias and the political Islamists into one command, but failed. The refusal to hand over Saif al-Islam to the central authority is one indication of the lack of control. The frequent clashes amongst the militia groups and then between the militias and the Libyan National Army are also signs of this failure.

In December, General Khalifa Hifter's forces fought against fighters en route to the airport in Tripoli. The National Army, under Hifter, is often derided as "bodyguards of Hifter," or as militias from the East (these are the words of Colonel Mukhtar Farnana, head of the militia in the west of Tripoli). If Libya is freed from Qaddafi and his sons, it has now to contend with Hifter and his male progeny. His son Belqasim Hifter and his grandson Saddam Hifter have taken to such shenanigans as armed robbery of the Aman Bank in Tripoli's Gurji neighborhood and an attack on Tripoli's Rixos Hotel. Liam Stack, in the *New York Times* (December 12, 2011), noted that Hifter has "emerged as the army's most influential officer" even though Yousef al-Manqoush is the official leader.

In this impasse, the Libyan authorities cannot name a proper army command. In early January, el-Keib's government proposed Yousef al-Manqoush, its Minister of Defense, as the Chief of Staff. The Coalition of Libyan Thwars (revolutionaries) and the Cyrenaica Military Council vetoed this decision. They wanted their own chap, Salah Salem al-Obeidi. Al-Manqoush, they said, has his roots in the Qaddafi establishment. Al-Obeidi, rather, is an Easterner.

Into this mess comes Abdel Hakim Belhaj, head of the Tripoli Military Council and a former leader of the Libyan Islamic Fighting Group. Belhaj has sued the UK and MI6 for its role in sending him and his wife back to Libya in 2004 to be tortured. He has no special fealty to the G7 and NATO. It was his armed column that spilled blood on the ground; NATO only fired from the skies, and the neoliberals did not join him on the battlefield. Belhaj has a real following in Libya, which is why it is assumed that the Muslim Brotherhood will put him forward as their electoral leader when elections inevitably take place in Libya. The Brotherhood is backed by Qatar, whose emir had similarly stroked the ambitions of political Islam's leaders from Tunisia to Egypt. The moves by Qatar and the popularity of Belhaj scared the neoliberals and the G7. Ali Tarhouni, speaking for the neoliberals, warned, "Anyone who wants to come to our house has to knock on our front door first." A "senior diplomat" from the Atlantic world carped, "Qatar is not being respectful, and there is a feeling that it is riding roughshod over the issue of the country's sovereignty." Political Islam is in a good position to take command of the Arab Spring in North Africa.

The rebellion from below has its own radical imagination. It will not be satisfied with the neoliberal phraseology of *transparency*, *empowerment*, *tolerance*, *rights* and *green jobs*. It does not want the verbiage of twenty-first century delusions, all the right words strung in the right order that offer little more than the right to vote, empowerment at the polls, transparency of consumerism and jobs that bring the green to a small minority of enfranchised neoliberals. That is inadequate. It has a much more plebian taste, but absent a working-class mass party, it seems to tend to the legions of political Islam.

But the rebellion from below might be constrained by the new electoral rules that emerged from the National Transitional Council in early January 2012. Those who could run in the elections to the General National Congress had to have "professional qualifications," had to have demonstrated "early and clear support for the February 17th Revolution," had to have no role in the Qaddafi regime and could not have received their university degree "without merit." These barriers would mean that most of the Libyan population is ineligible to stand for election, certainly the vast mass of the workers without "professional qualifications" would be barred from Democracy.

When Tripoli fell, the residents of the city hastened to create order through the creation of reconciliation committees (*lijan al-sulh*), and to form new neighborhood police forces. Disorder raged as the militia forces marched around, searching for spoils, but nonetheless it was already clear that the Libyan people were eager to forge a new life now that Qaddafi had done. One of their leaders, Isma'il al-Salabi, a well-regarded Islamist told Reuters, "The role of the executive committee [NTC] is no longer required because they are remnants of the old regime. They should all resign, starting from the head of the pyramid all the way down." This is the rebellion from below. It will not be silenced. What it says, on the other hand, might not be pleasant to the Atlantic powers or to the secular ear. That is the price of democracy.

Closings.

"Everything that is not new in a time of
innovation is pernicious."
—Louis Antoine de Saint-Just.

Several years ago, my friend Dilip Simeon and a group of other radical students sat with E. P. Thompson, the Marxist historian, in New Delhi. The Emergency was on, and Thompson had come to talk to the students about the repression and the fightback. Dilip was bemoaning the limits of "bourgeois democracy." Edward Thompson, according to Dilip, asked him to stop using the word "bourgeois" before "democracy." It was giving Edward Thompson a headache. The phrase demeaned democracy.

The impact of revolutionary developments is hard to predict.

The counter-revolution crushed the revolts of 1848, but it could not break its spirit nor its dynamic. The culture of feudalism perished in its aftermath, broken by the rise of new social identities. "Our age, the age of democracy, is breaking," wrote Frederick Engels in February 1848. A worker, pistol in hand, went into the French Chamber of Deputies and pronounced, "No more deputies, we are the masters." The counter-revolution was fierce. "The bourgeoisie, fully conscious of what it is doing, conducts a war of extermination against them," Marx pointed out. Nonetheless, 1848 opened up a new social horizon, against bondage and subservience, and a mid-point of struggle between the promise of an earlier revolution (1789) and the possibility of a later one (the Paris Commune of 1871). Europe could not return to its age of the lash and powdered wigs. That time was gone.

So many other revolutions have had a similar impact, breaking the back of older forms of social claustrophobia, but not immediately inaugurating new forms of social freedom. Russia's 1905 and 1917 strengthened the will of anti-colonial movements; Gandhi, then a lawyer in South Africa, wrote of the Russian revolution of 1905, "The present unrest in Russia has a great lesson for us. The Russian workers and all the other servants declared a general strike and stopped all work," and "it is not within the power of even the Czar of Russia to force strikers to return at the point of the bayonet. For even the powerful cannot rule without the cooperation of the ruled." If the Russian workers and peasants could strike out against their autocrats, so could the Indians and the Indonesians, the South Africans and the Persians. Gandhi's idea of non-cooperation comes via St. Petersburg.

The national liberation movements of the Third World project emerged head held high in the 1920s, and then walked off the stage of history in defeat by the 1980s. And yet, here too, a legacy of colonial heavy-handedness was dispatched as the countries committed to the Project sought to redress problems that they felt only they could answer (along these lines, Fanon wrote in 1961, "The Third World today faces Europe like a colossal mass whose project should be to try to resolve the problems to which Europe has not been able to find the answers"). Rates of inequality in the Global South belie any successes from this project, and yet it is the formidable example of the Third World era that provides sustenance to so many struggles that germinate in the South.

Closer to our time, the global uprisings of 1968 from Tokyo to Mexico City, from Paris to Karachi seemed not to have made much of an impact. The revolutionary dreams of the workers and students lay squandered at the wayside as young people turned in their slogans and bohemianism for the lure of personal advancement. And yet, the social and political impact of 1968 is formidable, not the least of which is the new horizon set for gender relations and for race relations. Many of the '68ers might have migrated to the world of corporations, and that has been the great limit of that revolt, but nonetheless they have not been able to turn back the new commitments to social equality.

Tunisia and Egypt are poised for modest electoral democracy. This is a major social shift in the Arab world. Of the many lessons that we have to take from the USSR's experiment and that of the national liberation State's attempts is that they badly misjudged the importance of democratic yearnings and democratic institutions. Qaddafi certainly provided transfer payments to the Libyan population with the oil wealth, so that Libya's people enjoy high human development indicators (the past ten years, however, have seen a decline in these payments). But such payments are no substitute for social and political dignity, as the emirs of the Gulf are finding amongst their restive populations. Elections are no panacea, but they set a new foundation. More will be demanded. New forms of popular engagement, new public spaces, new democratic dreams that far exceed the rancid constraints of neoliberalism.

The Arab lands will not be the same again.

There is an appropriate, although apocryphal story from the 1970s. Zhou Enlai the Chinese premier was asked what he thought of the 1789 French Revolution. He answered, "It is too soon to tell." What we know for sure is that the time of the neoliberal security state, of the governments of the possible, is now over. Even if such states remain, their legitimacy has eroded. The time of the impossible has presented itself. In Egypt, where the appetite for the possibilities of the future are greatest, the people continue to assert themselves into Tahrir Square and other places, pushing to reinvigorate a Revolution that must not die. They do not want to allow it to settle back into the possible forms, the neoliberal security state without Mubarak, the neoliberal security state that is also what Qaddafi had been erecting on the ruins of his attempt to create a national-liberation state. They want something more. For them the slogan is simple: Down with the Present. Long Live the Future. May it be so.

Acknowledgements.

"Singing in a cage is possible
And so is happiness."
— Mahmoud Darwish.

I would never have written about Libya had I not gone there in my youth, driven from Alexandria to Benghazi, watching the battlefields first of El Alamein and then Tobruk. Boyhood wonder at the halftracks and the tanks that remained on the side of the road from World War 2 made Libya a very special place for me. For this, and so much more, thanks to my father Pran Prashad (1924–1999), who inculcated in me in his own way a deep and abiding interest in the politics and potential of the Third World. Thanks as well to my mother, Soni Prashad (born 1929), brave traveller, undaunted spirit.

Friends in that area we know as the Arab world kept me informed and involved in the events of the Arab Spring and on the Libyan War. I am particularly grateful to a number of them whose emails and phone calls, writings and manifestos as well as conversations over dinner and lingering cups of coffee allowed me to learn hastily of details that would otherwise have gone right by me. Some of them are old friends, and others are new, some came to me first as students, and in the face of others, I will always be a student. Others who live elsewhere but have strong commitments to the region, and are experts in this or that aspect of it, have been invaluable to me. They include: Paul Amar, Zayde Antrim, Raymond Baker, Bassam Haddad, Toufic Haddad, Kifah Hanna, Adam Hanieh, Shafqat Hussain, Sam Husseini, Anjali Kamat, Sadri Khiari, Ron Kiener, Mahmood Mamdani, Seyed Mohammad Marandi, Qalandar Bux Memon, Raza Mir, Raza Naeem, Adam Shatz, Magid Shihade, Mayssun Sukarieh, Fawwaz Trabulsi and Haifa Zangana.

I learned a great deal from the reporting of, among others, Jon Lee Anderson, Ian Black, Owen Bowcott, C. J. Chivers, Alex Crawford, Patrick Cockburn, Orkhan Dzemal, Ahmad Val Ould Eddin, Pepe Escobar, Philippe Gelie, Toby Jones, Anjali Kamat, Shi Kewei, Zeina Khodr, Clifford Krauss, Franklin Lamb, Lotfi al Masoudi, Mahdi Nazemroaya, Kim Sengupta, Anthony Shadid, Paula Slier, Liam Stack and Feng Yunxian. I am indebted to the historian of Libya, Dirk Vandewalle and to my friends in the UN bureaucracy who fed me very useful information (particularly a friend in the UNHCR and another in the UNDP). I could not have done this without WikiLeaks, whose treasure trove sharpened my own interviews. The book comes without footnotes. As much as possible I indicate in the text itself where I have got material, with a nudge to a journalist or a State Department cable, to Vandewalle's book or to interviews with people in the United Nations or in this or that part of the Arab world.

When the Arab Spring took hold, Pratyush Chandra and Pothik Ghosh of *Radical Notes* did a long interview with me, which ran in two parts in their journal and then in *CounterPunch*. That was the spur to produce a series of essays for *CounterPunch*, which is so ably edited by Alexander Cockburn and Jeffrey St. Clair, and for my reports that appeared in *Frontline*, edited by my dear friend R. Vijayashankar. I am grateful to my editors for their confidence in my writing, and for their sensible suggestions. Many of the sentences in this book are drawn from the essays that appeared in these journals.

My thinking is sharpened by my interactions with such warm and wondrous people as Mona Ahmed Ali, Phil Armstrong, Bill Ayers, Vivek Bald, Prasenjit Bose, Shonali Bose, Jo Comerford, Bernardine Dohrn, Bill Fletcher, Craig Gilmore, Ruthie Gilmore, Andy Hsiao, Deepa Iyer, Rev. Jesse Jackson, Santita Jackson, Robin Kelley, Parag Khandhar, Bakari Kitwana, Amitava Kumar, Sunaina Maira, Naeem Mohaiemen, Clare Nader, Ralph Nader, Jeff Napolitano, Harish Patel, Prabir Purkayastha, Donna Riley, Najla Said, P. Sainath, James Thindwa and so many more.

Kate Khatib at AK decided that there was a book here, and edited it with great care. Lisa Armstrong, Zalia Maya and Rosa Maya indulged her assessment. Opinions in Delhi concurred, notably those of Prakash Karat, Brinda Karat and Sudhanva Deshpande. I am deeply grateful for the intellectual guidance and the encouragement from Aijaz Ahmad. Daisy Rockwell, *lapata*, allowed her remarkable painting to be on the cover, the original of which inspired me to get the book written as quickly as possible.

Index.

Symbols

9/11 126
1968 251
al-'Umar, Nasir 81

A

Abdel-Jalil, Mustafa 151–152, 201–202, 232–233, 237
Abdullah bin Abdul-Aziz Al Saud 35, 63, 67, 79, 164, 175
Abdullah, Sadeq 77
bin Abdullah, Youssef bin Alawi 182
Abdulmutallab, Umar Farouk 71
Abidi, Hasni 112
Abrahams, Fred 214
Achcar, Gilbert 157, 171
Afghanistan 39–40
    Libyan involvement in jihad 118
    NATO war on 195
    US invasion of 87
African Union 168, 175, 180–181, 188–192, 192, 193, 196, 197
Afro-Asian People's Solidarity Conference 21
Aguinaldo, Emilio 179
Abdul-Ahadwas, Faisal Ahmed 67
AhlulBayt Islamic Mission 76
Ahmad, Aijaz 6, 31
al-Ahmar, Ali Muhsin 70, 73, 74
al-Ahmar, Hamid 70
al-Ahmar, Hussein bin Abdullah 69–70
Akakoss 140
Akins, James 105
Aladdin (1992) 44
Alani, Mustafa 232
Albert II 12

Algeria 102, 209
    Civil War 118
Alhaiki, Mohamed Ali 184
al-Hakim, Mohsin 78
Ali, Abubakr 216
al-Alimi, Rashad 72
Ali, Tariq 162
Allen, Mark 133
Alliot-Marie, Michele 161
al-Mukhtar, Omar 132
Alooshe, Noy 58
Alwadi, Nada 184
Amar, Paul 19–20
Amazigh 114–115
American International Group 42
Amin, Idi 35
Amnesty International 74, 216, 218, 227, 230
Anderson, Jon Lee 205, 211
Anderson, Robert 46
April 6 Movement 15
Arab Banking Corporation 210
Arab Council for Human Rights 70
Arabi, Ahmed 53
al-Arabiyya 156–157
Arab League 7, 131, 155, 168, 176, 180–181, 182, 186, 187
The Arab Mind 44
Arab Organisation for Human Rights 217
Arab Organization for Human Rights 149
Arab Revolution (1950s) 11
Arab Socialist Party (Egypt) 19
Arab Spring 6, 7–8, 23, 38, 62, 88–90, 98–99, 160–161, 163, 246, 251
    and United States 21–22
    NATO/US cooptation of 235–236
    and Palestine 56
    Sanya Declaration (BRICS) 193–194

Araud, Gérard 198
Arbenz Guzmán, Jacobo 40
al-Aryan, Issam 29–30
al-Asad, Bashar 177, 178
al-Asiri, Abdullah 71
Asselborn, Jean 96
Atiyya, Ali 154
Atlantic powers 27–28, 47, 152, 160–162, 192. *See also* NATO
al-Attiya, Abdelrahman bin Hamad 137, 182, 188
al-Awlaki, Anwar 71, 73
al-Azima, Mutlaq bin Salem 183
Aziz, Mohamed Ould Abdel 189–190, 191
Azzam, Abdullah 118

B

Bahrain 6, 7, 64, 66, 75–83, 85–86, 88, 89, 171, 175, 176, 182–185
   as British Protectorate 77–78
   Pearl Square 76, 82, 88, 184
Bahrain Centre for Human Rights 6, 183
al-Baja, Fathi 225
Baker, James 39, 42, 47–48
Baker, Raymond 25
Bakoush, Abdul Hamid 103–104
Balfour, A. J. 236
Bamyeh, Mohammed 115
Bani, Omar Ahmed 203
Ban Ki-moon 186–187, 217, 228
Barak, Ehud 52
al-Barrak, 'Abd al-Rahman 81
al-Basha, Amal 70
Basic People's Congress 142
Basij-e Mostaz'afin 84

Bassiouni, Cherif 158, 184–185
BBC 157
BB Energy 239
Belgrave, Charles Dalrymple 77
Belhaj, Abdel Hakim 207, 246
Ben Ali, Leila 91–92
Ben Ali, Zein el-Abidine 14–15, 16, 17, 30, 35, 37, 64, 91–92, 161
Ben Bella, Ahmed 102
Bengadara, Farhat 140
Ben Halim, Mustafa 102, 107, 141
Ben Halim, Tarek 136, 139–140
Ben Jumaa, Mahmoud 226
Benotman, Noman 127
Bey, Husni 143
Biden, Joe 53
Bin Laden, Osama 117
bin Qumu, Abu Sufian Ibrahim 206–207
Bin Sabri, Ahmed 226–227
Bisharah, Abdullah 86
von Bismarck, Otto 238
al-Bizri, Afif 59
Black, Ian 149, 151
Blair, Tony 132
Bongo, Omar 176
Bouazizi, Mohamed 14, 17
Bouchard, Charles 212, 222
Bouchuiguir, Soliman 208
Boukhris, Fathi 165
Boulsayn, Hakim 226
Bourguiba, Habib 102
Bowcott, Owen 149
BP 239, 240
Braiga Company 138
Brazil 192, 239
BRICS 192–199, 238–239
   and Syria 198–199
Britain 77–78
Brown, Graham 106
Buhwaish, Rajab 102
Burns, Bill 50

Burundi 196
Bush, George H. W. 40, 120, 174
Bush, George W. 41, 87, 126, 163, 164

C

Calabresi, Massimo 164
Calderoli, Roberto 94
Cambodia 174
Cameron, David 155, 157, 170, 238, 244
Camp David 32
Carney, Jay 223
Carter Doctrine 47
Carter, Jimmy 84
Centre for Egyptian Women's Legal Assistance 21
Centre of Manual Workers of Egypt 15
Chad 111, 121–122
  Libyan war on 202
  Toyota War of 1987 with Libya 121–122
Chalgam, Mohammed Abderrahman 126
Challenger Ltd. 143
Charrani, Farj 165
China 192, 193, 195, 239
  economy of 198
Chivers, C. J. 158, 213
Chomiak, Laryssa 16
Churchill, Winston 99
CIA 40, 42, 133, 166, 202–203, 204, 207
Ciezadlo, Annia 13
Clinton, Bill 167
Clinton, Hillary 17, 43, 164, 176, 180, 232, 233
Coalition to Protect Journalists 217
Coca Cola 144
Cockburn, Patrick 98, 218, 227
Cohen, Roger 169
Cole, Juan 157, 200
Collins, Susan 132

Committee for the Defense of Insurance Funds 15
Communism 26–28, 28–29, 31, 59
  in Egypt 18–19
Congo 175, 176
Congo-Brazzaville 190
ConocoPhillips 239
Coordination Committee for the Defense of Worker Rights 15
COP15 195
credit crisis of 2007 93, 197–198
Credit Suisse First Boston 42
Cretz, Gene 138, 201
Cromer, Lord 53
Cuba 174

D

Daalder, Ivo 169
Dabbashi, Ibrahim 156, 215–216
Dahi, Omar 16
Darfur 175
al-Da'wah al-Islamiyah 26
Dawa Party 87
dawlaty.info 67
democracy 30, 31, 41, 44, 53, 61, 193, 209, 244, 247, 249, 251
de Noailles, Louis-Marie 232–233
al-Dighaili, Salwa 231
Djerejian, Edward 41
Dorda, Abu Zayd Umar 141
Drayton, William Henry 150
Dridi, Ibrahim 129
drones 72, 213
Dubai 82
al-Dusturieen 67

E

education 23

Egypt 5–6, 17–27, 29–30, 32–34, 67, 89, 93, 251, 252
  1967 War 18
  Armed Forces Supreme Council (and look for more) 54
  British colonial era 53
  Colonel's Coup 17
  food protests (1977) 10
  food protests (2010) 9, 12–13
  food subsidies 10
  IMF 10
  infitah ("openness") 10, 15
  labor 16
  Mahalla 12
  military 35–36
  peasant struggles 15–16
  political parties 18–19
  secret police 45
  sectarianism 25
  security state 18–19, 28
  social movement organizations 15, 34
  women 20–21
Egyptian Movement for Change (Kefaya) 15
Eisenhower, Dwight 101–102
Elaraby, Nabil 54, 188
ElBaradei, Mohamed 25, 32–33, 34, 42
el-Fortia, Muhammad 157
Eltahawy, Diana 218
Engels, Frederick 249
Engineers Against Sequestration 15
ENI 140, 239
Enron Corporation 42
Entelis, John 16
Erdogan, Recep Tayyip 178–179
Ereli, Adam 81
Ernst & Young 139
Escobar, Pepe 171
Europe 180
extraordinary rendition 41, 45, 49, 133, 229

F

Facebook 21, 22
Fahd bin Abdul Aziz 107
Fahim, Kareem 144
Fahmi, Ismail 33
al-Failaka al-Islamiya 116
Fakhrawi, Karim 184
Farkash, Safia 147
Farnana, Mukhtar 245
Farouk (Egypt) 17
fascism 31
Fatima (Libya) 208
al-Fattah Younis, Abdel 151–152, 155, 160, 200, 203, 204, 221
  assassination of 204
Fayyad, Ali 31
February 17 Movement 165, 211
Federation of Pensioners 15
Feltman, Jeffrey 82–83
Fituri, Ahmed 128
food crisis (2010) 13
Fox, Mark 83
France 223
  and Tunisan uprising 161
  Mediterranean Union 131, 162
Free Trade Area of the Americas protest (2003, Miami) 185
French Revolution 9, 20, 250, 252
Friedman, Thomas 48, 128
Frillici, Vincent 219

G

Gabon 176, 193
Gafez, Ali Hamid 213
al-Gallala, Jalal 238–239
Gandhi, Mahatma 250
Gates, Robert 71, 79–80, 159, 183, 223
Gaza Flotilla 207

Gazprom Neft 239
Gehani, Abdallah 166
Gelie, Philippe 223
General Agreement on Trade and Tariffs 192
Geneva Conventions 229
genocide 156, 157–158, 164, 167
Georgia 195
Germany 193
bin Ghalbon, Mohammed 208
Ghali, Boutros Boutros 33
Ghanem, Shukri 136–138, 145
Ghannouchi, Rashid 30
bin Ghashir, Ibrahim Yusuf 219–220
Gheriani, Mustafa 211
Ghoga, Abdul Hafiz 96–97, 120, 179, 204
Gilad, Amos 56
Gladiator (2000) 37
Global South 251
Goldman Sachs 136, 139–140
Goldrich, Ethan 130
Group of Fifteen (G15) 192
Group of Seven (G7) 192–193, 198, 234, 241
Guantanamo 206
Gulf Cooperation Council (GCC) 28, 73, 79, 85–88, 89, 181, 182–183, 185–188
 counterinsurgency in Bahrain 182–185
Gulf monarchies 7, 36, 89, 175, 252
Gulf Rapid Deployment Force 87
Gulf War (1991) 40

H

Haass, Richard 233
Habré, Hisséne 202

Hacham, David 52
al-Hadi, Abd al-Rab Mansur 73, 74
Abu Hajar, Youssef Ahmed Bashir 222
al-Halbous, Ibrahim 219
Halliday, Fred 65
Hamad bin Isa al-Khalifa 63, 75, 76, 77, 83, 183
el-Hamalawy, Hossam 41
Ham, Carter 171–172
Haq movement 75–76
Harakat an-Nahda 30
Haret Hreik 29
Hariri Group 157
Haroun, Fadlallah 226
al-Hasidi, Abdel-Hakim 206, 207
Hassanpour, Navid 22
al-Hattah, Abu Abd al-Rahman 119
al-Hawali, Safar 81
HB Group 143
Held, David 147
Henri-Levy, Bernard 162
Herati, Mahdi 207
Hess 239
Hezbollah 29, 31
Hifter, Khalifa Belqasim 97, 199–200, 200, 202–205, 204–205, 205, 220, 245
Hifter, Saddam 245
Holbrooke, Richard 39–40, 42
Hudson, Rock 103
humanitarian intervention 98–99, 164, 166, 168, 174–175, 193, 215, 229, 233, 236
Human Rights Watch 40, 74, 148, 157, 183, 214
hunger 9–10
al-Hurruj 140
Hussain, Abdul-Wahab 75–76
Hussein, Saddam 47–48, 84, 174, 229
Hussein, Salah 16

I

Ibrahim, Ahmed 130
Idris (Libya) 99–100, 103, 104–105, 112, 113, 205, 208
Imazighen 223
imperialism 65
India 192
  Communists 31
India-Brazil-South Africa (IBSA) 192
Indonesia 26–27
inequality 13
Institute for International Law 174
International Atomic Energy Agency 34
International Commission on Intervention and State Sovereignty 167
International Criminal Court (ICC) 153, 156, 170–171, 215–216, 228
International Crisis Group 191–192
International Legal Assistance Consortium 217
International Monetary Fund (IMF) 10, 11, 93, 134, 142, 192, 198, 241–243
  Food Price Index 9
Internet 22, 92
Iran 27, 50, 52, 58–62, 86–88
  1979 revolution 24, 28, 36, 47, 61, 66, 78, 83–84
  revisionism 46
Iraq
  1958 coup 28
  Communist Party 26
  insurgency 119–120
  invasion of Kuwait 26, 47–48
  US invasion 23, 49, 87, 163
  war with Iran 60, 84

al-Isawi, Ali Abd al-Aziz 136, 148–149, 201–202
al-Islah 69, 70
Islam. *See also* political Islam
Islamic Front for the Liberation of Bahrain 66, 85–86
Islamic Jihad 29
Islamic Liberation Front (Libya) 117
Islamic Salvation Front (FIS) 118
Islamic Umma Party 67
Islamophobia 94
Israel 44, 45–46, 51, 51–52, 54–55, 56–58, 59–60, 178, 242
  Koenig Memorandum 55
  Rothschild Boulevard protests, 2011 58
  and Syria 199
Italy 94, 131, 132
  bombardment of Italy 213
Ivory Coast 233–234

J

Jahjah, Dyab Abou 24
Jalloud, Abdessalam 109
Jamaatt al-Islamiyya 50
al-Jamal, Abdul Amir 78
James Baker Institute 41
Javadi, Yaghoob 7
Jawad, Ali 76
al-Jazeera 30, 157, 218
  Palestine Papers 62
Jerjir, Habib 35
Jiang Yu 178
Jibril, Mahmoud 136, 138, 139, 141, 146, 180, 182, 200–201, 204–205, 211, 218, 230, 232–233, 237, 240, 244
Jihad (Libyan group) 117
Johnstone, Diana 40
Joint Meeting Party (Yemen) 70

Jones, Toby 81, 182
Jum'ah, Abdullah S. 137
Jyllands-Posten 94

K

el-Kabir, Sadiq Amr 210
Karman, Tawakel 68–69,
    74–75
Kefaya 54
el-Keib, Abdurrahim
    232–233, 237, 245
Kemp, Geoffrey 84
al-Khalifa, Abd Allah bin
    Khalid 81
Khalifa, Ahmed 172
al-Khalifa, Hamad bin Isa.
    See Hamad bin Isa al-
    Khalifa
al-Khalifa, Isa bin Salman
    78
Khalifa Khanaish 109
Khalil, Azza 15
Khamenei, Hojatolislam Ali
    31, 85
Khan, Ismail 87
Khan, Samir 73
Kharroubi, Mustafa 109
al-Khatib, Abdul Ilah 194
al-Khatib, Ahmad 177
Khawaildi Hamidi 109
Kheir, Karen Aboul 25
Khmer Rouge 174
Khomeini, Ruhollah Musavi
    36, 84
el-Kikhia, Mansour Rashid
    208
Kimmerling, Baruch 57
Kissinger, Henry 83–84
Koh, Harold 212
Kosovo 215
Kouchner, Bernard 162,
    181
Koussa, Moussa 124–125,
    126, 129, 133, 134, 165,
    232
Krauss, Clifford 240
Krogh, Per 180

L

Lagarde, Christine 241
Lamb, Franklin 243
Lantos, Tom 125, 129
Lebanon 62, 63
the Left
    armed intervention and
        174
Lehman Brothers 42
Leyne, Jon 152–153
liberalism 22
al-Libi, Abu Layth 127
al-Libi, Ibn al-Shaykh 45
Libya 251
    1951 Constitution 113
    1969 revolution 6, 28,
        99–100, 102–103, 105,
        141, 200
    2006 protest in Benghazi 94
    2011 revolution 88–90
        African mercenaries
            95, 149, 219, 226
        and African Union
            188–192
        air war 153–154
        allegations of rape
            policies 216, 218
        allegations of war
            crimes 155–160,
            158–159, 218–219
        arms shipments to 222
        in Az Zawiya 155
        in al-Bayda' 149
        Benghazi 148–149,
            157, 160, 204
        in Benghazi 96
        BRICS criticism of
            NATO 196–197
        BRICS response
            192–199
        Central Bank of Beng-
            hazi 210
        and China 168,
            176–179
        civilian casualties
            212–215, 216–217, 225
        and civilians 171–172

and defections 138, 151–152, 153, 154, 200, 226
and France 161–162
and Global South 176
intervention 160–166
in Tripoli 224–226
al-Jazeera coverage of 218
Libyan Oil Company 210
military and 153–154
in Misrata 151–152, 154–155, 157–158, 160, 222, 244
National Transitional Council 98, 146, 155, 172, 175, 187, 200, 203–204, 210, 215, 218, 229, 247
and NATO 243
NATO bombardment 158, 166, 168, 172–173, 174, 186, 211–215, 216–218, 220–221, 224–225, 231
naval war 221
and neoliberalism 8, 209, 211, 230
"no-fly zone" 166–173, 186, 203
"no-fly zone" 153, 155, 179, 181–182
and oil 210, 238–240
and political Islam 206–207, 221
possibility of peaceful settlement 175, 191–192, 194
prisoners from 230
and Qatar 187–188
reaction of Gulf states 164–165
rebels 95–99, 134–135, 179–180, 203–204, 205–207, 245

refugee crisis 194
Resolution 1970 152–153, 222
Resolution 1973 133, 169, 171, 174, 177, 178, 190, 198, 216, 217, 222–223
and Russia 168, 176–178
SAS involvement 222
and Saudi Arabia 181
targeting of media 217–218
Tawergha 219
and tribal politics 115, 227
and Turkey 178–179
UN condemnation of regime 152
and Amazigh peoples 114–115
and political Islam 6, 94
involvement with insurgency in Iraq 119–120
Anglo-Libyan treaty in 1953 101
anti-Americanism 123, 130
Bevin-Sfora Plan 100
bombing of UTA Flight 772 125
British aid to Idris monarchy 100–101
Central Bank 8, 241
centralization of power, post 1969 108–110
and China 129
construction of national identity 114–115
and corruption 143–145, 147
currency 240–241
Days of Rage demonstration on February 17, 2011 93–95
diplomatic overtures 125–126, 129–130

discovery of oil 104
East vs. West 112–113
economic development under Qaddafi 105–107
food insecurity 143
foreign military intervention 96–98
General National Congress 247
geography of 106
human rights activists 6
Islamic unrest in 1989 117
Italian bombardment of 173–174, 213
Italian occupation of 100
Jamahiriya 109, 110, 146
literacy 106
Lockerbie bombing (Pan Am Flight 103), 125
media 149
military 122–123
National Economic Development Board 138
National Information Board 143
nationalization 106
National Oil Corporation 137
National Transitional Council 97, 151–152, 179, 197, 208–210
and neoliberalism 6, 92–93, 98, 124, 135–136, 142–143, 145–146, 165, 200–201, 242
and oil 98, 108, 132, 137–138, 140
oil 8
Old Guard 142, 237
and political Islam 111, 116–120
post 1969 land reform 106–107
and privatization 135, 138, 200–201
and "reform" 134–142, 145–146, 165

Revolutionary Command Council 122
Revolution Committee Movement 109
Riqaba Committee 143–144
security state 201
treaty of January 6, 1957 27
tribal politics 112, 115
Tripoli 6
UN sanctions 123, 125, 133
US bombing of, 1986 122
US influence over post WWII monarchy 102
Warfallah 151
and War on Terror 126–127, 202–203, 207
war with Chad 121–122, 202, 220
Wheelus Air Base 101
working-class 6
Libya Ahrar TV 187
Libya National Army 245
Libyan Central Bank 139, 140
Libyan Company for Distribution of Petroleum Products 138
Libyan Constitutional Union 208
Libyan Contact Group 187–188
Libyan Islamic Fighting Group (LIFG) 118–119, 127, 133, 203, 206, 207, 246
  1996 protest at Abu Selim prison 120
Libyan Islamic Movement (al-Harakat al-Islamiya al-Libiya). 206
Libyan League for Human Rights 208
Libyan National Army 202–203

Libyan National Salvation
  Front 202
Libyan Tmazight Congress
  208
Libya Youth Forum 135
Lieberman, Joseph 132
The Lion of the Desert
  (1981) 100
Lipton, David 50
Lizza, Ryan 169
Lloyd, Selwyn 163
Locklear, Samuel 173
Lungescu, Oana 190
Lupi, Emilio 101

M

"Ma Bi Marad" 102
Mabruk 140
Mack, David 243–244
Macmillan, Harold 163
Mahallah Committee for
  Workers' Consciousness
  15
Mahathir Mohamad 241
Mahfouz, Asmaa 20–21
al-Mahmudi, al-Baghdadi
  Ali 137–138
Maktab al-Khidamat 117
Mali 189, 227
Mamdani, Mahmood 167,
  168
Mandela, Nelson 37
al-Manqoush, Yousef 245
Mansouri, Ali Ounes 165
Mao Zedong 109
Marandi, Seyed Moham-
  mad 32
Marathon 239
March 9 Movement for the
  Independence of Univer-
  sities 15
March 20 Movement 15
Marinetti, Tommaso 173
Marxism 26–27
Marx, Karl 5, 250
al-Marzooq, Khalil Ibrahim
  63

Marzouki, Nadia 25
Mauritania 189–190
Mayouf, Abdeljalil 238
McCain, John 132
McKinsey & Company 139
Mediterranean
  strategic command of
  101–102
Mediterranean Union.
  See France, Mediterra-
  nean Union
Medvedev, Dmitry 196,
  197
Megally, Hanny 230
al-Megrahi, Abdelbaset 132
Mellita 140
al-Mesmari, Idris 94–95,
  231
Mesmari, Nuri 165, 166
el-Meyet, Ibrahim 145
MI6 133, 207
Milosevic, Slobodan 170
Misbach, Haji 26–27
al-Missned, Mozah bint
  Nasser 138
Mitterrand, Frédéric 161
Mladic, Ratko 150
Mohammed bin Nayef 68,
  71
Mohammed VI (Morocco)
  114
Mohammed V (Morocco)
  103
monarchy 64
Moneim, Ahmed 20
Montreux Convention 195
Moreno, Luis G. 52
Moreno-Ocampo, Luis
  216, 218
Mossadeq, Mohammad 40
Mourou, Abdelfattah
  24–25
Moussa, Amr 182,
  186–187, 188
MPLA 174
Mubadala Development 77
Mubarak, Gamal 13, 19, 20
Mubarak, Hosni 12, 13,

17, 18, 19, 22, 24, 25, 30, 33, 35–36, 37, 39, 40–41, 43, 44–45, 49–51, 52, 54, 95, 120
Muhammed as-Senussi 208
Muhammed bin Fahd bin Abdul Aziz al Saud 68
al-Mukhtar, 'Umar 100, 102
Mullah, Shweyga 145
Mullen, Mike 82–83, 159
al-Mundhir, Abu 118
Abu Munthir, Emir 133
al-Muqarayif, Muhammed Yusuf 117
Mushaima, Hassan 75
Muslim Brotherhood 6, 13, 18, 19, 23–24, 29–30, 32, 34, 36, 41, 44, 49, 50, 52, 63, 246
    Freedom and Justice Party 30

N

Naber, Nadine 21
Nader, Alireza 62
Nahda Party 24
al-Naimi, Haidar 184
Nasr, Vali 62
Nasser, Gamal Abdul 17, 18, 23, 48, 53, 59, 65
Nasserism 26, 33–34, 59, 60–61, 66, 78
National Conference for the Libyan Opposition 208
National Declaration of Reform 67
National Front for the Salvation of Libya 208
nationalization
    in Egypt 18
national liberation 250–251
National Liberation Front (FLN) 209
National Movement for the Liberation of the Azawad 227

National Oil and Gas Authority of Bahrain 77
National Oil Company 238
National Progressive Grouping Party (Egypt) 19
National Salvation Front for Libya (Inqat) 117
National Transitional Council. *See* Libya, National Transitional Council
NATO 6–7, 8, 97, 168, 192, 195, 196–197, 200, 201, 211, 228, 231, 234–235
    air war in Yugoslavia 195
    Istanbul Cooperation Initiative 181, 187
Nayed, Aref Ali 239
Nayef bin Abdul Aziz al-Saud 67, 68, 73, 86, 87
Nayid, 'Arif 244
neoliberalism 32, 33, 34, 41, 92–93, 124, 147, 205, 236–237, 246–247, 252
    Egypt 19–20
Netanyahu, Benjamin 56, 58
New York Times 199, 238
NGOs 147
Nguesso, Denis Sassou 190
Nigeria 193
Non-Aligned Movement (NAM) 192
al-Nour 30
Nour, Ayman 6, 33
nuclear weapons 233

O

Obama, Barack 17, 21, 44, 56, 128–129, 163, 164, 168–169, 169, 170, 176, 234, 244
    2009 Cairo speech 39
Obeidi, Amal 110
al-Obeidi, Salah Salem 245
Ocampo, Luis Moreno 228

Occidental Petroleum 77
Odebrecht 239
Ogwu, U. Joy 152–153
oil 7, 8, 11–12, 45–48,
   60–61, 77–78, 83, 89, 104,
   137–138, 140, 162–163,
   210, 238–240
Okello, Henry Oryem 189
Oman 66, 79
OMV 239
OPEC 26, 137
Operation Odyssey Dawn.
   See Libya, 2011 Revolu-
   tion, NATO bombard-
   ment
Orientalism 44
Owen, David 96
Oxford Group 139

P

Pahlavi, Mohammad Reza
   59, 60, 83
Pakistan 39–40
Palestine 23, 51, 51–52, 54,
   55, 56–57, 58, 62
Palestinian Centre for Hu-
   man Rights 217
Paris Commune 250
Pasha, Twefik 53
Patai, Raphael 44
Patterson, Anne 42
Patton Boggs 218–219, 240
Pelt, Adrian 113
Peninsula Shield 87.
   See Gulf Cooperation
   Council (GCC)
People's Front for the Lib-
   eration of the Occupied
   Arab Gulf 65–66
Perónism 18
Perseus 42
Petraeus, David 50, 72
Petrobras 239
petro-dollars 11–12
Petroleum Institute 237
Philippines, US invasion
   of 179

Phillips, Sarah 71
Pillay, Navi 96, 149
political Islam 8, 25–27,
   111, 116–120, 118, 246
Pol Pot 174
Porteous, Tom 148
Power, Samantha 164, 235
Pritchard, Evans 100
Puri, Manjeev Singh 176

Q

Qaddafi, Aisha 144
Qaddafi Foundation 151
Qaddafi, Hannibal 144–145
Qaddafi, Mohammed 144
Qaddafi, Muammar 7–8,
   8, 45, 63, 89–90, 92–99,
   99, 102–103, 124, 133,
   140, 141, 142–143, 143,
   146, 164, 165, 175, 197,
   200, 202, 205, 209, 215,
   220, 237
   1993 assassination at-
      tempt 115
   and Africa 189, 191
   and Amazigh 114–115
   assassination attempts in
      1990s 119
   death 97, 227–231
   and Eastern Libya 94
   Green Book 110, 116
   and Islam 116–117,
      120–121
   lifestyle 144
   Nasserism 116
   and nationalism 130–131
   and NATO 170–171, 173
   and political Islam
      126–127
   political philosophy
      108–110, 132–133
   and populism 107–109
   reaction to 2011 rebel-
      lion 150
   reading habits 128–129
   and tribal politics
      112–114

Qaddafi, Mutassim 111, 132, 144
Qaddafi, Sa'adi 95, 96, 144
Qaddafi, Saif al-Islam 8, 110, 111, 123, 126, 127, 135–136, 138, 140, 141, 146, 148, 151, 175, 200–201, 207, 221, 227, 229–230, 242, 245
    PhD Dissertation 146–147
al-Qaeda 45, 127, 176, 206–207
al-Qaeda in the Arabian Peninsula (AQAP) 65, 71
al-Qaeda in the Maghreb (the AQIM 127
al Qaradawi, Yusuf 24, 25, 63
Qassim, Isa Ahmed 78
Qatar 7, 35, 82, 160, 187–188, 226, 239, 243, 246
Qatar Petroleum 239
Qattan, Ahmed bin Abdulaziz 181
Quinn, Anthony 100
Qunayfid, Mustafa 119
al-Qurmezi, Ayat 75, 76

R

al-Rahila 138
Rajab, Nabeel 79, 184
Rasmussen, Anders Fogh 234–235
Reagan, Ronald 84, 85, 202
real estate 12
Regional Workers' Union of Tunis 35
Repsol 140
Republican National Convention (2000, Philadelphia) 185
revisionist powers 58–60
revolution 155–156, 232, 249–252

Revolution of 1848 249–250
Ricciardone, Francis 12–13
Rice, Condoleezza 128–129
Rice, Susan 164, 176, 216
Rishmawi, Mona 230
Roberts, Hugh 171
Rommel, Erwin 99
Roosevelt, Theodore 52–53
Ross, Dennis 219
Rovera, Donatella 216, 229–230
Rugunda, Ruhakana 196
Russia 192, 193, 195, 196, 239
    revolutions in 250
Rwanda 167

S

Saad, Amer 149
Saadawi, Bashir 210
Saad Party 184
Sachs, Jeffery 140
Sadat, Anwar 10, 17, 18, 19, 33, 48, 59–60
Sadiki, Larbi 10
al-Sadiq, Abu Abdullah. See Belhaj, Abdel Hakim
al-Sadr, Baqir 26, 26–27
Sadr Movement 29, 87
al-Sa'idi, Sami 118
el-Said, Karima 21
al-Salabi, Isma'il 247
Salam, Nawaf 186
Saleh, Ahmed Ali 70, 73
Saleh, Ali Abdullah 65, 66, 68–69, 70–74, 176
Saleh, Ammar 73
Saleh, Khaled 73
Saleh, Yahya 73
al-Sallabi, Ali 127
Salman, Ali 76, 78, 80
Salwa al-Dighaili 94
Salwa, Fathi Terbil 93, 231
al-Sansusi, Sayyid Muhammed bin Ali 112
Sarkozy, Nicolas 17, 131,

132, 157, 161, 162, 166, 170, 180, 238, 244
Satterfield, David 63
Saud al-Faisal 63, 182
Saudi Arabia 17, 35, 36, 57, 60, 60–61, 64–68, 66, 83, 160, 164, 181–182
"Days of Rage" protest, March 2011 on March 11 67
monarchy 7, 66
Saudi National Guard 67
al-Saud Inc. 66
saudireform.com 67
Sawani, Youssef 151
Sawiris, Naguib 19–20
Sayyid Abdallah Abed Al Senussi 104
Scahill, Jeremy 185
Schmitt, Eric 158, 213
Scobey, Margaret 42, 49, 50
Seche, Stephen 72
Senussi, Abdullah 95, 96, 120, 129, 203
sha'b (the people) 24–25
Shadid, Anthony 144
Shah. See Pahlavi, Mohammad Reza
Shalgham, Abdel Rahman 153
al-Shaltami, Muhammad Farhat 91
al-Shanuka, Sayed 157
al-Sharara 138
Sharawy, Helmi 15
Shariati, Ali 27
Sharif, Ibrahim 75
Sharp, Gene 22
Shebani, Ahmed 242
Shegunts, Aram 239
al-Sheikh, Ali Jawad 184
Shi'a 61–63, 67, 78–80, 81
The Shia Revival 62
Shiglabu, Rajab 136
Shkal, Albarrani 244
shock and awe 212
shock therapy 140, 143

Simeon, Dilip 249
Skaf, Aline 145
Socialist Liberal Party (Egypt) 19
Soliman, Azza 21
Soros, George 128
Sourani, Raji 217
South Africa 37, 174, 190, 192, 193
South Ossetia war over, 2008 195
Sri Lanka 176
Stack, Liam 245
Stavrianos, L. S. 18
St. John, Roland Bruce 131
Stork, Joe 183
Sudan 117
Suez Canal 54, 62
bin Sulayman, Fathy 119
Suleiman, Kareem 41
Suleiman, Omar 19, 43, 45, 49, 50, 52, 53, 53–54, 127
Syria 88, 149–150, 176, 177–178, 198–199
Syrian Revolution General Commission 177

T

Tafuri, David 240
Tahrir Square 17, 20, 45, 53, 89, 252
al-Tajer, Mohammed 77
Talal bin Abdulaziz 67
Tantawi, Mohammed Hussein 49, 50–51, 54, 55, 163
Tappin, John 102
Tarhouni, Ali 210, 240, 246
Tatneft 239
Tattanaki, Hassan 143
Tatweer Petroleum 77
Tayib, Mohammed Sayed 67
Taylor, Charles 110
Tenasil, Walid 244
Terbil, Fateh 120, 148

al-Thani, Hamad bin Khalifa 165
Thatcher, Margaret 85
al-Thawra 29
Third World Project 26
Thompson, E. P. 249
Timoney, John 185
Tobruk (1967) 103
de Tocqueville, Alexis 147
Toner, Mark 150
Total 140, 239
Touré, Amadou Toumani 189
Trabelsi, Belhassen 161
Trabulsi, Fawwaz 31
Traoré, Moussa 189
Tripoli Military Council 246
al-Tubal, Abdel Basat 226
Tunisia 5, 14–15, 16–17, 30–31, 89, 91–92, 93, 161, 251
    food protests (2010) 9
    Redayef protests 17
    relations with Libya 102
    trade unions 34–35
    treaty of January 6, 1957 27
Turki al-Faisal 57, 185–186
Turner, Mike 173

U

al-Udeid Air Base 82
Uganda 189
Ullman, Harlan 212
ummah 8
UN 230
Union Générale Tunisienne du Travail or UGTT 34
United Arab Emirates 86, 182
United Arab Republic 21
United Kingdom 162–163
    SAS 222
United Nations 7, 55–56, 57, 97, 149, 155, 158, 167, 168, 176–177, 180–181, 190, 192. *See also* Libya, 2011 revolution, Resolution 1970, Resolution 1973
    Human Rights Council 201
    Security Council 84, 193, 199
United States 223
    1986 bombing of Libya 122
    AFRICOM 128, 243
    and Syria 199
    arms deals 83
    consumers 11–12
    economy of 198
    entry into Libyan conflict 163–164
    export of crowd control techniques 185
    extraordinary rendition 19
    Fifth Fleet 82, 83
    foreign aid 45, 51
    global hegemony 45
    media 157
    military 47
    power in Middle East/ Northern Africa 38–43
    Presidential Study Directive on Mass Atrocities (PSD-10) 234–235
    State Department 133, 150, 158, 163, 178, 202, 205–206, 218
    support for Chad 202
    USAID 11
USS Cole 71
USSR 28, 66

V

Vandewalle, Dirk 107, 122
Veba 140
Vietnam 174
Viotti, Maria Luiza Riberio 177
Vitol 239

W

Waad Society 76
Wa'atassemo Foundation 144
Wade, James 212
Wafa 76
Wallstrom, Margot 216
Walzer, Michael 175
Ward, William 128
War on Terror 7, 48–49, 72, 92, 126–127, 195, 229
al-Wasat 184
weapons of mass destruction 125
al-Wefaq 6, 61, 62, 63, 76, 78, 80, 82, 83, 184
Weinstein, Jeremy 164
Wen Jiabao 198
Wenzel, Robert 210
WikiLeaks 49, 91–92
Wisner, Frank 38–43, 44, 50, 53, 163
Wisner, Frank Sr. 40
al-Wohaibi, Abdul Aziz Mohammed 67
women 31
  in Yemen 71
  liberation of 20–21
Women for Change (Mesreyat Maa al-Tagheer) 15
Women Journalists Without Chains 68–69
Workers' Communist Party (Tunisia) 17
Workers for Change 15
World Amazigh Congress 114
World Bank 11, 33, 192
World Economic Forum 14–15
World Muslim League 26, 27
WTO 195

Y

Yemen 7, 63, 64, 65, 66, 68–75, 89, 171, 175–176
  Britain protectorate 81
  Marxists 66
  Taghyir Square 69
Yemeni Socialist Party 69
Yom Kippur War (1973) 51, 59
Yugoslavia
  NATO intervention in 215
Yunis, Abu Bakr 109

Z

al-Zahf al-Akhdar 142
Zakaria, Fareed 128
al-Zawahiri, Ayman 29, 127
Zelikow, Philip 235
Zetkin, Clara 31
Zhou Enlai 252
Ziu, Mahdi 96
Zuma, Jacob 176, 188, 190, 195, 196–197

Support AK Press!

AK Press is one of the world's largest and most productive anarchist publishing houses. We're entirely worker-run and democratically managed. We operate without a corporate structure — no boss, no managers, no bullshit. We publish close to twenty

books every year, and distribute thousands of other titles published by other like-minded independent presses from around the globe.

The Friends of AK program is a way that you can directly contribute to the continued existence of AK Press, and ensure that we're able to keep publishing great books just like this one! Friends pay a minimum of $25 per month, for a minimum three month period, into our publishing account. In return, Friends automatically receive (for the duration of their membership), as they appear, one free copy of every new AK Press title. They're also entitled to a 20% discount on everything featured in the AK Press Distribution catalog and on the website, on any and every order. You or your organization can even sponsor an entire book if you should so choose!

There's great stuff in the works — so sign up now to become a Friend of AK Press, and let the presses roll!

Won't you be our friend? Email friendsofak@akpress.org for more info, or visit the Friends of AK Press website:

http://www.akpress.org/friends.html